Building Secure PHP Applications

A Comprehensive Guide to Protecting Your Web Applications from Threats

Satej Kumar Sahu

Building Secure PHP Applications: A Comprehensive Guide to Protecting Your Web Applications from Threats

Satej Kumar Sahu
Bangalore, Karnataka, India

ISBN-13 (pbk): 979-8-8688-0931-6   ISBN-13 (electronic): 979-8-8688-0932-3
https://doi.org/10.1007/979-8-8688-0932-3

Copyright © 2024 by Satej Kumar Sahu

This work is subject to copyright. All rights are reserved by the Publisher, whether the whole or part of the material is concerned, specifically the rights of translation, reprinting, reuse of illustrations, recitation, broadcasting, reproduction on microfilms or in any other physical way, and transmission or information storage and retrieval, electronic adaptation, computer software, or by similar or dissimilar methodology now known or hereafter developed.

Trademarked names, logos, and images may appear in this book. Rather than use a trademark symbol with every occurrence of a trademarked name, logo, or image we use the names, logos, and images only in an editorial fashion and to the benefit of the trademark owner, with no intention of infringement of the trademark.

The use in this publication of trade names, trademarks, service marks, and similar terms, even if they are not identified as such, is not to be taken as an expression of opinion as to whether or not they are subject to proprietary rights.

While the advice and information in this book are believed to be true and accurate at the date of publication, neither the authors nor the editors nor the publisher can accept any legal responsibility for any errors or omissions that may be made. The publisher makes no warranty, express or implied, with respect to the material contained herein.

    Managing Director, Apress Media LLC: Welmoed Spahr
    Acquisitions Editor: Melissa Duffy
    Development Editor: James Markham
    Coordinating Editor: Gryffin WInkler

Cover designed by eStudioCalamar

Cover image by Li Zhang @ Unsplash.com

Distributed to the book trade worldwide by Apress Media, LLC, 1 New York Plaza, New York, NY 10004, U.S.A. Phone 1-800-SPRINGER, fax (201) 348-4505, e-mail orders-ny@springer-sbm.com, or visit www.springeronline.com. Apress Media, LLC is a California LLC and the sole member (owner) is Springer Science + Business Media Finance Inc (SSBM Finance Inc). SSBM Finance Inc is a **Delaware** corporation.

For information on translations, please e-mail booktranslations@springernature.com; for reprint, paperback, or audio rights, please e-mail bookpermissions@springernature.com.

Apress titles may be purchased in bulk for academic, corporate, or promotional use. eBook versions and licenses are also available for most titles. For more information, reference our Print and eBook Bulk Sales web page at http://www.apress.com/bulk-sales.

Any source code or other supplementary material referenced by the author in this book is available to readers on GitHub (https://github.com/Apress). For more detailed information, please visit https://www.apress.com/gp/services/source-code.

If disposing of this product, please recycle the paper

This book is dedicated to my parents and sister.

Table of Contents

About the Author xxi

About the Technical Reviewer xxiii

Acknowledgments xxv

Introduction xxvii

Chapter 1: Introduction to PHP Application Security 1

What Is Application Security? 1

    Protection of Software Applications 2

    Identification of Vulnerabilities 2

    Lifecycle Approach 3

    Security Testing 4

    Secure Development Practices 4

    Authentication and Authorization 4

    Data Protection 5

    Incident Response 5

    Compliance and Regulations 6

Importance of Security 6

Role of Application Developer in Security 7

Understanding the PHP Security Landscape 13

    Core PHP Security 14

    Framework-Specific Security 15

    Ecosystem Security 15

TABLE OF CONTENTS

- The Impact of Security Vulnerabilities in PHP Applications 15
  - Data Breaches 16
  - Financial Loss 16
  - Reputation Damage 16
  - Operational Disruption 17
  - Legal Consequences 17
  - User Impact 17
  - Mitigation Costs 18
  - Long-Term Impact 18
  - Damage Beyond the Application 18
  - Operational Inefficiency 19
- Common Attack Vectors and Threats 19
  - Phishing Attacks 19
  - Malware 19
  - Denial-of-Service (DoS) and Distributed Denial-of-Service (DDoS) Attacks 20
  - SQL Injection 20
  - Cross-Site Scripting (XSS) 20
  - Cross-Site Request Forgery (CSRF) 21
  - Man-in-the-Middle (MitM) Attacks 21
  - Social Engineering 21
  - Insider Threats 21
  - Zero-Day Vulnerabilities 22
  - Credential Theft 22
  - IoT Vulnerabilities 22
  - Cryptojacking 22
  - Supply Chain Attacks 23
  - Advanced Persistent Threats (APTs) 23

TABLE OF CONTENTS

Principles of Secure PHP Application Development 23
    Security by Design 24
    Secure Coding Practices 25
    Authentication and Authorization 25
    Session Management 26
    File Uploads 27
    Error Handling and Logging 27
    Security Updates and Patch Management 28
    Secure Communication 28
    Security Testing and Code Reviews 29
    Incident Response Plan 29
Summary 30

Chapter 2: PHP Core Security 31

The Great PHP Update Debate 32
Why Does PHP Version Matters? 33
    Security Updates 33
    End of Life (EOL) 34
    Best Practices 35
    Performance and Efficiency 36
    Compatibility 37
    Vendor and Application Support 38
Secure PHP Configuration 40
    php.ini 41
    Directives 42
    Per-Directory Configuration 42
    Runtime Configuration 42
    Extensions 43

TABLE OF CONTENTS

    Security 43

    Common Settings 43

    Error Reporting ("display_errors", "error_reporting")..........................44

    "expose_php = Off" 45

    "error_reporting = E_ALL"..46

    "display_errors = Off"..47

    "display_startup_errors = Off" 47

    "log_errors = On"..48

    "error_log = /valid_path/PHP-logs/php_error.log" 48

    "ignore_repeated_errors = Off"...49

    File Inclusion ("allow_url_fopen", "allow_url_include")......................50

    SQL Injection Prevention ("magic_quotes_gpc", "mysqli") 50

    File Uploads ("upload_max_filesize", "post_max_size")..................51

    "file_uploads = On"...52

    "upload_tmp_dir = /path/PHP-uploads/"..53

    "upload_max_filesize = 2M"..53

    "post_max_size = 5M" 54

    "max_file_uploads = 2" 55

    Session Management ("session.cookie_secure", "session.cookie_httponly")..56

Session Data Storage and Management...57

    session.save_path...57

    session.name 57

Session Initialization and Handling 57

    session.auto_start...57

    session.use_trans_sid...58

Session Cookie Configuration 58

    session.cookie_domain...58

    session.cookie_secure..58

TABLE OF CONTENTS

    session.cookie_httponly 58
    session.cookie_samesite 59
Session Security Enhancements 59
    session.use_strict_mode 59
    session.use_cookies and session.use_only_cookies 59
    session.cookie_lifetime 59
Additional Security Measures 60
    session.cache_expire 60
    session.sid_length 60
    session.sid_bits_per_character 60
    session.hash_function and session.hash_bits_per_character 60
    Access Controls ("open_basedir", "disable_functions") 61
    "enable_dl = Off" 61
    "disable_functions = " 62
    "disable_classes = ..." 63
Other PHP General Settings 63
    doc_root and open_basedir 64
    include_path 65
    extension_dir 65
    mime_magic.magicfile 66
    allow_webdav_methods 66
    session.gc_maxlifetime 67
    session.referer_check = /application/path 67
    memory_limit = ... 68
    max_execution_time = ... 68
    report_memleaks = On 69
    track_errors = Off 69
    html_errors = Off 70

TABLE OF CONTENTS

Input Validation and Sanitization Techniques 71
    Preventing Injection Attacks 72
    Mitigating Data Exposure 72
    Safeguarding Against Parameter Manipulation 72
    Defending Against Cross-Site Scripting (XSS) 72
    Blocking Cross-Site Request Forgery (CSRF) Attacks 73
    Enhancing Data Integrity 73
    Preventing Application Logic Abuse 73
    Strengthening Database Security 73
    Ensuring Compliance 73
    Minimizing Attack Surfaces 74
    Maintaining User Trust 74
    Facilitating Future Development 74
    Data Filtering and Validation Functions 74
    Regular Expressions 75
    Allowed List and Denied List 76
    Escape Output 76
    Parameterized Queries 77
    Cross-Site Request Forgery (CSRF) Tokens 77
    Content Security Policy (CSP) 79
    HTTP Security Headers 80
    File Upload Validation 80
    Input Sanitization 82
    Prevention of SQL Injection 83
    Mitigation of Cross-Site Scripting (XSS) 83
    Preventing Cross-Site Request Forgery (CSRF) 83
    Protection Against Data Tampering 84
    Defense Against File Upload Exploits 84

TABLE OF CONTENTS

    Reducing Attack Surface 84
    Enhanced User Experience 84
    Compliance with Security Best Practices 85
    Long-Term Maintenance and Security 85
    Stripping HTML Tags 85
    Filtering Special Characters 86
    Using "htmlspecialchars()" for Output Escaping 86
    Preventing SQL Injection with Prepared Statements 86
    Handling File Uploads Securely 87
    Filtering User-Generated URLs 87
    Removing or Escaping Control Characters 88
Handling Sessions and Cookies Securely 88
    Cookies 89
    Sessions 89
Secure File Handling and Uploads 110
    Limit File Types 114
    Rename Uploaded Files 114
    Use a Secure Directory 115
    Set Appropriate Permissions 115
    Validate File Size 115
    Use a Randomized Upload Path 116
    Prevent Double Extensions 116
    Validate and Sanitize File Names 116
    Regularly Clean the Uploads Directory 117
    Implement an Authentication and Authorization System ... 117
Securing Database Operations in PHP 117
    Use Prepared Statements (Parameterized Queries) 119
    Input Validation and Sanitization 119

TABLE OF CONTENTS

    Authentication and Authorization 120

    Limit Database Privileges 120

    Protect Database Credentials 120

    Validate User Input for Query Parameters 120

    Regularly Update and Patch 121

    Error Handling 121

    Logging and Monitoring 122

    Secure Your Environment 122

    Data Encryption 122

Summary 123

Chapter 3: Web Security for PHP Applications 125

Principles of Web Application Security 126

    Defense in Depth 127

    Least Privilege 129

    Input Validation 131

    Secure Coding Practices 132

    Authentication and Authorization 133

    Secure Session Management 137

    Custom Middleware or Access Control Lists (ACL) 138

    Encryption 140

    Error Handling 145

    Session Management 145

    Web Application Firewalls (WAFs) 146

    Regular Security Testing 147

    Patch Management 149

    Data Validation 150

    Security Headers 151

    Security by Design 152

TABLE OF CONTENTS

Incident Response Plan 153
User Education 155
Vendor Security 157
Protecting Against Cross-Site Scripting (XSS) Attacks 161
Output Encoding 164
Content Security Policy (CSP) 165
Input Validation 165
Use Prepared Statements (Database Queries) 166
Avoid Dynamic JavaScript Generation 166
HTTP-Only Cookies 166
Use Security Libraries 167
Regular Security Testing 167
Security Training 167
Mitigating Cross-Site Request Forgery (CSRF) Attack 168
Unauthorized Actions 168
Data Manipulation 168
Financial Loss 169
Data Exposure 169
Authentication Bypass 169
Session Hijacking 169
Reputation Damage 170
Legal and Compliance Issues 170
Summary 174

Chapter 4: Framework Security 177
Introduction to Laravel Security Features 178
Cross-Site Request Forgery (CSRF) Protection 178
Cross-Site Scripting (XSS) Protection 183
SQL Injection Protection 186

TABLE OF CONTENTS

    Authentication and Authorization 189

    Session Security 199

    File Upload Security 205

    Middleware for Additional Protection 212

    HTTPS and Secure Configuration 216

Secure Configuration and Deployment in Laravel 224

    Protecting Sensitive Information 224

    Preventing Security Vulnerabilities 224

    Enforcing HTTPS for Secure Communication 225

    Implementing HTTP Strict Transport Security (HSTS) 225

    Maintaining Production-Ready Environments 225

    Enhancing Overall Application Security 226

Protecting Routes, Middleware, and Controllers 232

    1. Access Control and Authorization 233

    2. Input Validation and Sanitization 233

    3. Defense Against Attacks and Security Policies 233

    4. Logging and Monitoring 234

Security Best Practices 238

    Role-Based Access Control (RBAC) 239

    Middleware 239

    Policies 239

    Authorization in Controllers 239

    Middleware Parameters 240

    Error Handling 240

    Route Grouping 240

Securing Laravel Database Operations 241

Summary 246

TABLE OF CONTENTS

Chapter 5: Security Standards and Best Practices.......................... 249

OWASP Top Ten: Key Web Application Security Risks.. 251
- Injection (SQL, NoSQL, OS) 251
- Cross-Site Scripting (XSS).. 251
- Broken Authentication 252
- Insecure Direct Object References (IDOR) 252
- Security Misconfigurations.. 252
- Sensitive Data Exposure.. 253
- Missing Function-Level Access Control... 253
- Cross-Site Request Forgery (CSRF)... 254
- Using Components with Known Vulnerabilities 254
- Unvalidated Redirects and Forwards... 255

Secure Coding Practices and Code Reviews.. 255
- Secure Coding Practices in PHP 256
- Input Validation and Sanitization 256
- Password Handling... 257
- Session Management 257
- Error Handling 258
- File Upload Security... 258
- Cross-Site Request Forgery (CSRF) Tokens 259
- Data Validation and Sanitization.. 259
- Secure Password Recovery.. 260
- Content Security Policy (CSP) 260
- Database Connection Security 260
- Session Security... 261
- SSL/TLS Usage 261
- Secure Coding Practices in Laravel... 262
- Middleware for Authentication and Authorization 262

xv

TABLE OF CONTENTS

    Use Laravel's Authentication System 263
    Validation with Requests 263
    Authorization with Policies and Gates 264
    Use Eloquent ORM Safely 264
    Cross-Site Request Forgery (CSRF) Protection 265
    Secure Session Management 265
    Content Security Policy (CSP) 266
    Use Dependency Injection 266
    Database Migrations and Seeders 266
    Use HTTPS 267
    Code Reviews 267
    Peer Reviews 269
    Static Code Analysis 269
    Security Linters and Scanners 270
    Checklist-Based Reviews 270
    Automated Testing 270
Security-Related Packages in Laravel 271
    Laravel Bouncer (for Authorization) 271
    Laravel Sanctum (for API Authentication) 272
    Laravel Debugbar (for Debugging and Profiling) 273
    Laravel Scout (for Full-Text Search) 274
    Laravel Telescope (for Monitoring and Debugging) 275
    Laravel Nova (for Admin Panel) 276
    Spatie Laravel Activitylog (for Activity Logging) 277
    Intervention Image (for Image Handling) 278
    Laravel Dusk (for Browser Testing) 278
    Laravel Medialibrary (for Media Management) 279

TABLE OF CONTENTS

Secure Authentication and Authorization Mechanisms 280
    Importance of Secure Authentication and Authorization 280
    Secure Authentication and Authorization in PHP 281
    Laravel Sanctum (for API Authentication) 282
    Laravel Passport (for OAuth2) 283
    Laravel Breeze (for Starter Kits) 284
    Laravel Fortify (for Custom Authentication) 284

Security Testing and Vulnerability Assessments 291
    Importance of Security Testing and Vulnerability Assessments 291
    Security Testing and Vulnerability Assessment Practices: 292
    Static Application Security Testing (SAST) 292
    Dynamic Application Security Testing (DAST) 292
    Dependency Scanning 293
    Container Image Scanning 293
    Security Headers 294
    Automated Security Testing in CI/CD 294

Secure Deployment and DevOps Considerations 299
    General Secure Deployment and DevOps Considerations 300
    PHP and Laravel-Specific Deployment Considerations 303
    Secure Deployment Code Practices (Example Using Ansible) 305
    General Secure Deployment Code Practices 307

Summary 314

Chapter 6: Protocol Security **315**
    Securing HTTP Communications: SSL/TLS and HTTPS 315
    HTTPS 320
    SSL (Secure Sockets Layer) and TLS (Transport Layer Security) 323
    Usage of SSL/TLS/HTTPS in the Context of PHP Application 327

TABLE OF CONTENTS

Web Server Configurations 327

Forced HTTPS in Laravel 330

HSTS (HTTP Strict Transport Security) 330

Mixed Content Handling 331

Laravel Mix 331

Testing 332

Securely Handling User Input and Data Transmission 332

Code Samples and Examples in Laravel 334

Securing API Communication: OAuth, JWT, and API Security Best Practices 337

Code Samples and Examples in Laravel 340

Implementing Transport Layer Security (TLS) for Email Communication 342

Key Reasons for Implementing TLS for Email Communication 342

Confidentiality 342

Configuring Laravel for TLS Email Communication 343

Summary 345

Chapter 7: Incident Response and Security Monitoring 347

Developing an Incident Response Plan 348

Identifying Stakeholders 348

Define Incident Severity Levels 349

Establish Communication Channels 351

Create an Incident Response Team (IRT) 354

Document PHP Application Architecture 356

Implement Monitoring and Logging 359

Define Incident Response Procedures 361

Test Incident Response Plan 363

Incident Reporting and Escalation 366

Post-incident Analysis and Improvement 368

Training and Awareness 371

TABLE OF CONTENTS

Legal and Regulatory Compliance 373
Incident Communication and Escalation Procedures 377
    Define Communication Channels 377
    Designate Communication Roles 377
    Incident Reporting Process 378
    Internal Communication Procedures 378
    External Communication Procedures 378
    Incident Severity Classification 379
    Escalation Matrix 379
    Response Time Objectives (RTOs) and Service-Level Agreements (SLAs) ... 379
    Incident Notification Templates 379
    Training and Awareness 380
    Documentation and Post-incident Analysis 380
    Legal and Regulatory Compliance 380
Forensic Analysis and Post-incident Analysis 381
Implementing Security Monitoring and Intrusion Detection Systems 384
Summary 386

Chapter 8: Future Trends in PHP Application Security 389

Emerging Security Threats and Attack Techniques 389
Advancements in Security Tools and Technologies 391
The Role of AI and Machine Learning in PHP Application Security 393
Integrating LLMs and Generative AI Technologies into PHP Application
Security 395
Securing Microservices and Serverless Architectures 397
    Implement Proper Authentication and Authorization 397
    Secure Communication Channels 397
    Apply the Principle of Least Privilege 398
    Implement Defense in Depth 398

TABLE OF CONTENTS

Monitor and Logging...398
Continuous Vulnerability Management..399
Secure Deployment and Configuration...399
Implement Rate Limiting and Throttling..399
Container and Function Security..399
Security Testing and Compliance...400
Summary..400

Index...403

About the Author

As an experienced software engineer, architect, and security enthusiast with over a decade of industry experience, **Satej Kumar Sahu** has dedicated his career to building robust and secure applications. Throughout his journey, he has encountered numerous challenges and witnessed the evolving landscape of PHP application security. With a passion for sharing knowledge and empowering fellow developers, he has decided to write this book as a comprehensive guide to PHP application security. Drawing from practical experiences, industry best practices, and a deep understanding of PHP development, his goal is to equip readers with the skills and insights needed to build secure and resilient PHP applications in today's threat landscape. He is excited to contribute to the community and help developers create secure software that withstands the ever-present risks of the digital world.

About the Technical Reviewer

Aravind Medamoni is a full-stack web application developer, mobile application developer, and software developer, currently living in Hyderabad. He has a Bachelor of Science in Computer Science from JNTUH. He is both driven and self-motivated and constantly experimenting with new technologies and techniques. He is very passionate about full-stack development and strives to better himself as a developer, and the development community as a whole, having proficiency in Java, Kotlin, Python, Dart, PHP, JavaScript, Node.js, Flutter, Android, Angular, React JS, Vue.js, Spring, MongoDB, and SQL. Aravind worked as a Tech Lead at OpenStackDC for one year as a Backend and Android Developer. Now he is working as a full-stack developer in Nisum. He also trained a lot of students to start their career in the software domain. He won a national-level hackathon in his career. Feel free to connect with him through aravindmedamoni@gmail.com.

Acknowledgments

I would like to dedicate this book to my parents for always believing in and having patience with me while I pursued my interest in technology and for giving me the freedom to explore and try different things. Also, thanks to my sister Lipsa for always being beside me whenever I needed her. I would like to thank all my teachers for being with me during my journey, Runish for the foundational mentoring support at the start of my career, Mindfire Solutions for my first career opportunity, and to all with whom I have had an opportunity to interact and learn from. Last but not least, I would like to thank Melissa for the awesome opportunity to write my second book and the wonderful team at Apress for all their support without whom this book would not have been possible.

Introduction

Today, we are seeing a major shift in how web applications are being built and particularly the importance of the "shift left" paradigm. With the shift left focus on security, there is increased responsibility on developers to build security in their design and code from the start. The stakes are too high to ignore, given the variety of compliance-specific industries we work across.

With this in mind, the book starts to give web application developers insight into the context of security in web applications, particularly in PHP.

There are a variety of applications a developer works in starting from green field projects, existing projects, hybrid ones (Kubernetes and OpenShift), and cloud native. To understand this and gain practical insights, the book focuses on security aspects which need to be understood and implemented while building core applications which do not use any frameworks, then proceeds to the security protocols behind various processes which help us build web applications, and finally security practices prevalent in enterprise frameworks like Laravel.

Software development lifecycle has many phases and security needs to be built into each phase from the very start. The book gives practical insights into discussing security with stakeholders, understanding the context of security in different phases like development, testing, deployment, infrastructure as cloud, cloud security, and maintenance.

The book finally details the future of security and some of the helpful tools which will be part of the developer lifecycle. There are concepts and code recipes shared throughout the book which are helpful not only for learning but also while working on real-world projects.

CHAPTER 1

Introduction to PHP Application Security

In this chapter, we will be discussing the general nature of application security and its importance in the context of PHP. In the security ecosystem, software engineers play a crucial role, and we will learn about their responsibilities in this evolving space of security-based development. Then we will touch base on the impact of security vulnerabilities while building PHP applications, learn about common attack vectors and threats. Finally, we will learn how to employ the principles of secure application development in PHP.

What Is Application Security?

Application security, often abbreviated as AppSec, is a crucial aspect of information security that focuses on protecting software applications from security threats and vulnerabilities. It encompasses a wide range of practices, tools, and methodologies designed to ensure the confidentiality, integrity, and availability (the CIA triad) of an application and its data.

How do we correlate this from a developer's perspective? As a developer, we are involved in the development of applications. While this is the simplest approach, there are other layers which come into effect when thinking about the practical world. Since this application would

CHAPTER 1   INTRODUCTION TO PHP APPLICATION SECURITY

not just be present in our laptops and would eventually be deployed and used throughout the world, security of the application becomes very important.

To give a simpler example, consider a castle. We can compare a castle to the application which we have built with its richness, beauty, and features. It's a delight to the world for people to visit.

But there's more to it than meets the eye. When viewed from the top, we see the different layers of sections and perimeters built while building the castle. I lay much stress on the word *while* and not after the castle was built. This adds the security aspect to it.

Let us discuss some additional context around application security.

Protection of Software Applications

Application security primarily deals with safeguarding software applications, including web applications, mobile apps, desktop software, and server-side applications, from various security risks and potential attacks. These applications hold many of the important assets for us like the intellectual property for our business, valuable user data of our customers which can be used or rather misused for a variety of purposes, and access to important resources like a nuclear plant which has tremendous potential but a liability when in the hands of the wrong person.

Identification of Vulnerabilities

A vulnerability is a weakness or flaw in a system, process, software, or network that can be exploited by a threat actor (such as a hacker) to gain unauthorized access, cause harm, or perform malicious activities. Vulnerabilities can result from various issues including design flaws, errors in code, misconfigurations, etc. Identifying and addressing vulnerabilities is crucial for maintaining the security and integrity of systems and data.

It involves identifying and addressing vulnerabilities within the application's code, configuration, and design that could be exploited by malicious actors. Common vulnerabilities include SQL injection, cross-site scripting (XSS), cross-site request forgery (CSRF), and insecure authentication mechanisms. We will discuss these more in the coming chapters.

Lifecycle Approach

Application security is not a one-time task; it's an ongoing process that spans the entire software development lifecycle (SDLC). It is a multistep end-to-end process integral to all parts and processes inherent to the system and has to be iterative to understand the current security environment and see that our system evolves to safeguard against them in a proactive stance. It starts from the initial design and continues through development, testing, deployment, and maintenance phases.

In the development stage, the application developer adds security in the code, configuration, CI/CD pipeline, and any other infrastructure part of the development environment like cloud, third-party APIs, etc. Once the development phase is done or many times while the development phase is continuing in iterative steps, the Quality Assurance (QA) team validates and tests the applications from a 360-degree outlook to consider the application for security and performance, taking into consideration the enterprise guidelines laid for the organization. Once the QA team approves it, then the application has to be deployed to production. Before that, the enterprise security team runs through all the design processes, templates, standards, and security guidelines and comes with feedback for the application. This whole process goes on iteratively since the application builds new features and there are new security hacks which have been shared in the security community which need to be validated against our application.

CHAPTER 1   INTRODUCTION TO PHP APPLICATION SECURITY

Security Testing

One of the fundamental components of application security is security testing. This includes activities such as quality assurance testing, penetration testing, vulnerability scanning, code review, and security-focused quality assurance to detect and rectify vulnerabilities. These are handled by many teams within an enterprise organization but also sometimes by a small team capable of such skills in a startup environment.

Secure Development Practices

Promoting secure coding practices is a key aspect of application security. We as developers need to follow guidelines and best practices to write code that is resistant to common vulnerabilities. These guidelines have been the result of many years of improvement and shared knowledge of working engineers, communities, and experts through incremental learning from mistakes and hacks from different parties both internal and external.

These guidelines vary from organization to organization, since each organization has their unique business model and domain and has different security requirements. An application related to the defense of a country will have a more extended and different set of guidelines than a web application catering to blogs for users. These guidelines and practices have always to be updated to be current in the security environment and with the evolving nature of the business model.

Authentication and Authorization

Authentication ensures we verify the users are who they say they are, while authorization ensures what the users are allowed to do. Both are crucial for the security of an application, ensuring that the application employs strong authentication mechanisms to verify the identity of users and enforces appropriate authorization to control access to data and features.

CHAPTER 1 INTRODUCTION TO PHP APPLICATION SECURITY

There are various industry standard protocols for implementing authentication and authorization. Some authentication protocols and frameworks to be named are password-based authentication, multifactor authentication (MFA), OAuth (Open Authorization), OpenID Connect, Kerberos, SAML (Security Assertion Markup Language), LDAP (Lightweight Directory Access Protocol), and JWT (JSON Web Token). Similarly, some authorization protocols and frameworks are OAuth 2.0, RBAC (Role-Based Access Control), ABAC (Attribute-Based Access Control), ACL (Access Control List), SAML, JWT, etc. We will explore some of these in the coming chapters to know more about them.

Data Protection

Protecting sensitive data is crucial. This involves encrypting data during transmission to ensure it can't be intercepted or read by unauthorized parties. Access controls are implemented so only authorized users can access the data. Additionally, secure storage practices are used to protect data at rest, ensuring it remains safe from breaches. These measures collectively help maintain the integrity and confidentiality of sensitive information.

Incident Response

An incident response plan is a structured approach outlining the steps to detect, respond to, and recover from security incidents or breaches. It ensures a systematic and efficient reaction to minimize damage and restore normal operations. A well-defined incident response plan is essential. This plan enables quick detection of security incidents or breaches, allowing for immediate action. It outlines procedures to contain the threat, preventing further damage, and provides steps to mitigate the impact. By having this plan in place, organizations can respond effectively to security incidents, minimizing potential harm and ensuring a swift recovery.

Compliance and Regulations

Compliance refers to adhering to laws, regulations, and industry standards relevant to an organization's operations. Regulations are the specific rules and guidelines established by governing bodies to ensure legal and ethical conduct. Ensuring compliance with relevant security regulations, industry standards, and legal requirements is critical. This involves aligning the application with the specific rules and guidelines based on its use case and the nature of the data it handles, thereby maintaining legal and operational integrity.

Importance of Security

In today's interconnected digital landscape, application security is of paramount importance. Neglecting it can lead to data breaches, financial losses, reputational damage, and legal consequences. Therefore, organizations must integrate robust application security practices into their development processes to mitigate risks and protect their applications and users from cyber threats.

Security is a critical aspect of building software applications, as it ensures the protection of sensitive data, maintains user trust, and prevents malicious attacks. In the context of banking, for example, applications must safeguard financial information. A breach can lead to severe financial losses for both individuals and institutions. The 2019 Capital One breach, where over 100 million credit card applications were compromised, highlights the devastating impact of inadequate security measures.

CHAPTER 1 INTRODUCTION TO PHP APPLICATION SECURITY

In the realm of healthcare, securing patient data is equally vital. Health records contain sensitive information that, if exposed, can lead to identity theft and privacy violations. The 2015 Anthem Inc. data breach, which exposed the personal information of nearly 80 million individuals, underscores the importance of robust security protocols in healthcare applications.

Data protection is another crucial area. Applications across various industries handle vast amounts of personal and sensitive data. Without proper security measures, this data is vulnerable to unauthorized access and misuse. The 2017 Equifax breach, which affected 147 million people, revealed the catastrophic consequences of poor data security practices.

Security in applications also involves ensuring compliance with regulations such as the General Data Protection Regulation (GDPR) and the Health Insurance Portability and Accountability Act (HIPAA). These regulations mandate stringent data protection measures to safeguard user information and ensure privacy. Failure to comply can result in hefty fines and legal repercussions, as seen in the case of Google, which was fined $57 million for GDPR violations in 2019.

Role of Application Developer in Security

Application developers play a critical role in ensuring the security of software applications. While security is often seen as the responsibility of security professionals, the development team has a significant influence on the security posture of an application.

With the use of modern practices in development, the practice of shift left where instead of giving the task of security to another team, some of these security responsibilities are expected of the developer. "Shift left" is a concept in the field of application security that emphasizes moving security practices and considerations earlier in the software development lifecycle (SDLC), specifically to the left side of the timeline. In the context

CHAPTER 1   INTRODUCTION TO PHP APPLICATION SECURITY

of application developers, "shift left" means involving developers in security activities and decisions as early as possible in the development process. This approach helps identify and address security issues sooner, reducing the cost and effort required to fix them later in the development cycle or after deployment.

Let's delve into the concept of "shift left" from a security perspective for application developers. The idea is simple but powerful: integrating security measures early in the software development process, rather than treating it as an afterthought. By doing so, we can build more secure applications from the ground up.

Firstly, early engagement is key. Imagine starting a project by sitting down with security experts to discuss the potential risks and vulnerabilities specific to your application. This proactive approach allows you to identify security goals, conduct threat modeling, and perform risk assessments at the planning stage. It's like laying a solid foundation for a building – essential for stability and safety.

Next, secure coding practices become part of your everyday workflow. Think of it as learning to cook with fresh ingredients; you start by using secure coding techniques to prevent common vulnerabilities like SQL injection, cross-site scripting (XSS), and cross-site request forgery (CSRF). By writing secure code from the beginning, you ensure your application is robust and resilient against attacks.

Integrating security tools into your development pipeline is another crucial step. Tools like static application security testing (SAST), dynamic application security testing (DAST), and interactive application security testing (IAST) provide real-time feedback. It's akin to having a seasoned chef tasting your dish at every step, ensuring it's perfect before it reaches the customer.

Security training for developers is equally important. By educating yourself about common security threats and attack vectors, you become better equipped to make informed, security-conscious decisions. Think of it as attending a cooking class where you learn new techniques and safety practices, making you a more skilled and cautious chef.

Regular code reviews within your team help catch security issues early. Peer feedback and insights from security experts can identify vulnerabilities before they become costly to fix. It's like having a fellow chef taste your dish and suggest improvements before you serve it.

Incorporating security checks into your Continuous Integration/Continuous Deployment (CI/CD) pipeline ensures that every code change is scrutinized for security flaws. This automated testing process acts like a quality control checkpoint, ensuring that security is maintained at every stage of development.

Secure design principles are also vital. During the design phase, make architectural decisions that prioritize security, such as data flow management, authentication methods, and access controls. It's like designing a restaurant with safety features in mind, ensuring a safe environment for both staff and customers.

Engaging in threat modeling exercises helps you identify potential security threats and vulnerabilities specific to your application. This proactive approach allows you to design appropriate security controls and countermeasures early. It's like anticipating kitchen hazards and implementing safety measures before they cause accidents.

Defining security requirements alongside functional requirements ensures that security is a fundamental aspect of your application's design and development. This holistic approach is akin to considering nutritional value alongside taste when creating a new dish, ensuring it's both delicious and healthy.

Finally, collaboration is crucial. Working closely with security professionals and other stakeholders ensures that security concerns are effectively addressed and that everyone understands their role in maintaining security. It's like running a successful restaurant where the chef, kitchen staff, and management work together seamlessly to deliver a great dining experience.

By embracing the "shift left" approach, developers can build applications that are not only functional and innovative but also secure from the outset. This proactive mindset fosters a culture of security, ultimately leading to more resilient and trustworthy software.

The shift left approach acknowledges that addressing security solely at the end of the development process or after deployment is inefficient and less effective at mitigating security risks. By involving developers early, integrating security into development workflows, and fostering a security-conscious culture, organizations can build more secure applications and reduce the likelihood of security incidents and breaches.

Now that we have understood what shifting left means in the security context, let us understand some of the key roles and responsibilities application developers have in application security:

1. Secure Coding Practices: Developers should follow secure coding practices to write code that is resistant to common security vulnerabilities. This includes input validation, output encoding, proper error handling, and avoiding risky coding patterns.

2. Vulnerability Identification and Remediation: Developers should be proactive in identifying and fixing security vulnerabilities in their code during development. They can use static analysis tools, code reviews, and security testing techniques to detect and address issues like SQL injection, XSS, CSRF, and more.

CHAPTER 1   INTRODUCTION TO PHP APPLICATION SECURITY

3. Secure Authentication and Authorization: Developers are responsible for implementing secure authentication and authorization mechanisms to ensure that only authorized users can access certain functionalities and data. They should avoid hard-coding credentials, use strong password hashing, and employ multifactor authentication where necessary.

4. Data Encryption: When handling sensitive data, developers should ensure that data is properly encrypted during transmission and storage. This includes using HTTPS for web applications and employing encryption algorithms for data at rest.

5. API Security: If the application interfaces with other services or APIs, developers should implement secure API design and authentication practices to prevent unauthorized access or data leakage.

6. Security Frameworks and Libraries: Utilizing well-established security libraries and frameworks can help developers implement security features more effectively. These libraries often have built-in security mechanisms and can help developers avoid reinventing the wheel.

7. Third-Party Component Security: Developers should carefully assess the security of third-party components, libraries, and APIs they integrate into their applications. Keeping these components up to date with security patches is crucial.

8. Security Training and Awareness: Developers should receive training in security best practices and stay up to date with the latest security threats and trends. This knowledge helps them make informed decisions during development.

9. Secure Deployment Practices: Developers often play a role in configuring and deploying applications. Ensuring that servers and databases are properly configured and access controls are appropriately set is part of their security responsibility.

10. Collaboration with Security Teams: Developers should collaborate with security professionals within their organization to understand security requirements, undergo security reviews, and address security findings promptly.

11. Code Reviews and Peer Feedback: Regular code reviews within development teams can help identify and correct security issues early in the development process. Peer feedback can be valuable for improving code security.

12. Incident Response: Developers should be familiar with the organization's incident response plan and know how to respond to security incidents promptly.

13. Testing and Quality Assurance: Participating in security testing activities, such as penetration testing and vulnerability scanning, helps developers identify and resolve security weaknesses.

CHAPTER 1 INTRODUCTION TO PHP APPLICATION SECURITY

Incorporating security practices into the development process from the beginning is essential for building resilient and secure applications. Developers who are security-aware and actively engage in security efforts contribute significantly to reducing the risk of security breaches and ensuring the safety of the application and its users.

Understanding the PHP Security Landscape

PHP, a popular server-side scripting language, is widely used in web development to create dynamic websites and web applications. However, like any technology, PHP is not without its security challenges. Understanding the PHP security landscape is crucial for developers, administrators, and anyone responsible for building and maintaining PHP-based applications.

PHP as a programming language does not and cannot stand alone and be foolproof within the security ecosystem. Securing PHP applications involves a multifaceted approach that encompasses core PHP security practices, framework-specific security considerations, and the broader security ecosystem. Understanding and addressing vulnerabilities and risks within each context is essential to building robust and resilient PHP applications. By adopting best practices and staying informed about evolving security threats, developers can enhance the security of their PHP applications and protect both their data and users from potential security breaches.

Let's delve a bit into each of these three contexts as shown in Figure 1-1.

Chapter 1 Introduction to PHP Application Security

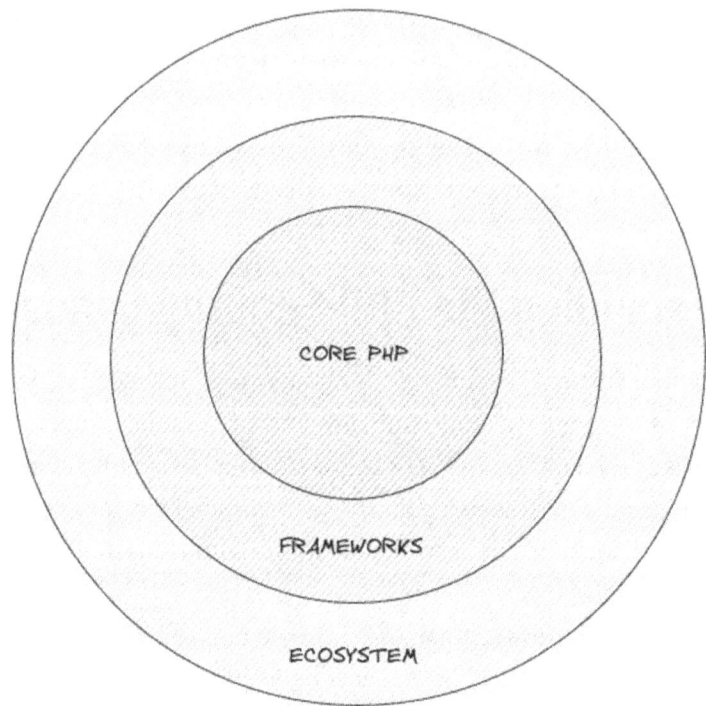

Figure 1-1. *PHP security landscape*

Core PHP Security

We can build an entire application, including a web server using just core PHP language constructs. Each of them has their challenges in terms of their limitations, potentials, and use case. As history stands, we have seen in the past many PHP applications built using simple code constructs without any framework to assist. With such an approach, a developer needs to know about what are the various attack vectors which can be used for different aspects like authentication, upload, etc. It becomes very challenging to also keep up to date with the nitty gritties as the digital world evolves.

Framework-Specific Security

Frameworks work on a different level. They handle some of the security aspects of different components through configurations and provide patches to address new security issues. They also handle the security aspects which come into play when integrating different components like your PHP application interacting to your database through secure channels which we will touch more in the coming chapters.

Ecosystem Security

While PHP and the supporting frameworks exist, they have to exist in the wider digital world which has its own dynamics. For example, PHP can run on an operating system like Linux, and Linux has its own security aspects to deal with. Similarly, there are other components like HTTP 1/2/3, TCP layers, and various others which we will discuss in the coming chapters.

The Impact of Security Vulnerabilities in PHP Applications

When we talk about the impact of security vulnerabilities in PHP applications, it's important to understand the breadth and depth of the potential consequences. These vulnerabilities can affect organizations in numerous ways, ranging from data breaches to operational inefficiencies. Let's explore these impacts in detail, enriched with real-world examples to bring the concepts to life.

Data Breaches

Data breaches are among the most damaging consequences of security vulnerabilities in PHP applications. When attackers exploit these vulnerabilities, they gain unauthorized access to sensitive data. This data can include user credentials, personal information, financial data, and confidential business information.

Consider the infamous Yahoo data breaches of 2013 and 2014, which exposed the personal information of over three billion accounts. The fallout included a significant loss of user trust, legal repercussions, and a hefty financial impact, ultimately affecting Yahoo's sale price during its acquisition by Verizon.

Financial Loss

Security vulnerabilities can lead to substantial financial losses. These losses occur due to several factors such as remediation costs, application downtime, and fines for noncompliance with regulations like GDPR.

For instance, the Target data breach in 2013 resulted in an estimated $162 million in expenses for the company. These costs included compensation to affected customers, legal fees, and the implementation of enhanced security measures.

Reputation Damage

A security breach can severely damage an organization's reputation. Rebuilding trust after such an incident can be challenging and time-consuming.

Take the example of Equifax, which suffered a massive data breach in 2017, exposing sensitive information of 147 million people. The breach led to a significant loss of consumer trust and long-lasting damage to Equifax's reputation, highlighted by extensive media coverage and scrutiny.

Operational Disruption

Security vulnerabilities can disrupt normal operations. These disruptions might include application unavailability due to attacks or exploits and resource diversion to handle security incidents.

A notable case is the WannaCry ransomware attack in 2017, which affected numerous organizations worldwide, including the UK's National Health Service (NHS). The attack caused significant operational disruptions, delaying medical treatments and services.

Legal Consequences

Security vulnerabilities can result in severe legal problems for organizations. These issues include regulatory fines and lawsuits from affected individuals or entities.

For example, the GDPR fine imposed on British Airways in 2018 after a data breach resulted in a proposed fine of £183 million. This incident underlines the importance of complying with data protection laws to avoid substantial financial penalties.

User Impact

Security vulnerabilities directly impact users by potentially leading to identity theft, financial loss, and privacy invasion.

The data breach at Adobe in 2013 exposed the personal data of 38 million users. This incident resulted in numerous users experiencing unauthorized access to their accounts and identity theft, emphasizing the importance of robust security measures.

Mitigation Costs

Organizations must invest in mitigating security vulnerabilities, which includes implementing security measures, conducting penetration testing, and providing security training.

For instance, after the Sony Pictures hack in 2014, the company invested heavily in improving its cybersecurity infrastructure and training its employees, which was a costly but necessary endeavor to prevent future breaches.

Long-Term Impact

The repercussions of security incidents can have long-lasting effects, such as loss of market share, increased regulatory scrutiny, and resource reallocation.

Post-breach, companies like Equifax have faced increased scrutiny and more stringent compliance requirements, which necessitate ongoing investments in security and compliance measures.

Damage Beyond the Application

Security vulnerabilities can extend their impact beyond the application itself, affecting the entire IT infrastructure and supply chain.

The 2018 attack on the software company, SolarWinds, demonstrated how vulnerabilities in one company's software could compromise multiple organizations, including government agencies and private enterprises, through interconnected systems.

CHAPTER 1   INTRODUCTION TO PHP APPLICATION SECURITY

Operational Inefficiency

Insecure applications lead to operational inefficiencies due to continuous monitoring and emergency response efforts required to address security threats.

Organizations like the NHS faced operational inefficiencies during the WannaCry attack, where emergency responses took precedence over routine operations, leading to significant disruptions and inefficiencies.

Common Attack Vectors and Threats

As technology advances, cybersecurity threats and attack vectors continue to evolve. Understanding these common attack vectors is crucial for safeguarding systems and data. Let's review a more detailed overview of these threats, incorporating real-world examples and subheadings to create a narrative that is both informative and engaging.

Phishing Attacks

Phishing involves tricking individuals into revealing sensitive information or clicking malicious links. Attackers use deceptive emails, websites, or messages to impersonate trusted entities, such as banks or social media platforms. This method is alarmingly effective; for instance, the 2016 phishing attack on John Podesta, Hillary Clinton's campaign chairman, led to the leak of thousands of private emails, demonstrating the far-reaching impact of such schemes.

Malware

Malware, short for malicious software, includes viruses, worms, Trojans, and ransomware. These programs infiltrate systems to steal data or cause damage. One notable example is the WannaCry ransomware attack in 2017, which infected over 200,000 computers across 150 countries, crippling healthcare systems and businesses by encrypting data and demanding ransom payments.

Denial-of-Service (DoS) and Distributed Denial-of-Service (DDoS) Attacks

DoS attacks overwhelm a target system or network, rendering it inaccessible to users. DDoS attacks involve multiple compromised devices to amplify the scale of the attack. In 2016, the Dyn DNS DDoS attack disrupted major websites like Twitter, Netflix, and Reddit, highlighting how DDoS attacks can cripple online services and cause widespread disruption.

SQL Injection

SQL injection attacks exploit poorly sanitized user inputs to manipulate SQL queries, allowing attackers to access, modify, or delete database data. The 2014 breach of AT&T's network, where attackers used SQL injection to access sensitive customer information, underscores the importance of proper input validation and parameterized queries.

Cross-Site Scripting (XSS)

XSS attacks inject malicious scripts into web applications, which are executed by unsuspecting users. This can lead to cookie theft, session hijacking, or website defacement. A well-known incident occurred in 2005 with the Samy worm on MySpace, which used XSS to spread rapidly and compromised over a million user profiles.

Cross-Site Request Forgery (CSRF)

CSRF attacks trick users into performing actions on a website without their consent, often leading to unauthorized transactions or data manipulation. Implementing anti-CSRF tokens and secure coding practices are essential defenses. The attack on GitHub in 2012, which exploited CSRF to delete user repositories, highlights the potential damage of such vulnerabilities.

Man-in-the-Middle (MitM) Attacks

MitM attackers intercept communications between two parties to eavesdrop, modify data, or impersonate one party. Secure communication protocols like HTTPS and public key infrastructure (PKI) are critical for protection. The 2013 NSA surveillance scandal, involving extensive MitM techniques, revealed the importance of robust encryption and secure communications.

Social Engineering

Social engineering manipulates individuals to disclose confidential information, such as passwords or access codes. Techniques include pretexting, baiting, and tailgating. The 2011 RSA breach, where attackers used social engineering to gain access to secure data, shows how human vulnerabilities can be exploited.

Insider Threats

Insider threats involve malicious or negligent actions by employees, contractors, or business partners. These insiders may steal data, compromise systems, or inadvertently cause breaches. The Snowden leaks in 2013, where Edward Snowden exposed NSA surveillance activities, illustrate the significant risk posed by insider threats.

Zero-Day Vulnerabilities

Zero-day vulnerabilities are undisclosed software flaws that attackers exploit before developers can create patches or updates. Regular software updates and vulnerability assessments help protect against these threats. The Stuxnet worm, discovered in 2010, exploited multiple zero-day vulnerabilities to sabotage Iran's nuclear program, showcasing the potential impact of such attacks.

Credential Theft

Attackers steal usernames and passwords through keyloggers, brute-force attacks, or password guessing. Multifactor authentication (MFA) and strong password policies are essential defenses. The LinkedIn breach in 2012, which exposed over 117 million user credentials, highlights the critical need for robust authentication measures.

IoT Vulnerabilities

Internet of Things (IoT) devices often lack robust security measures, making them prime targets for attackers. Vulnerabilities in IoT devices can lead to privacy breaches, network compromise, or distributed attacks. The Mirai botnet attack in 2016, which leveraged IoT devices to execute a massive DDoS attack, underscores these risks.

Cryptojacking

Cryptojacking involves hijacking devices to mine cryptocurrencies without the owner's consent. Attackers leverage the processing power of compromised systems for financial gain. The widespread cryptojacking campaign in 2018, which infected thousands of websites and servers, demonstrated the growing threat of this malicious activity.

CHAPTER 1   INTRODUCTION TO PHP APPLICATION SECURITY

Supply Chain Attacks

Supply chain attacks target the software supply chain, compromising products or services before they reach users. Attackers may inject malware or backdoors into software updates. The 2020 SolarWinds attack, where hackers inserted malware into a software update, affecting numerous government and private organizations, exemplifies the severe impact of supply chain compromises.

Advanced Persistent Threats (APTs)

APTs are long-term, targeted attacks conducted by skilled adversaries. These attackers maintain persistence in a compromised network for extended periods, exfiltrating sensitive data or conducting espionage. The APT attack on Sony Pictures in 2014, attributed to North Korean hackers, resulted in significant data loss and operational disruption, highlighting the danger of such sophisticated threats.

Understanding these common attack vectors and threats is essential for implementing effective cybersecurity measures. Organizations must adopt a proactive approach, including regular security assessments, employee training, and the deployment of security tools to mitigate these risks and protect their digital assets. By staying informed and vigilant, developers and security professionals can better safeguard systems against evolving cyber threats.

Principles of Secure PHP Application Development

In today's digital age, developing secure PHP applications is not just a best practice; it's a necessity. Security vulnerabilities can lead to data breaches, financial losses, and damage to an organization's reputation.

CHAPTER 1   INTRODUCTION TO PHP APPLICATION SECURITY

As developers, it's our responsibility to build resilient applications by following security best practices throughout the development lifecycle. Let's explore some key principles of secure PHP application development, sharing insights and practical examples along the way.

Security by Design

When starting a new project, it's essential to incorporate security into the application's design from the outset. This approach is much more effective and cost-efficient than trying to add security measures later.

- Secure Architecture: Before diving into coding, take a step back and consider how your application will be structured. For example, if you're designing an e-commerce site, think about how to securely handle payment processing and customer data. Using microservices can help isolate different parts of your application, reducing the potential impact of a security breach.

- Threat Modeling: At the planning stage, we need to identify potential threats to the application. Imagine you're developing a social media platform; a threat model might reveal risks such as unauthorized data access or account takeovers. By understanding these risks early, we can prioritize security measures to address them.

CHAPTER 1   INTRODUCTION TO PHP APPLICATION SECURITY

Secure Coding Practices

Writing secure code is fundamental to PHP application security. It's like cooking a meal with fresh, high-quality ingredients – essential for a good outcome.

- Input Validation: We should always validate and sanitize user inputs. For instance, if our application accepts email addresses, using PHP's filter functions to ensure the input is a valid email format can prevent malicious data from causing harm.

- Output Encoding: When displaying user-generated content, using output encoding functions like "htmlspecialchars()" helps prevent XSS attacks by ensuring that user input is treated as plain text, not executable code.

- Parameterized Queries: Avoiding dynamic SQL queries that include user inputs is crucial. Instead, we should use prepared statements to interact with the database. This method effectively protects against SQL injection attacks, which have caused major breaches in the past, such as the one that hit Heartland Payment Systems in 2008.

Authentication and Authorization

Controlling access to our application's resources is crucial. It's like having a secure lock on your front door – only authorized people should get in.

- Strong Password Policies: Implementing strong password policies that require complex passwords and regular updates helps protect user accounts from being easily hacked.

- Multifactor Authentication (MFA): Adding MFA is like having an extra lock on your door. Even if someone steals a password, they'd still need a second factor to gain access. Google's use of MFA has significantly reduced phishing attacks on its accounts.

- Least Privilege Principle: We should grant users only the permissions they need. If our application has different user roles, ensuring each role has the minimum necessary access limits the damage if an account is compromised.

Session Management

Proper session management is vital to keeping user sessions secure.

- Secure Session Tokens: Using secure and random session tokens can prevent session hijacking. Regenerating session IDs upon login adds an extra layer of security.

- Session Timeout: Implementing session timeouts to automatically log users out after a period of inactivity protects accounts from unauthorized access if someone leaves their device unattended.

- Session Storage: Storing session data securely on the server, not on the client side, prevents unauthorized access.

File Uploads

Allowing users to upload files can introduce security risks if not handled correctly.

- File Type Verification: Ensuring uploaded files match expected formats is crucial. For example, if our application accepts image uploads, verifying that the file is indeed an image and not a disguised executable is important.

- File Storage: Storing uploaded files in a directory that isn't directly accessible from the Web and using a secure method to serve files prevents direct access to potentially harmful content.

Error Handling and Logging

How we handle errors can make a big difference in security.

- Custom Error Pages: Displaying generic error messages to users while hiding sensitive information that could help an attacker understand our application's inner workings is a best practice.

- Security Logging: Keeping logs of security-related events and monitoring them regularly can help us detect and respond to potential threats before they cause significant damage.

Security Updates and Patch Management

Keeping our software up to date is like regular maintenance for our car – it keeps things running smoothly and securely.

- Vulnerability Assessments: We need to regularly scan our application and its dependencies for known vulnerabilities. Tools like OWASP Dependency-Check can help us stay on top of this.

- Security News: Staying informed about the latest security advisories and vulnerabilities related to our technology stack helps us react quickly to new threats.

Secure Communication

Ensuring that data transmitted between clients and our PHP application is secure is crucial.

- HTTPS: We should always use HTTPS to encrypt data in transit. This protects sensitive information, such as login credentials and personal data, from being intercepted.

- HTTP Security Headers: Implementing headers like Content Security Policy (CSP) and Strict Transport Security (HSTS) enhances security. These headers provide additional protection against various attack vectors.

Security Testing and Code Reviews

Regular testing and reviews are essential to maintaining a secure application.

- Penetration Testing: Conducting regular penetration tests to identify vulnerabilities and weaknesses in our application's security is a proactive approach that helps us fix issues before they can be exploited.

- Code Reviews: Regularly reviewing code for security issues, involving peers or security experts, helps catch potential security flaws early and improves the overall security posture of our application.

Incident Response Plan

Having a plan in place for when things go wrong is crucial.

- Plan Documentation: Documenting the steps to follow during a security incident, including communication and remediation procedures, ensures a quick and efficient response.

- Training: Training our team to recognize and respond to security incidents, and conducting regular drills, ensures everyone knows their role and can act swiftly during an actual incident.

CHAPTER 1   INTRODUCTION TO PHP APPLICATION SECURITY

Summary

In this chapter, we explored the importance of securing PHP applications against various threats and vulnerabilities. It emphasizes the need for a security-first approach in the development process, starting with threat modeling and implementing secure architecture. It highlights key security practices such as secure coding, authentication, session management, and file upload handling. It also covers essential aspects of communication security, vulnerability management, and incident response planning. The main takeaways are that building secure PHP applications requires proactive measures, continuous learning, and adaptation to emerging threats.

CHAPTER 2

PHP Core Security

PHP is one of the most widely used programming languages in the world, and as such, it is also susceptible to security threats. This chapter will cover the security considerations related to the PHP core and provide practical guidance for securing PHP code. As a result, it is essential for developers to take appropriate measures to ensure the security of their PHP applications. From secure PHP configuration to secure file handling, this chapter will cover everything you need to know to build a safe and secure PHP application. By the end of this chapter, readers will have a solid foundation in PHP security and be able to write their own secure code.

As discussed in the previous chapter, we will be focusing on Core PHP and later delve into frameworks and ecosystems. Figure 2-1 shares the three concentric circles which illustrate the layered security approach to protecting web applications. At the core is Core PHP, representing the foundation of code that requires protection from vulnerabilities and attacks. The second layer, Frameworks and Libraries, supports Core PHP with additional layers of security, such as input validation, authentication, and authorization. The outermost circle represents the Ecosystem, encompassing external factors like HTTP protocols, third-party integrations, and user interactions. This ecosystem requires protection from common web attacks, such as SQL injection, cross-site scripting (XSS), and denial-of-service (DoS) attacks.

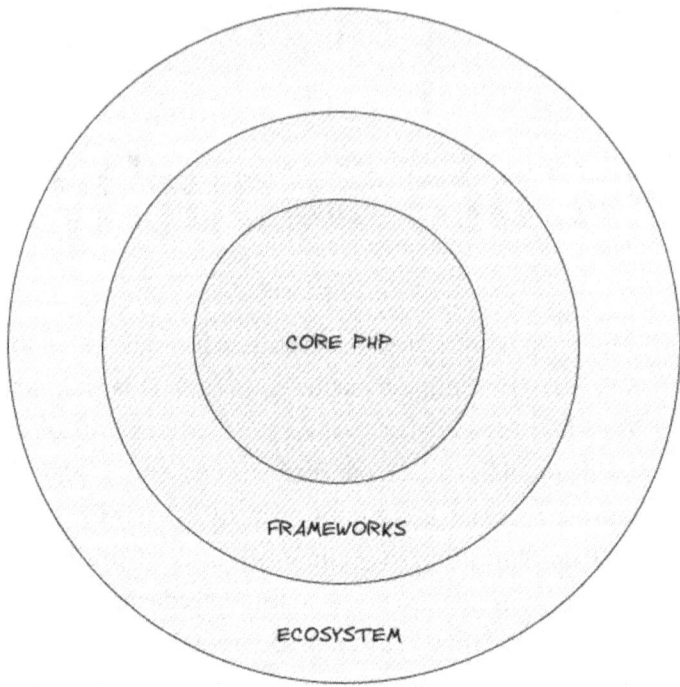

Figure 2-1. *Web development in layers: a visual representation*

The Great PHP Update Debate

Imagine you're running a popular restaurant, but you've been using a recipe book from ten years ago. You think it's still good, but little do you know, some of the ingredients are actually poisonous! That's what happens when your website uses an outdated version of PHP.

Why Does PHP Version Matters?

The PHP version you are using is critically important from a security perspective. The PHP development team continually releases new versions to address security vulnerabilities and improve the overall security of the language. Let's discuss a few reasons why keeping your PHP version up to date is crucial.

Security Updates

Let's delve into the importance of security updates, particularly in the context of PHP versions. One of the primary reasons for updating to newer PHP versions is the inclusion of security patches. These patches address vulnerabilities that have been discovered in previous versions. By running an outdated PHP version, we are essentially leaving our web application exposed to these known security issues, which can be exploited by malicious actors.

Think of it this way: just as you wouldn't leave the doors of your house unlocked if you knew there had been break-ins in the neighborhood, you shouldn't leave your web server vulnerable to attacks that have known solutions. Keeping PHP up to date is like reinforcing the locks and adding security cameras; it's an essential measure to ensure that your server is protected against known threats.

Moreover, staying current with PHP updates doesn't just protect you from existing vulnerabilities; it also helps mitigate the risks associated with new types of attacks. Cybersecurity is an ever-evolving field, and attackers are constantly finding new ways to exploit software. By regularly updating PHP, you benefit from the latest security research and improvements made by the community and the developers maintaining the language.

Also updating PHP can also help maintain compliance with industry standards and regulations. Many compliance frameworks require that you keep your software up to date to ensure the security of sensitive data. By neglecting updates, you not only risk the security of your application but also potential legal and financial repercussions.

Another point to consider is the impact on your reputation. If your web application is compromised due to running an outdated PHP version, it can lead to data breaches, loss of customer trust, and damage to your brand's reputation. In today's digital age, news of security breaches spreads quickly, and customers are increasingly aware of the importance of data security. Demonstrating that we take security seriously by keeping our software updated can enhance your credibility and trustworthiness.

End of Life (EOL)

Let's explore the concept of End of Life (EOL) for PHP versions and why it is crucial for us to stay informed about the support lifecycle of the software we are using. PHP, like many other software products, has a limited support lifecycle. This means that each version of PHP is actively maintained and supported for a certain period, after which it reaches its EOL.

When a PHP version reaches its EOL, it no longer receives official updates. This includes not only feature enhancements and bug fixes but also, most critically, security patches. Security patches are essential as they address vulnerabilities that have been discovered in the software. If we continue to use an EOL PHP version, we are missing out on these crucial updates.

Imagine this scenario: we have a robust security system for our house, but over time, new types of locks and alarms are developed to counter more advanced burglary techniques. If we don't update our security system, it becomes easier for burglars to break in. Similarly, by using an EOL PHP version, our application remains exposed to vulnerabilities that have been identified but not patched, making it an easy target for attackers.

Moreover, using an EOL version can have significant implications for compliance and legal responsibilities. Many regulatory frameworks require organizations to use supported and up-to-date software to protect sensitive data. By running an unsupported PHP version, we may be in violation of these requirements, which could result in fines, penalties, or legal action.

Relying on an EOL PHP version can also impact the performance and reliability of our web application. As new PHP versions are released, they often include optimizations and improvements that enhance the performance and stability of our application. Sticking with an outdated version means we are not benefiting from these enhancements, which could affect our application's efficiency and user experience.

The broader PHP community and third-party developers often stop supporting older versions once they reach EOL. This means that we might find it increasingly difficult to get help, find compatible libraries, or integrate with other modern software solutions.

Best Practices

Let's discuss the importance of adhering to best practices when it comes to using PHP, particularly regarding security. New PHP versions frequently introduce improvements and changes in security best practices. These updates are crucial for maintaining the security and integrity of our web applications.

New PHP versions often include enhancements in default settings. These default settings are configured to provide better security out of the box, reducing the need for us to manually tweak configurations to achieve a secure setup. By staying current with PHP updates, we ensure that our applications automatically benefit from these improved defaults.

Newer PHP versions deprecate insecure features. Deprecation is a critical process where features that are no longer considered safe or efficient are phased out. Continuing to use outdated features can leave our application vulnerable to attacks that exploit these weaknesses. By updating to the latest PHP version, we avoid relying on these deprecated, insecure features, thus reducing our risk exposure.

Modern security mechanisms are regularly adopted in new PHP versions. These mechanisms might include improvements in encryption algorithms, better session management, and more robust input validation techniques. Using the latest PHP version ensures that we can leverage these advanced security measures to protect our applications and data more effectively.

By keeping our PHP version up to date, we are better positioned to comply with security guidelines and standards. Many security frameworks and compliance requirements evolve over time to incorporate the latest best practices. Using the latest PHP version helps us stay aligned with these evolving standards, making it easier to achieve and maintain compliance.

Performance and Efficiency

Let's explore the performance and efficiency benefits of using the latest PHP versions. Beyond security enhancements, new PHP versions often bring significant performance improvements. These improvements can indirectly enhance security by making your application more resilient to certain types of attacks. Faster and more efficient code execution is one of the key benefits of updating PHP. With each new version, the PHP development team optimizes the core engine to run code faster and use fewer resources. This can lead to noticeable improvements in the speed and responsiveness of your web application.

Improved performance can help mitigate the risk of resource exhaustion attacks. These attacks, such as denial-of-service (DoS) attacks, aim to overwhelm your server by consuming excessive CPU, memory, or bandwidth. When your PHP code runs more efficiently, it requires fewer resources to handle each request. This means your server can handle a higher volume of traffic without becoming overloaded, making it harder for attackers to succeed in resource exhaustion attempts.

Better performance also contributes to a smoother user experience. Faster page load times and quicker response rates can significantly enhance user satisfaction and engagement. In today's fast-paced digital environment, users expect web applications to be quick and responsive. Keeping your PHP version up to date ensures that you can meet these expectations and provide a positive user experience. Efficiency improvements in new PHP versions often include enhanced memory management and optimized functions. These enhancements can reduce the likelihood of memory leaks and other issues that can degrade performance over time. By running the latest PHP version, you benefit from these optimizations, ensuring that your application remains stable and performs well under varying loads.

Compatibility

Let's consider the compatibility challenges that can arise when upgrading PHP, alongside the need to maintain a balance between security and compatibility. While newer PHP versions offer numerous benefits, they can sometimes introduce compatibility issues with older code or deprecated functions. Addressing these issues is crucial to ensure the smooth operation of your web application. Upgrading PHP can lead to situations where certain functions or features your application relies on have been deprecated or removed. This can cause parts of your application to break or behave unexpectedly. It's essential to thoroughly test your application in a staging environment before deploying a new PHP version to production. This testing phase allows you to identify and address any compatibility issues that may arise.

Maintaining a balance between security and compatibility requires careful planning and proactive management. While it's tempting to delay updates to avoid the hassle of fixing compatibility issues, relying on outdated PHP versions due to compatibility concerns is not a sustainable long-term strategy. Outdated versions not only leave your application vulnerable to security threats but also miss out on performance improvements and new features.

A sustainable approach involves regularly updating and refactoring your code base to support newer PHP versions. This might include replacing deprecated functions with their modern equivalents, optimizing your code for better performance, and ensuring that your application adheres to current best practices. Refactoring your code base can be a significant undertaking, but it pays off in terms of improved security, performance, and maintainability.

Adopting a proactive stance toward compatibility involves staying informed about upcoming PHP changes and preparing your application in advance. PHP's official documentation and community resources provide valuable insights into changes introduced in new versions. By keeping an eye on these resources, you can anticipate potential issues and plan your updates accordingly. Additionally, we think leveraging automated testing can help streamline the process of identifying compatibility issues. Writing unit tests and integration tests for your application ensures that you can quickly detect when an update causes problems. Automated tests provide a safety net, allowing you to make changes with confidence and reducing the risk of introducing new bugs.

Vendor and Application Support

Let's explore the importance of staying current with PHP versions, especially in the context of vendor and application support. Many applications and content management systems (CMS) have specific PHP version requirements to function correctly and securely. Keeping our

PHP version up to date is crucial for ensuring compatibility and taking advantage of the latest features and security improvements.

Applications and CMS platforms often specify the minimum and recommended PHP versions for their software. These requirements are set to ensure that the software runs efficiently and securely. By adhering to these version requirements, we can avoid potential issues that might arise from using an unsupported PHP version. This ensures that the features and functionalities of the application or CMS work as intended, providing a smooth user experience. Staying up to date with PHP versions also means we can leverage the latest features introduced in newer versions. These features can include improvements in performance, security, and developer productivity. For instance, new PHP versions might offer enhanced syntax, better error handling, or more efficient functions, all of which can contribute to writing cleaner and more maintainable code.

Security improvements in newer PHP versions are another critical aspect. Vendors and application developers often release updates and patches that depend on the security enhancements provided by the latest PHP versions. By keeping our PHP version current, we ensure that our applications benefit from these security improvements, reducing the risk of vulnerabilities and potential exploits. Running a supported PHP version ensures that we can receive timely support and updates from the vendors of the applications and CMS platforms we use. If we encounter issues or need assistance, vendors are more likely to provide support if our environment meets their version requirements. Using an outdated PHP version can lead to difficulties in obtaining support, as vendors may not address issues related to unsupported versions.

In the context of a CMS, using an up-to-date PHP version can enhance the overall security and performance of our website. Content management systems like WordPress, Joomla, and Drupal regularly update their platforms to take advantage of the latest PHP features and security patches. By keeping PHP updated, we ensure that our CMS runs optimally and securely, protecting our website and its data. Maintaining an up-to-date

PHP version is essential for ensuring compatibility with the software and applications we use. It allows us to take advantage of the latest features and security improvements while ensuring that we can receive timely support from vendors. Regularly updating PHP should be a key part of our strategy to maintain a secure, efficient, and well-supported application environment.

Secure PHP Configuration

PHP configuration refers to the settings and parameters that control the behavior and functionality of the PHP scripting language on a web server. As a server-side scripting language commonly used for web development, PHP can be configured to suit the specific requirements of a web application. These configuration settings are typically defined in configuration files and can be adjusted at both the server level and the application level.

Understanding and implementing secure PHP configuration is crucial for maintaining the security and performance of our web applications. By configuring PHP properly, we can mitigate potential vulnerabilities and ensure that our server operates efficiently. One important aspect of PHP configuration is setting appropriate error reporting levels. Displaying errors on a production server can expose sensitive information to attackers. Instead of displaying errors, it's essential to log them, which helps in troubleshooting without compromising security.

For example, imagine you have a web application that processes user data. If an error occurs and the application displays the error message, it might reveal the structure of your database or other sensitive details. By logging the error instead, you can keep this information secure while still being able to diagnose and fix the issue.

Figure 2-2 describes key aspects around PHP configuration.

CHAPTER 2 PHP CORE SECURITY

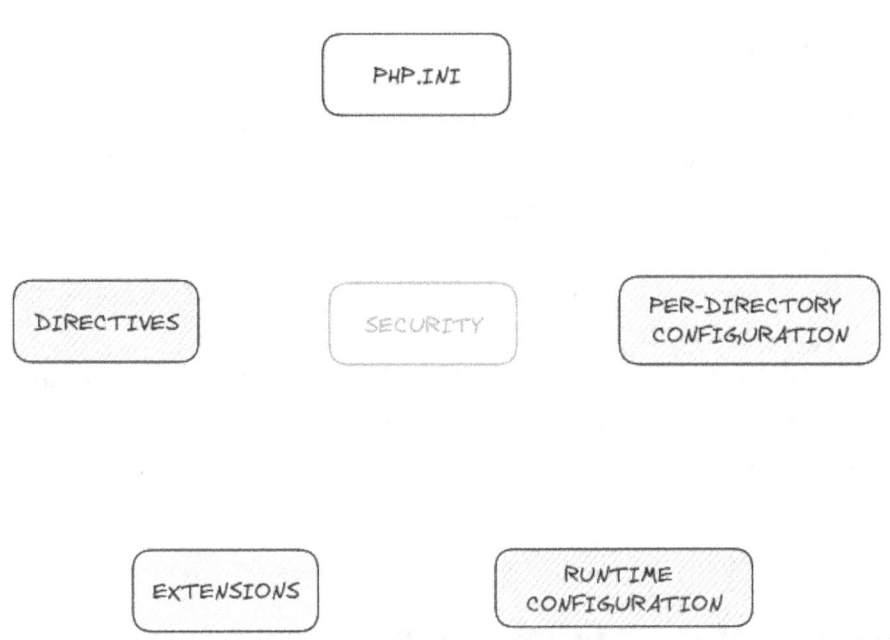

Figure 2-2. *Key aspects around PHP configuration relevant to security*

php.ini

Let's dive into secure PHP configuration, a key aspect of ensuring our web applications run smoothly and safely. Think of PHP configuration as the instructions we give to our PHP server on how it should behave. The primary configuration file for PHP is called "php.ini." This file contains a wide range of settings that affect how PHP operates, including error reporting, resource limits, security features, and extensions (modules). We can find the php.ini file on our web server, usually located in a directory like /etc/php/ on Linux or C:\php\ on Windows.

Directives

PHP configuration settings are referred to as directives. These directives control various aspects of PHP, such as memory limits, file upload limits, error display, database connections, and more. Each directive has a name, a value, and a scope (e.g., global, per-directory, or per-script). We can change the values of these directives in the php.ini file or in our application code using the ini_set() function.

Imagine we're running a lemonade stand, and we need to decide how much sugar to use per gallon. The directive is like a recipe instruction: "Use two cups of sugar per gallon." If we want a sweeter lemonade just for one batch, we can adjust this instruction for that batch only, much like using ini_set() for a specific script.

Per-Directory Configuration

In addition to the global php.ini file, we can also have per-directory PHP configuration settings in a .htaccess file for Apache web servers or a .user.ini file in some environments. These per-directory settings can override global settings for specific directories or applications.

Think of it as making different rules for different rooms in our house. The kitchen might have a rule to keep the fridge door closed, but the living room has a rule to always keep the curtains open. Similarly, per-directory configurations let us customize PHP settings for different parts of our application.

Runtime Configuration

We can also adjust PHP configuration dynamically during runtime using functions like ini_set() or by modifying the configuration array, $_SERVER['PHP_INI_USER']. Imagine we're playing a video game, and we can change the difficulty level mid-game. Using ini_set() is like changing the game's settings on the fly to make it easier or harder as we play.

Extensions

PHP can be extended with various modules and extensions to enable specific features or functionalities. Some extensions are included by default, while others need to be explicitly enabled or installed. These extensions may have their own configuration settings.

Think of extensions as adding new tools to our kitchen. We might start with a basic set of pots and pans (default extensions), but if we want to make pasta, we might need to add a pasta maker (an additional extension). Each new tool might come with its own set of instructions.

Security

PHP configuration is crucial for maintaining the security of our web application. We can control features like register_globals, open_basedir, and disable dangerous functions to enhance security.

For example, imagine our lemonade stand has a security system. We set rules like "Don't let strangers behind the counter" (disabling dangerous functions) and "Only mix ingredients in the kitchen" (setting open_basedir). These rules help keep our lemonade stand (and our PHP application) safe.

Common Settings

Some common PHP configuration settings include display_errors (to control error reporting), max_execution_time (to limit script execution time), memory_limit (to restrict memory usage), and many others. Picture our lemonade stand again. display_errors is like deciding whether to put up a sign saying "Oops, we're out of lemons!" in front of customers. max_execution_time is like setting a timer for how long we let the lemonade mix. memory_limit is like limiting the number of lemons we can use in one go.

Understanding PHP configuration helps us optimize the performance and security of our web applications, ensuring they work as expected. However, we should be cautious when modifying configuration settings, as misconfigurations can lead to security vulnerabilities or unexpected behavior in our applications. Now that we have a basic understanding of what configurations are in PHP and how they work, let's focus on how some of these configurations help us enhance security. For a more extensive look at all available configurations, we can always refer to the PHP manual.

The PHP manual can be referred for an extensive look at all available configurations.

PHP configurations play a significant role in enhancing the security of web applications. Properly configuring PHP settings can help protect your application against various security threats and vulnerabilities. Let's discuss some specific examples of how PHP configurations can improve security.

Error Reporting ("display_errors", "error_reporting")

Properly configuring error reporting settings can help prevent sensitive information from being exposed to potential attackers. By setting display_errors to "Off" and configuring error_reporting to report only essential errors, you can ensure that error messages do not leak critical information about your application, such as database credentials or server paths.

For example: Imagine your website is a shop with a back office where staff work. If the office door (error reporting) is left wide open and anyone can see inside, customers might accidentally see sensitive information like employee schedules or stock levels. By closing the door (setting display_errors to "Off") and only allowing essential staff inside (using error_reporting wisely), you keep this information secure.

```
expose_php                  = Off
error_reporting             = E_ALL
display_errors              = Off
display_startup_errors      = Off
log_errors                  = On
error_log                   = /valid_path/PHP-logs/php_error.log
ignore_repeated_errors      = Off
```

Example:

```php
display_errors = Off
error_reporting = E_ALL & ~E_NOTICE & ~E_WARNING
```

Let's go through each of the PHP configuration settings in Figure 2-3 in the context of their security implications.

"expose_php = Off"

Setting expose_php to "Off" is a security best practice. When exposed, PHP information, such as the PHP version and server information, can be visible in HTTP response headers. This information can be exploited by attackers to identify potential vulnerabilities or outdated software. By turning off the exposure of PHP, you make it more challenging for attackers to gather information about your server's configuration.

For example: Imagine your house number (PHP version) is prominently displayed on your front door. If a thief knows which houses have outdated security systems based on house numbers, they can target those houses. By hiding your house number (setting expose_php to "Off"), you make it harder for thieves to figure out your security setup.

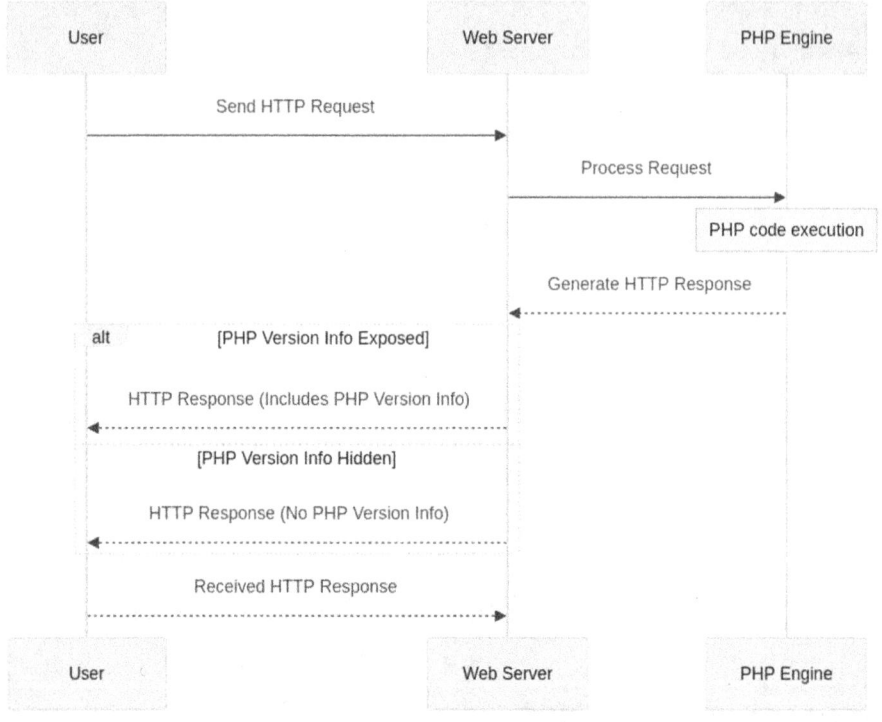

Figure 2-3. *Request-response sequence displaying PHP version info exposure*

"error_reporting = E_ALL"

This setting configures the level of error reporting. Setting it to "E_ALL" is quite permissive and will report all types of errors, including notices and warnings. While it's valuable for development and debugging, in a production environment, you might want to reduce error reporting to a more minimal level (e.g., error_reporting = E_ERROR) to avoid revealing potentially sensitive information. Reducing error reporting can help prevent the disclosure of detailed error messages that could be used by attackers to gain insight into your application's structure.

For example: Imagine you're running a restaurant and during training sessions (development), you allow your staff to discuss all mistakes openly to improve service (error reporting set to "E_ALL"). However, during dinner service with customers present (production), you only want to address critical issues that need immediate attention (error reporting set to "E_ERROR") to maintain a professional and secure environment, preventing customers from overhearing any internal problems.

"display_errors = Off"

This setting controls whether PHP should display error messages in the browser. Setting display_errors to "Off" in a production environment is crucial for security. When errors are displayed in the browser, it can potentially reveal sensitive information about your code, such as file paths and variable values. Turning off the error display ensures that such details are not exposed to users or attackers.

For example: Imagine your website is a restaurant kitchen. During staff training (development), you might discuss mistakes openly to learn from them. But during a busy dinner service (production), you wouldn't want customers (users) to see or hear these discussions, as it could reveal sensitive information about your operations. By turning off error display (display_errors = Off), you keep such details hidden from view, maintaining a professional and secure environment.

"display_startup_errors = Off"

Similar to display_errors, display_startup_errors controls whether PHP should display errors that occur during the startup of PHP scripts (e.g., in the PHP configuration files). Keeping this setting as "Off" is recommended for security to prevent exposure of errors that could contain sensitive information related to server configuration.

For example: Imagine your website is a restaurant and the kitchen setup (PHP startup) is crucial for the day's operation. During the setup phase, mistakes might happen, but you wouldn't want the customers (users) to see the kitchen staff (server configuration errors) sorting out these issues. By keeping display_startup_errors set to "Off", you ensure that any initial setup problems are not exposed to the public, maintaining a secure and professional appearance.

"log_errors = On"

Enabling log_errors is a security best practice. When set to "On," PHP will log errors to a file specified by error_log (which is the next setting). Logging errors is essential for security and troubleshooting, as it allows you to track and review errors without exposing them to end users. It provides a record of issues that can be used for analysis and debugging while keeping the information secure from prying eyes.

Imagine your website is a school, and when something goes wrong, the teacher writes it down in a private notebook (error log). This way, the teacher can review the problems later and find solutions without the students (users) knowing about the issues. By keeping log_errors set to "On," you ensure that problems are documented securely for later analysis and fixing, without exposing sensitive information to the users.

"error_log = /valid_path/PHP-logs/php_error.log"

This setting determines the path to the error log file where PHP errors will be written. It's important for security to specify a valid and secure path. The specified directory and file should only be accessible to authorized personnel. Avoid placing error logs in web-accessible directories to prevent attackers from potentially accessing them.

CHAPTER 2   PHP CORE SECURITY

Imagine your website is a library, and the error log is a special book where the librarian (server) writes down any problems. You wouldn't leave this book on a public table where anyone can read it. Instead, you keep it in a secure office where only the librarian (authorized personnel) can access it. By setting error_log to a secure path, you ensure that only trusted individuals can see and review the problems.

"ignore_repeated_errors = Off"

When set to "Off," ignore_repeated_errors means that PHP will report repeated errors. This can be valuable for identifying patterns of errors that may indicate a potential security issue. In a security context, you might want to leave this setting as "Off" to ensure that repeated errors are not ignored, allowing you to investigate and address potential security vulnerabilities.

Imagine your website is a school, and every time a student reports the same problem, the teacher writes it down in a notebook (error log). If the teacher ignored repeated reports (setting ignore_repeated_errors to "On"), they might miss a bigger issue, like a broken swing in the playground. By keeping this setting "Off," the teacher can see if the same problem is reported multiple times and can take action to fix it, ensuring a safer environment for everyone.

The configuration settings you've provided demonstrate best practices for enhancing the security of a PHP environment. They help in reducing the exposure of sensitive information, logging errors for review and analysis, and ensuring that important errors are not ignored, which can be crucial for identifying security issues.

CHAPTER 2   PHP CORE SECURITY

File Inclusion ("allow_url_fopen", "allow_url_include")

These settings control whether PHP can include files from remote locations via URLs. Allowing remote file inclusions can be a significant security risk, as it can be exploited to execute arbitrary code on the server. By setting both allow_url_fopen and allow_url_include to "Off," you prevent PHP from including files from external sources.

Imagine your website is a school's computer lab. If you let students download and run any software from the Internet (allowing remote file inclusion), it could introduce viruses or malicious programs. By setting allow_url_fopen and allow_url_include to "Off," you're ensuring that only approved and safe software from within the school's network can be used, keeping the computers secure.

Example:

```php
allow_url_fopen = Off
allow_url_include = Off
```

SQL Injection Prevention ("magic_quotes_gpc", "mysqli")

While magic_quotes_gpc is deprecated in newer PHP versions, it used to automatically escape data from external sources (e.g., form inputs) to help prevent SQL injection attacks. Modern PHP applications should use prepared statements and parameterized queries with extensions like mysqli or PDO (PHP Data Objects) to prevent SQL injection.

Imagine your website is a restaurant, and customers (users) place orders by writing their choices on paper slips (form inputs). If you simply take these slips and pass them directly to the chef (database), someone might write something harmful or misleading (SQL injection). Instead, you can use a special translator (prepared statements) to read the slips and ensure everything is safe and understandable before the chef sees them. This way, you prevent any harmful or misleading orders from reaching the kitchen.

Example (for older PHP versions):

```php
magic_quotes_gpc = Off
```

File Uploads ("upload_max_filesize", "post_max_size")

Configuring the maximum file size and handling of file uploads is essential to prevent malicious file uploads. By setting appropriate limits on upload_max_filesize and post_max_size, you can prevent users from uploading oversized files that could potentially harm your server or application.

Imagine your website is a community art gallery where people can submit their artwork (file uploads). If you let anyone bring in huge sculptures (oversized files), it could overcrowd the gallery and cause problems. By setting size limits on submissions, like allowing only paintings up to a certain size, you ensure the gallery remains manageable and secure. Similarly, setting upload_max_filesize and post_max_size ensures that uploads are within a safe and manageable size.

```
file_uploads            = On
upload_tmp_dir          = /path/PHP-uploads/
upload_max_filesize     = 2M
post_max_size           = 5M
max_file_uploads        = 2
```

Example:

```php
upload_max_filesize = 5M
post_max_size = 8M
```

Let's go through each of the PHP configuration settings in the figure above in the context of their security implications.

"file_uploads = On"

This setting controls whether file uploads are allowed in your PHP application. Setting it to "On" enables file uploads, while "Off" disables them.

Enabling file uploads without proper validation and controls can introduce significant security risks. It opens the door to potential file upload vulnerabilities, including allowing malicious files to be uploaded to your server.

If file uploads are necessary for your application, you should implement strong validation, including checking file types, limiting file size, and storing uploaded files in a secure location. Additionally, consider using the move_uploaded_file() function to store uploaded files securely.

For example, imagine your website is a school art contest where students can submit their drawings (file uploads). If you allow any type of drawing without checking, someone might submit inappropriate or harmful content (malicious files). To keep the contest safe, you need to check that the drawings are appropriate (valid file types), not too large (file size limits), and stored safely in a secure gallery (secure location). Using the move_uploaded_file() function is like having a secure process to move and store the drawings where only authorized staff can access them.

"upload_tmp_dir = /path/PHP-uploads/"

This setting specifies the temporary directory where uploaded files are stored before they are moved to their final destination.

If the specified temporary directory is not properly secured, it can be a potential target for attackers. Malicious users could upload files that, even if not executed, might cause other security issues in the temporary directory.

Ensure that the upload_tmp_dir directory is properly configured and secured. It should not be accessible via the Web, and access permissions should be restricted to the PHP process for read and write operations.

For example, imagine your website is a delivery service where packages (files) are temporarily stored in a sorting area (temporary directory) before being delivered to their final destination. If the sorting area is not secure, anyone could tamper with the packages, causing problems. To prevent this, you secure the sorting area so only authorized staff (PHP process) can access and handle the packages, ensuring they are safe until they reach their final destination.

"upload_max_filesize = 2M"

Have you ever thought about how much space a single file can take up on a website? That's where the upload_max_filesize setting comes in. It's like setting a cap on the size of files that people can upload to your site.

Imagine if you allowed people to upload files without any size limits. Someone might try to upload a massive video file or a huge image, which could hog your server's resources and slow everything down. It's like letting someone bring a giant suitcase onto a small boat – it could cause the boat to tip over!

From a security standpoint, limiting file sizes can help prevent your server from being overwhelmed. Just like how we wouldn't want someone to bring an oversized bag onto an airplane for safety reasons, we don't want excessively large files taking up all the server's resources.

We can set an appropriate value for upload_max_filesize based on our website's needs and available resources. For instance, a common setting is 5MB (upload_max_filesize = 5M), which is enough for most images and documents but not so large that it would cause problems.

Think of your website as a photo contest. If you let people upload giant posters instead of regular photos, it could overwhelm your system. By setting a size limit, you ensure that everyone can participate without causing any issues.

"post_max_size = 5M"

This setting specifies the maximum size of POST data that PHP will accept. It's an important configuration for maintaining the security and performance of your application.

Imagine if someone tries to send an enormous amount of data to your website all at once. This could overload your server, slow down your site, or even crash it. Limiting post_max_size is like setting a limit on how much cargo a truck can carry to prevent it from being overloaded.

By limiting post_max_size, we help prevent potential denial-of-service (DoS) attacks. This control ensures that no one can send excessively large amounts of data through POST requests, which could disrupt your application.

We can set post_max_size to an appropriate value based on the expected usage of our application. It's important to find a balance – the limit should be high enough to handle legitimate requests but not so high that it could be abused. For example, if our application involves users submitting forms with text and images, a value like 8MB might be appropriate.

Think of your website as an online application form for a contest. If someone tries to submit an entry with an unusually large amount of data, it could clog up the system. By setting a reasonable limit on the size of the data people can submit, you keep the system running smoothly and prevent abuse.

"max_file_uploads = 2"

This setting controls the maximum number of files that a single form can upload. It's crucial for preventing abuse and ensuring your server remains responsive.

Imagine if someone tried to upload a hundred files at once. This could overwhelm your server, using up valuable resources and potentially crashing your application. Limiting the number of file uploads is like setting a limit on how many items a person can bring through airport security at one time to ensure smooth operations.

By limiting the number of files that can be uploaded in a single request, we help prevent potential abuse and resource exhaustion attacks. This control ensures that no one can overload the system with too many files at once.

We can set max_file_uploads to an appropriate value based on our application's needs. The limit should be high enough to accommodate legitimate use cases but not so high that it could be abused. For example, if our application typically requires users to upload only a few files at a time, setting max_file_uploads = 2 might be a good balance.

Think of your website as a photo contest where people can upload their best pictures. If someone tries to upload dozens of photos at once, it could overwhelm the contest system. By limiting the number of uploads to a manageable amount, you ensure everyone can participate without causing issues.

These PHP configuration settings related to file uploads and file processing play a significant role in your application's security. By configuring them carefully and applying proper validation and security controls in your code, you can mitigate potential security risks associated with file uploads and POST data handling.

Session Management ("session.cookie_secure", "session.cookie_httponly")

Proper configuration of session settings is vital for preventing session hijacking and related attacks. By enabling session.cookie_secure and session.cookie_httponly, we can ensure that session cookies are only sent over secure (HTTPS) connections and cannot be accessed via JavaScript, respectively. Let's discuss each of these settings and their security implications.

```
session.save_path                    = /path/PHP-session/
session.name                         = myPHPSESSID
session.auto_start                   = Off
session.use_trans_sid                = 0
session.cookie_domain                = full.qualified.domain.name
#session.cookie_path                  = /application/path/
session.use_strict_mode              = 1
session.use_cookies                  = 1
session.use_only_cookies             = 1
session.cookie_lifetime              = 14400 # 4 hours
session.cookie_secure                = 1
session.cookie_httponly              = 1
session.cookie_samesite              = Strict
session.cache_expire                 = 30
session.sid_length                   = 256
session.sid_bits_per_character       = 6 # PHP 7.2+
session.hash_function                = 1 # PHP 7.0-7.1
session.hash_bits_per_character      = 6 # PHP 7.0-7.1
```

Session Data Storage and Management

session.save_path

This setting determines the directory where session data is stored on the server. We can ensure this directory is adequately protected and not accessible to unauthorized users to prevent exposure of sensitive session data. Think of this setting as a secure vault where session information is kept. Only authorized personnel should have the key to this vault to ensure the safety of the data inside.

session.name

By changing the session name from the default ("PHPSESSID"), we can make our application less predictable and reduce the risk of session fixation attacks. Imagine giving each visitor a unique, secret name tag instead of a common one that everyone knows. This makes it harder for intruders to impersonate legitimate users.

Session Initialization and Handling

session.auto_start

Setting this to "Off" is generally recommended. We can avoid sessions starting automatically on every page to reduce security implications, especially if our application doesn't need sessions on all pages. It's like keeping a door unlocked even when it's not in use. Keeping it locked (off) when unnecessary enhances security.

session.use_trans_sid

By disabling trans-sid (setting it to "0"), we can prevent session IDs from being exposed in URLs, making them less vulnerable to session fixation attacks and less visible in logs. Avoid writing sensitive information on a postcard (URL). Instead, keep it inside an envelope (cookie).

Session Cookie Configuration

session.cookie_domain

Setting this to a fully qualified domain name can help prevent session cookies from being accessible on subdomains, thus restricting the session cookie's scope. This is like ensuring your house keys (session cookies) only work for your house (domain) and not any of your neighbors' houses (subdomains).

session.cookie_secure

By enabling this setting, we can ensure that session cookies are only transmitted over secure (HTTPS) connections, preventing eavesdropping on session data. It's like sending sensitive information through a secure, encrypted channel rather than an open one.

session.cookie_httponly

We can prevent session cookies from being accessed via JavaScript by enabling this setting, reducing the risk of cross-site scripting (XSS) attacks. Think of it as making sure only the server can read the keys (cookies), not the client-side scripts.

session.cookie_samesite

Setting the "Strict" value for the SameSite attribute helps prevent cross-site request forgery (CSRF) attacks by limiting when cookies are sent with cross-origin requests. It's like ensuring a key is only used within the house and not passed around outside.

Session Security Enhancements

session.use_strict_mode

By enabling strict mode, we can ensure that session data is not shared between HTTP and HTTPS, enhancing protection against session hijacking and data leakage. Think of it as using different keys for different doors, ensuring that a key for a less secure door (HTTP) can't open a more secure one (HTTPS).

session.use_cookies and session.use_only_cookies

By enabling the use of cookies for session management, we can ensure more secure handling of sessions compared to URL-based sessions. Using only cookies ensures sessions can't be manipulated through other means. It's like storing a key in a secure, hidden place (cookie) rather than carrying it openly (URL).

session.cookie_lifetime

Setting a short session cookie lifetime reduces the window of opportunity for attackers to hijack sessions if they manage to steal a session ID. This is like setting an expiration date on a passkey to ensure it can't be used indefinitely if stolen.

Additional Security Measures

session.cache_expire

We can prevent the storage of potentially sensitive session data for extended periods by setting a reasonable cache expiration time. Think of it as regularly updating the security codes to ensure old ones can't be used.

session.sid_length

Increasing the session ID length to 256 characters enhances security by making it more difficult for attackers to guess valid session IDs. It's like using a long, complex password instead of a short, simple one.

session.sid_bits_per_character

By using 6 bits per character for session IDs in PHP 7.2 and later, we can increase the complexity of session IDs, improving security. This is akin to making each character in a password more complex, making it harder to guess.

session.hash_function and session.hash_bits_per_character

In PHP 7.0–7.1, configuring the hash function and bits per character for session ID generation can enhance the security of the session ID generation algorithm. It's like choosing a more advanced encryption method to ensure better protection of keys.

By configuring these PHP session settings according to best practices, we can significantly reduce the risk of session hijacking, session fixation, and cross-site scripting attacks. This helps enhance the overall security of our application and protects sensitive user data.

Example:

```php
session.cookie_secure = 1
session.cookie_httponly = 1
```

Access Controls ("open_basedir", "disable_functions")

PHP allows you to restrict file and function access. "open_basedir" can limit the directories where PHP scripts can read or write files, and "disable_functions" can prevent the execution of potentially dangerous functions.

```
enable_dl            = Off
disable_functions    = system, exec, shell_exec, passthru, phpinfo, show_source, highlight_file, popen, proc_open, fopen_with_path, dbmopen, dbase_open, putenv, move_uploaded_file, chdir, mkdir, rmdir, chmod, rename, filepro, filepro_rowcount, filepro_retrieve, posix_mkfifo
disable_classes      =
```

Let's examine each of the PHP configuration settings we've provided in the context of security implications.

"enable_dl = Off"

We should set enable_dl to "Off" generally, and this is considered a good security practice. By doing so, we reduce the risk of arbitrary code execution through untrusted extensions.

By disabling dynamic loading of extensions at runtime, we prevent potential security risks associated with malicious users uploading or loading their own extensions, which may contain harmful code.

Imagine your website is a secure facility, and extensions are like tools that workers can bring in. Allowing dynamic loading of extensions (tools) is like letting anyone bring their own tools, which could be dangerous. By setting enable_dl to "Off," we ensure that only pre-approved, secure tools (extensions) are used within the facility.

"disable_functions = "

This setting allows us to specify a list of PHP functions that are prohibited from being executed. We've listed several functions that can be used for executing system commands or potentially compromising the server. The listed functions are system, exec, shell_exec, passthru, phpinfo, show_source, highlight_file, popen, proc_open, fopen_with_path, dbmopen, dbase_open, putenv, move_uploaded_file, chdir, mkdir, rmdir, chmod, rename, filepro, filepro_rowcount, filepro_retrieve, and posix_mkfifo.

By disabling these functions, we can prevent the execution of potentially dangerous operations. For example, disabling functions like system, exec, and shell_exec helps protect against command injection vulnerabilities. Disabling move_uploaded_file can prevent unauthorized file uploads or the overwriting of important files. However, it's important to use this setting judiciously as it can impact the functionality of our application. We should have a clear understanding of the implications before disabling any functions.

Imagine your website is a secure lab. Allowing dangerous functions like system and exec is akin to allowing potentially harmful chemicals into the lab without restrictions. By disabling these functions, we ensure that only safe, controlled substances are used, protecting the lab from accidental or intentional harm. Similarly, disabling move_uploaded_file is like ensuring only authorized personnel can move and handle important documents to prevent misplacement or unauthorized changes.

"disable_classes = ..."

This setting allows us to specify a list of PHP classes that are prohibited from being instantiated. It's similar in concept to disable_functions but for classes instead of functions.

The security implications of disabling specific classes depend on the context and the purpose of our application. By restricting the use of certain classes that might pose a security risk if abused, we can enhance the security of our application. However, we should be cautious when using this setting, as it may impact the functionality of our application or libraries that rely on these classes.

Imagine your website is a secure factory, and classes are like specialized machines that workers can use. Allowing any machine to be used without restriction could lead to misuse or accidents. By disabling specific machines (classes) that are deemed dangerous or unnecessary for the workers, we can ensure a safer working environment. However, it's important to ensure that essential operations are not disrupted by these restrictions.

Example:

```php
open_basedir = /var/www/html
disable_functions = exec, shell_exec, system
```

Other PHP General Settings

Some other general settings which are important to configure for the security of your PHP setup are shared below.

```
doc_root                  = /path/DocumentRoot/PHP-scripts/
open_basedir              = /path/DocumentRoot/PHP-scripts/
include_path              = /path/PHP-pear/
extension_dir             = /path/PHP-extensions/
mime_magic.magicfile      = /path/PHP-magic.mime
variables_order           = "GPCS"
allow_webdav_methods      = Off
session.gc_maxlifetime    = 600
```

Let's discuss each of the PHP configuration settings in the description above in the context of their security implications.

doc_root and open_basedir

doc_root sets the document root directory where PHP scripts are allowed to access files, while open_basedir restricts PHP scripts to operate within specific directories.

These settings help contain PHP scripts within a specific directory structure, reducing the risk of unauthorized file access. If not configured properly, it's possible for an attacker to use directory traversal attacks to access sensitive files or execute arbitrary code on the server. Properly setting open_basedir can prevent scripts from accessing system files or directories outside the designated paths, enhancing security.

Imagine your website is a large office building. The doc_root setting is like defining which areas of the building employees can work in. Without these restrictions, employees might wander into sensitive areas (like the server room) that they shouldn't access. Setting open_basedir is like placing security guards at the doors of restricted areas, ensuring that employees only operate within their designated zones.

include_path

include_path specifies the directories where PHP will search for included or required files.

If the include path includes directories that contain sensitive files, an attacker might exploit it to include malicious files. We should take care to avoid including directories that are not under our control, as this could lead to security vulnerabilities.

Imagine your website is a library. The include_path setting is like specifying which shelves the librarian should look at when finding a book. If the shelves contain harmful books (malicious files) or books that should not be accessed by just anyone (sensitive files), an attacker could misuse this access. Ensuring that the librarian only searches trusted shelves (directories) helps maintain the security of the library.

extension_dir

extension_dir sets the directory where PHP looks for extensions (shared libraries that extend PHP's functionality).

If an attacker can manipulate this setting, they might be able to load and execute malicious extensions, compromising server security. It's crucial to ensure that this directory is secure and that only trusted extensions are used.

Imagine your website is a restaurant kitchen, and extension_dir is the storage room where chefs keep their cooking tools (extensions). If anyone could place their own tools in the storage room, they might bring in dangerous or inappropriate items (malicious extensions). By securing the storage room and ensuring only trusted chefs can add tools, we can maintain a safe kitchen environment.

mime_magic.magicfile

mime_magic.magicfile specifies the path to a MIME magic file used for MIME type detection.

If an attacker can control or manipulate this file, they could potentially trick the server into misidentifying the type of a file, which may lead to security vulnerabilities such as code execution.

Imagine your website is a factory, and the mime_magic.magicfile is like the quality control manual that tells workers how to identify different materials. If someone could alter the manual, they might mislabel harmful substances as safe, leading to potential accidents. By ensuring the manual is securely stored and only accessible to trusted personnel, we maintain the safety and accuracy of the factory operations.

allow_webdav_methods

allow_webdav_methods controls whether WebDAV methods are allowed in PHP scripts.

Allowing WebDAV methods could expose your application to security risks associated with WebDAV, such as unauthorized file access and manipulation. It's generally recommended to set this to "Off" unless you have a specific need for WebDAV methods.

Imagine your website is a secure document storage facility. Allowing WebDAV methods is like giving external parties the ability to directly access and manipulate the documents stored in the facility. This could lead to unauthorized access and potential data breaches. By setting allow_webdav_methods to "Off," we ensure that only authorized and necessary methods are used for accessing and manipulating files.

CHAPTER 2   PHP CORE SECURITY

session.gc_maxlifetime

session.gc_maxlifetime specifies the maximum lifetime of a session in seconds.

Setting this value too high can lead to long-lived sessions that are susceptible to session hijacking or fixation attacks. Properly configuring this setting ensures that sessions expire after a reasonable time, reducing the risk of unauthorized access to user sessions.

Imagine your website is a hotel, and session.gc_maxlifetime is like the duration a guest can stay in a room without renewing their booking. If guests are allowed to stay indefinitely, unauthorized individuals might exploit this to occupy rooms (sessions) without proper authorization. By setting a reasonable checkout time, we ensure that rooms (sessions) are vacated and unauthorized access is minimized.

Some more security configurations: In addition to the aforementioned configurations, here are a few more which are essential for extra security setup.

```
session.referer_check   = /application/path
memory_limit            = 50M
max_execution_time      = 60
report_memleaks         = On
track_errors            = Off
html_errors             = Off
```

session.referer_check = /application/path

This setting allows you to specify a referer check for session validation. It restricts the session to be accessible only if the HTTP Referer matches the specified value.

Using session.referer_check can be a security measure to prevent session fixation and session hijacking attacks. It limits access to a session only to requests originating from a specific application path. This can help protect against unauthorized access to sessions from external sources.

Imagine your website is a secure building, and session.referer_check is like a security guard checking the ID of anyone entering. The guard only allows access to those with valid IDs from your building, preventing outsiders from gaining unauthorized access.

Example configuration:

session.referer_check = /application/path

memory_limit =

memory_limit sets the maximum amount of memory that a PHP script can allocate. It's typically used to prevent PHP scripts from consuming excessive server resources.

Setting an appropriate memory_limit is essential for security because it helps prevent resource exhaustion attacks. If a script can't allocate unlimited memory, attackers can't easily overwhelm the server by consuming all available memory. However, setting it too low can affect the proper functioning of your application, so it should be balanced with your application's needs.

Imagine your website is a cafeteria with limited seating (memory). Setting a limit ensures that no single group can occupy all the seats, allowing fair access to all customers and preventing overcrowding.

Example configuration:

memory_limit = 128M

max_execution_time =

max_execution_time determines the maximum amount of time (in seconds) a PHP script is allowed to run before it's terminated.

Limiting script execution time can help prevent denial-of-service (DoS) attacks where an attacker submits scripts that run indefinitely and consume server resources. However, setting it too low might disrupt legitimate script execution. It should be configured based on your application's requirements.

Think of your website as a meeting room. Setting a maximum meeting time ensures that meetings don't run indefinitely, allowing others to use the room and preventing a single meeting from monopolizing the space.

Example configuration:

max_execution_time = 30 // 30 seconds

report_memleaks = On

This setting controls whether PHP reports memory leaks when a script ends.

Enabling report_memleaks can help in debugging memory-related issues and identifying potential security vulnerabilities in your code. It doesn't have a direct security impact but can aid in identifying and fixing vulnerabilities related to memory usage.

Imagine your website as a factory. Reporting memory leaks is like having inspectors who identify and report leaks in machinery, helping maintain the factory's efficiency and safety.

Example configuration:

report_memleaks = On

track_errors = Off

track_errors determines whether PHP records errors in the variable $php_errormsg.

Keeping track_errors off by default is generally a good practice because it minimizes the exposure of error messages in your application, reducing the risk of information leakage. If error messages contain sensitive information or stack traces, keeping them out of the error log can enhance security.

Think of your website as a secure communication system. Turning off track_errors ensures that error messages aren't broadcasted, preventing sensitive information from being overheard by unauthorized parties.

Example configuration:

track_errors = Off

html_errors = Off

When html_errors is off, error messages are displayed as plain text instead of formatted HTML.

Disabling html_errors is a good practice from a security perspective because it reduces the risk of cross-site scripting (XSS) attacks. If error messages are displayed as HTML, they might be used by attackers to inject malicious scripts into the error output. Keeping it off ensures that error messages are not processed as HTML.

Imagine your website is a bulletin board. Disabling html_errors is like ensuring that notes pinned to the board are plain text, preventing anyone from adding harmful code that could affect others reading the board.

Example configuration:

html_errors = Off

Properly configuring these PHP settings is crucial for maintaining the security of your web application. It's important to understand the potential security implications and apply the principle of least privilege to restrict access and operations to only what is necessary for your application's functionality. Additionally, regular security audits and testing can help identify and address vulnerabilities related to these settings.

These are just a few examples of how PHP configuration settings can enhance the security of your web application. However, it's essential to keep in mind that security is a multifaceted concern, and proper coding practices, regular updates, and other security measures are also crucial for a robust defense against threats which we will touch upon further. Regularly reviewing and adjusting PHP configuration settings in accordance with best practices and the specific requirements of your application is a fundamental aspect of web application security.

Input Validation and Sanitization Techniques

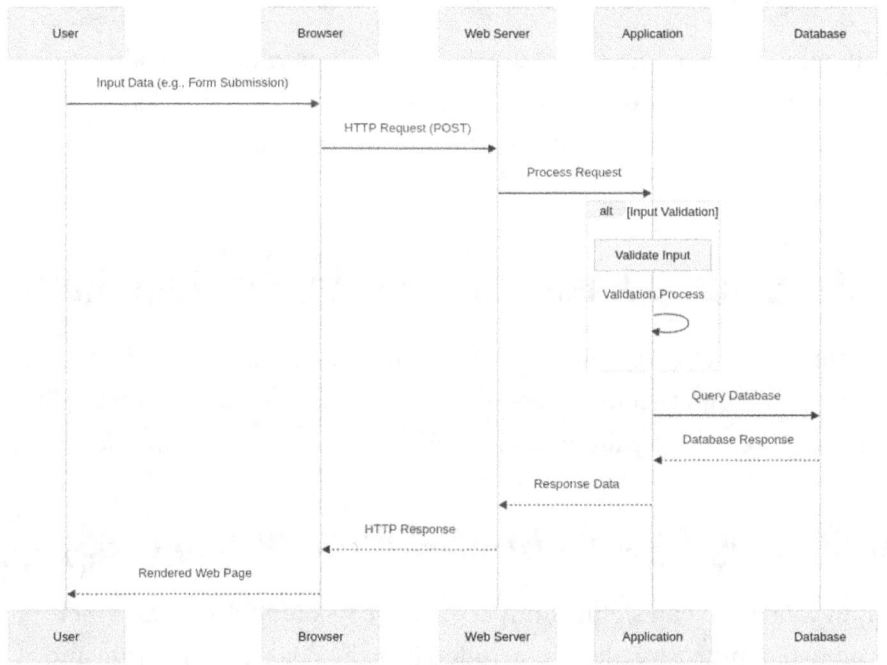

Figure 2-4. *Context of input validation in the request-response cycle*

Input validation is of paramount importance in security, particularly in PHP, because it serves as a crucial defense against a wide range of security vulnerabilities and attacks. Here's why input validation is significant, especially in the context of PHP.

Preventing Injection Attacks

Input validation helps protect against injection attacks, such as SQL injection and cross-site scripting (XSS). By validating and sanitizing user input, you ensure that attackers cannot inject malicious code or payloads into your application.

Mitigating Data Exposure

Validating input helps control the data that enters your application. This reduces the risk of sensitive information exposure, such as database credentials, that could be leaked in error messages or through vulnerabilities.

Safeguarding Against Parameter Manipulation

Proper input validation prevents parameter manipulation attacks, where attackers attempt to manipulate query parameters, such as changing the value of "user_id" to gain unauthorized access to another user's data.

Defending Against Cross-Site Scripting (XSS)

Input validation can significantly reduce the risk of XSS attacks, which occur when untrusted data is included in web pages. By validating and escaping output, you prevent malicious scripts from executing in users' browsers.

Blocking Cross-Site Request Forgery (CSRF) Attacks

Utilizing anti-CSRF tokens and validating requests can help thwart CSRF attacks. Properly validated input ensures that requests come from trusted sources.

Enhancing Data Integrity

Input validation improves data integrity by ensuring that the data your application processes is accurate and adheres to predefined standards, preventing data corruption.

Preventing Application Logic Abuse

Input validation helps prevent attackers from exploiting application logic, such as submitting negative values for shopping cart quantities or bypassing access controls.

Strengthening Database Security

Protecting against SQL injection through input validation safeguards your database and data from unauthorized access and manipulation.

Ensuring Compliance

In many industries, regulatory compliance standards, such as GDPR and HIPAA, require data protection measures, including proper input validation. Neglecting validation can result in noncompliance and potential legal consequences.

CHAPTER 2   PHP CORE SECURITY

Minimizing Attack Surfaces

Reducing the attack surface of your application by validating and sanitizing input minimizes the opportunities for attackers to exploit vulnerabilities, making your application more resilient to attacks.

Maintaining User Trust

A secure application that validates input and protects user data builds trust with your user base. Security breaches and data leaks can have severe reputational and financial consequences.

Facilitating Future Development

Proper input validation simplifies the development process by ensuring that data received by your application is reliable. It reduces the chances of unexpected behaviors and security incidents.

In the context of PHP, input validation is a fundamental aspect of web security. PHP applications often handle a large volume of user input and are thus prime targets for attackers. Proper input validation in PHP helps prevent vulnerabilities that could lead to data breaches, unauthorized access, and other security incidents. Therefore, it's crucial to implement thorough and effective input validation as a fundamental security measure in your PHP applications.

Now, we will dive into a few input validation techniques for PHP in a more explicit and detailed manner, focusing on their security implications.

Data Filtering and Validation Functions

Use PHP's built-in "filter_var()" and "filter_input()" functions to validate and filter input data. These functions allow you to specify the type of data you're expecting, such as email addresses or integers. If the input doesn't

CHAPTER 2   PHP CORE SECURITY

match the expected format, they return "false." Imagine you're checking if a toy fits into the correct-shaped hole. This function makes sure the email fits the right shape. These functions help prevent vulnerabilities like SQL injection and XSS by ensuring that input adheres to specific formats and data types.

Example:

```php
$email = filter_var($_POST['email'], FILTER_VALIDATE_EMAIL);
if ($email === false) {
    // Invalid email address
}
```

Regular Expressions

Regular expressions (regex) provide powerful pattern-matching capabilities. You can use them to define and validate input against complex patterns. For example, you can validate a date in the YYYY-MM-DD format using regex. Regex allows you to enforce strict input patterns, reducing the risk of data manipulation and exploitation. It's like using a stencil to see if your drawing matches the right pattern, like making sure a date looks like "2023-12-31".

Example:

```php
if (preg_match('/^\d{4}-\d{2}-\d{2}$/', $_POST['date'])) {
  // Valid date
}
```

75

Allowed List and Denied List

Allowed list involves explicitly specifying allowed characters or patterns, while a denied list identifies disallowed characters or patterns. Whitelisting is the more secure approach. Allowed list ensures that only expected characters are allowed, reducing the risk of code injection and other attacks. This is like a teacher only letting students with proper uniforms (letters and numbers) enter the classroom.

Example (allowed list):

```php
if (preg_match('/^[a-zA-Z0-9]+$/', $_POST['username'])) {
    // Valid username
}
```

Escape Output

Although not input validation, escaping output is vital for preventing XSS. Use functions like "htmlspecialchars()" to escape user-generated content before displaying it in HTML, ensuring that any HTML or JavaScript in the content is treated as plain text. Properly escaped output prevents malicious scripts from being executed within the context of your web application. Imagine you're wrapping your food before putting it in the fridge so it stays clean and safe. This keeps the website safe from bad stuff.

Example:

```php
echo htmlspecialchars($_POST['user_input'], ENT_QUOTES, 'UTF-8');
```

Parameterized Queries

When interacting with databases, use parameterized queries or prepared statements with PDO or MySQLi. This separates SQL code from user input, effectively preventing SQL injection. Parameterized queries eliminate the risk of SQL injection by ensuring that user input is treated as data, not executable code. It's like having separate slots for food and drinks in your lunchbox so they don't mix and make a mess. This keeps data safe and separate.

Example with PDO:

```php
$stmt = $pdo->prepare("SELECT * FROM users WHERE username = :username");
$stmt->bindParam(':username', $_POST['username']);
$stmt->execute();
```

Cross-Site Request Forgery (CSRF) Tokens

Cross-site request forgery (CSRF) is an attack where an attacker tricks a user into unknowingly making an unwanted request to a web application while the user is authenticated. To illustrate a CSRF attack in a PHP application using a sequence diagram, we can depict a scenario where an attacker exploits the victim's session to perform an unwanted action. Figure 2-5 is a simplified sequence diagram.

CHAPTER 2 PHP CORE SECURITY

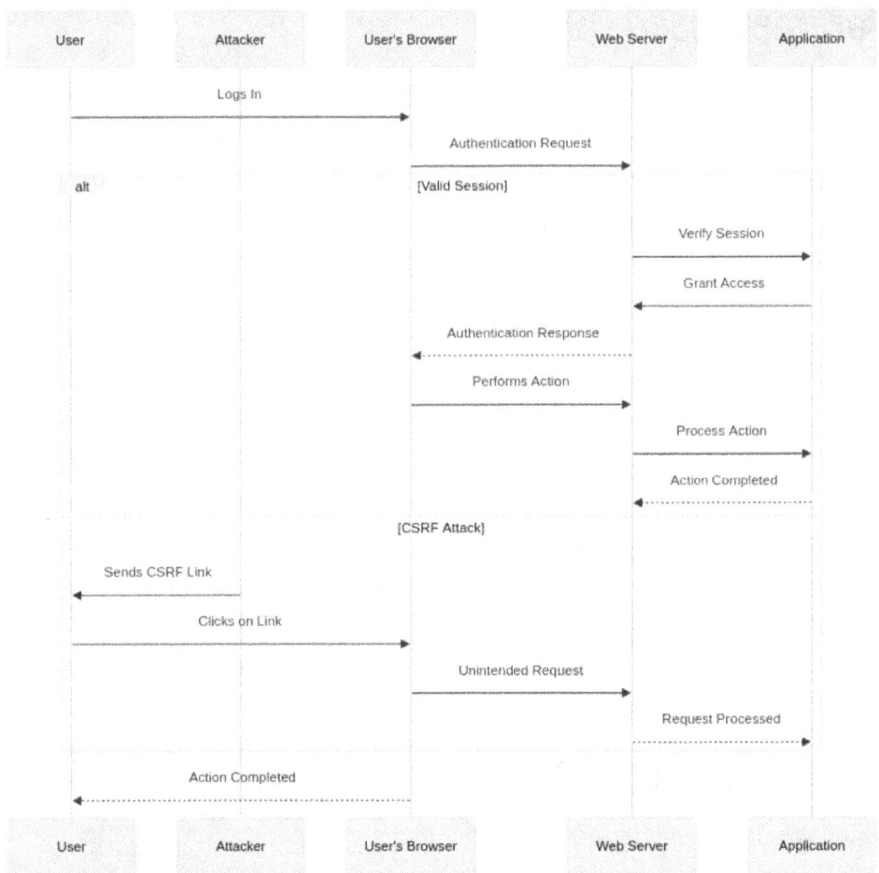

Figure 2-5. *Request-response cycle showcasing the context of CSRF*

Include anti-CSRF tokens in forms to verify the source of requests. This protects your application from CSRF attacks by confirming that the request originated from an expected source. CSRF tokens ensure that only trusted sources can make requests to your application, preventing unauthorized actions. It's like a secret handshake that only your friends know, so only they can play in your yard.

Example:

```php
// In the HTML form
<input type="hidden" name="csrf_token" value="<?php echo
generateCSRFToken(); ?>">

// In the PHP code
if ($_POST['csrf_token'] !== $_SESSION['csrf_token']) {
    // Invalid CSRF token
}
```

Content Security Policy (CSP)

Implement CSP headers to specify which sources are allowed for loading content like scripts, styles, and images. This mitigates the risk of XSS attacks by limiting the domains from which content is loaded. CSP helps protect your application against XSS by controlling the sources from which scripts can be executed. Imagine your parents only letting you eat food from your own kitchen and one trusted store. This keeps you safe from bad food.

Example:

```php
header("Content-Security-Policy: default-src 'self'; script-src 'self' cdn.example.com");
```

CHAPTER 2 PHP CORE SECURITY

HTTP Security Headers

Set HTTP security headers, such as X-Content-Type-Options, X-Frame-Options, and X-XSS-Protection, to improve overall security. These headers prevent content type sniffing, clickjacking, and XSS attacks. These headers add an extra layer of protection by instructing the browser to behave securely and resist certain types of attacks. These are like road signs that tell cars (browsers) to drive safely and follow the rules.

Example:

```php
header("X-Content-Type-Options: nosniff");
header("X-Frame-Options: DENY");
header("X-XSS-Protection: 1; mode=block");
```

File Upload Validation

If your application allows file uploads, validate file types and use a whitelist of allowed file extensions. Store uploaded files in a separate directory with restricted permissions to prevent arbitrary file execution. Validating file uploads prevents the execution of malicious code and restricts uploads to known safe formats. It's like only letting certain toys into your playroom, making sure they're safe and allowed.

Example:

```php
$allowedExtensions = ['jpg', 'png', 'gif'];
$fileExtension = pathinfo($_FILES['file']['name'], PATHINFO_EXTENSION);
if (!in_array($fileExtension, $allowedExtensions)) {
    // Invalid file type
}
```

These explicit and detailed input validation techniques are fundamental to building secure PHP applications. They help prevent a wide range of security vulnerabilities and protect your application and its users from potential threats and attacks. Always follow best practices and stay up to date with security standards to maintain a robust defense against security risks.

CHAPTER 2 PHP CORE SECURITY

Input Sanitization

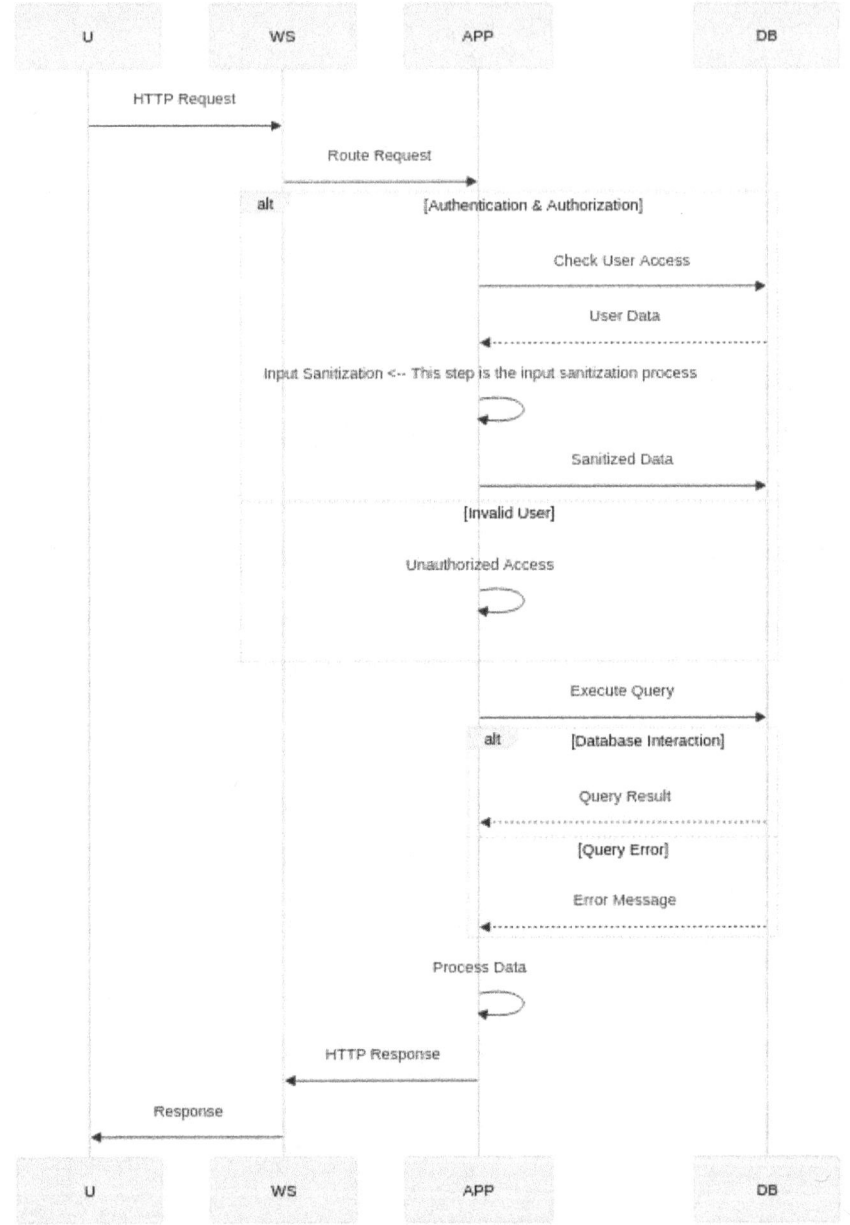

Figure 2-6. *Request-response cycle showing input sanitization context*

Input sanitization is of critical importance in web application security in PHP as it serves as a crucial defense mechanism against various security threats. Input sanitization involves cleansing and validating user-supplied data to ensure that it adheres to expected formats, data types, and security standards. Below are some reasons input sanitization is important in PHP and web application security.

Prevention of SQL Injection

One of the most common and severe security threats is SQL injection. Attackers attempt to manipulate SQL queries by injecting malicious code into input fields, which, if not properly sanitized, can lead to unauthorized access to, modification, or deletion of data in the database.

Input sanitization techniques like parameterized queries and data filtering can prevent SQL injection by ensuring that user input is treated as data, not executable code.

Mitigation of Cross-Site Scripting (XSS)

Cross-site scripting attacks involve injecting malicious scripts into web pages, which are then executed in the browsers of unsuspecting users. Input fields that accept unfiltered user input are common attack vectors for XSS. Input sanitization, such as escaping output using functions like "htmlspecialchars()", helps ensure that user-generated content is treated as plain text rather than code. This prevents the execution of malicious scripts.

Preventing Cross-Site Request Forgery (CSRF)

CSRF attacks trick users into performing actions on a website without their knowledge or consent. These attacks often manipulate data via authorized user sessions. Proper input validation and verification, including anti-CSRF tokens in forms, help ensure that requests are only accepted from trusted sources, reducing the risk of CSRF attacks.

CHAPTER 2   PHP CORE SECURITY

Protection Against Data Tampering

Users may attempt to manipulate input data sent to the server in various ways. For instance, they might attempt to submit negative values or unauthorized data. Input sanitization ensures that the data received is valid and within expected boundaries, safeguarding the integrity of your application's data.

Defense Against File Upload Exploits

If your application accepts file uploads, proper input validation helps prevent malicious file uploads. Users might try to upload files with executable code or dangerous content. Validating file types, checking file extensions, and storing uploaded files in secure locations protect your server from file-related vulnerabilities.

Reducing Attack Surface

Web applications are exposed to a wide range of inputs from users, and each input field represents a potential attack vector. Input sanitization reduces the attack surface by ensuring that only valid and expected data is processed, thereby minimizing opportunities for attackers.

Enhanced User Experience

While the primary focus of input sanitization is security, it can also contribute to a better user experience. Validating and providing feedback on input data can help users understand the requirements, resulting in smoother interactions with your application.

CHAPTER 2   PHP CORE SECURITY

Compliance with Security Best Practices

Proper input sanitization is a fundamental best practice in secure web application development. Adhering to these best practices ensures that your application aligns with industry standards and security regulations.

Long-Term Maintenance and Security

Developing a robust input sanitization strategy as part of your application's architecture simplifies maintenance and future security updates. It creates a solid foundation that is easier to maintain and secure against evolving threats.

Input sanitization is a cornerstone of web application security, including PHP. It helps protect against a wide range of security threats, including SQL injection, XSS, CSRF, data tampering, and file-related exploits. Incorporating strong input validation and sanitization practices into your PHP application is critical for safeguarding your data, users, and the overall security of your web application.

Below are a few techniques to sanitize inputs in PHP.

Stripping HTML Tags

We can use the strip_tags() function to remove HTML and PHP tags from user input. This helps prevent cross-site scripting (XSS) attacks by neutralizing any potentially harmful HTML or script tags. Imagine we're making a sandwich, and strip_tags() is like removing any dangerous or harmful ingredients before we eat it.

```php
$cleanedInput = strip_tags($_POST['user_input']);
```

Filtering Special Characters

We can use filter_var() with the FILTER_SANITIZE_STRING filter to remove or escape special characters from input. Think of this as a special cleaner that scrubs away any yucky stuff from our food before we eat it.

```php
$cleanedInput = filter_var($_POST['user_input'], FILTER_SANITIZE_STRING);
```

Using "htmlspecialchars()" for Output Escaping

While not technically input sanitization, it's essential to mention that we should use htmlspecialchars() when displaying user-generated content in HTML. This function escapes special characters to prevent XSS. It's like wrapping our food in clean paper before putting it on our plate to keep it safe and clean.

```php
echo htmlspecialchars($_POST['user_input'], ENT_QUOTES, 'UTF-8');
```

Preventing SQL Injection with Prepared Statements

When dealing with user input in database queries, we should use prepared statements (e.g., with PDO or MySQLi). These statements automatically escape and sanitize input data to prevent SQL injection. This is like having a special lunchbox with separate compartments so our food doesn't mix and make a mess.

```php
$stmt = $pdo->prepare("INSERT INTO users (username) 
VALUES (:username)");
$stmt->bindParam(':username', $_POST['username']);
$stmt->execute();
```

Handling File Uploads Securely

When users upload files, it's crucial to sanitize and validate the file names and extensions to prevent directory traversal or arbitrary file execution. Imagine we're letting friends bring toys to a playdate, but we check to make sure they only bring safe toys.

```php
$allowedExtensions = ['jpg', 'png', 'gif'];
$fileExtension = pathinfo($_FILES['file']['name'], 
PATHINFO_EXTENSION);
$fileExtension = strtolower($fileExtension); // Ensure 
it's in lowercase
if (!in_array($fileExtension, $allowedExtensions)) {
    // Invalid file type
}
```

Filtering User-Generated URLs

If our application allows users to input URLs, we can use filter_var() with the FILTER_VALIDATE_URL filter to ensure the URLs are in a valid format. It's like making sure the addresses our friends give us are real places we can visit.

```php
$cleanedURL = filter_var($_POST['url'], FILTER_
VALIDATE_URL);
if ($cleanedURL === false) {
    // Invalid URL
}
```

Removing or Escaping Control Characters

We can use a regular expression to remove or escape control characters from user input. This is like taking out any funny symbols from our drawings to make sure they're nice and clear.

```php
$cleanedInput = preg_replace('/[[:cntrl:]]/', '',
$_POST['user_input']);
```

Handling Sessions and Cookies Securely

Before delving into the security aspects of sessions and cookies, we will try to understand the inner workings of them in a web application context in PHP.

Cookies and sessions are fundamental concepts in web applications that help maintain user state and enable personalized experiences. Let's understand them.

Cookies

Imagine cookies as small pieces of information that a website stores on your computer when you visit it. These cookies are like little notes that the website leaves on your computer, and they can contain various details, like your preferences or items you've added to a shopping cart.

- Example 1: Think of cookies as a shopping list you use when you visit an online store. You add items to your list, and when you return to the store, your list is still there, showing the things you wanted to buy. This is similar to how cookies store your preferences and keep you "logged in" on websites.

- Example 2: When you visit a news website, it remembers if you like to see sports news or business news first. It's as if the website says, "Oh, this person prefers sports news," and it shows you that content. This is done using cookies, which remember your preferences.

Sessions

Sessions are like virtual rooms where a website keeps track of your activities while you're using it. They help the website remember who you are and what you're doing as you click around. Sessions are temporary and exist only while you're on the website.

- Example 1: Imagine you're at a library and you're reading a book. The librarian gives you a special card, and as long as you have that card, you can keep reading and picking up where you left off. That card is like your session, allowing the website to remember what you're doing while you're on the site.

CHAPTER 2   PHP CORE SECURITY

- Example 2: Suppose you're using an online banking website. When you log in, the website creates a session for you. It keeps track of your account balance, recent transactions, and other information as you move from one page to another. This makes it easy for you to manage your finances without having to log in again each time.

Cookies are like little notes websites leave on your computer to remember your preferences and actions over a more extended period, even after you leave the site. Sessions are like temporary rooms websites create to keep track of what you're doing while you're actively using the site. Together, cookies and sessions help make your web experience more personalized and efficient.

CHAPTER 2   PHP CORE SECURITY

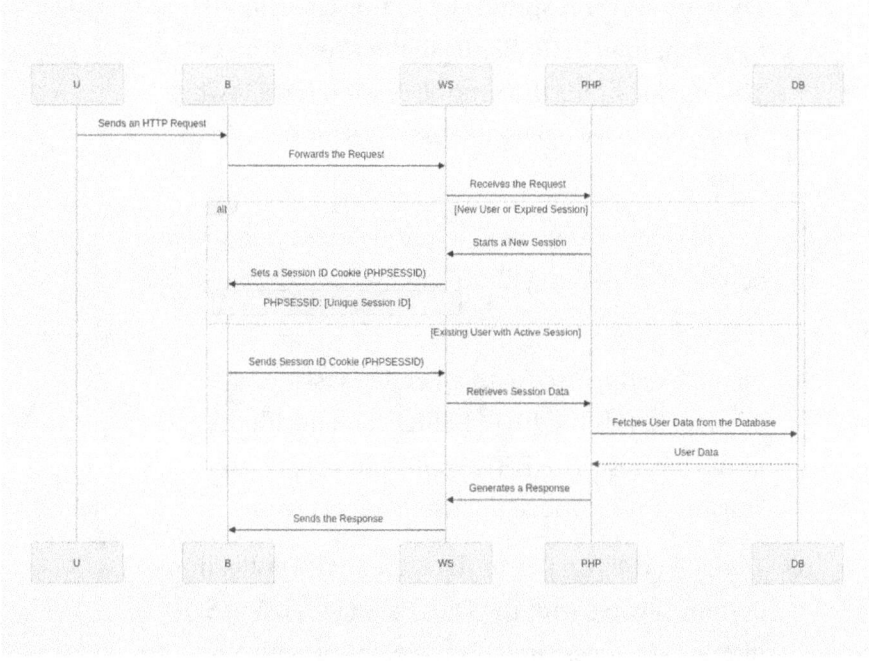

Figure 2-7. *Request-response cycle showing the use of cookies and session*

Below are a few steps happening in Figure 2-7:

1. User (U) initiates an HTTP request.

2. Browser (B) forwards the request to the Web Server (WS).

3. The Web Server (WS) routes the request to the PHP Application (PHP).

4. In the case of a new user or an expired session, the PHP application starts a new session using session_start(). This function generates a unique session ID (e.g., PHPSESSID) and creates a server-side data structure to store session data.

91

CHAPTER 2   PHP CORE SECURITY

5. The web server responds by setting a session ID cookie named PHPSESSID in the user's browser. This cookie holds the unique session ID, allowing the server to associate the user's requests with their session.

6. The PHPSESSID value is a unique identifier, which could be something like 57fcb0843d4d7269c69b450f7f2c7853.

7. For an existing user with an active session, the browser sends the PHPSESSID cookie with the user's request. The PHP Application (PHP) uses this session ID to retrieve the user's session data.

8. To fetch additional user data, the PHP application communicates with the Database (DB) using SQL queries. The session ID is typically passed as a parameter to identify the user's session data in the database.

9. The database responds with the requested user data, such as user preferences, shopping cart items, or login status.

10. The PHP application generates a response based on the user's session data and the requested page or action.

11. The web server sends the response back to the user's browser.

CHAPTER 2 PHP CORE SECURITY

For setting and managing sessions, PHP provides several functions:

1. session_start(): This function initializes a new session or resumes an existing session.

2. session_id(): You can use this function to get or set the current session ID.

3. setcookie(): This function is used to set cookies, including the PHPSESSID session cookie.

4. $_SESSION: A superglobal array that stores session variables and their values. You can use this array to store and retrieve data specific to a user's session.

Now that we have refreshed the basics, lets touch upon the secure ways to handle both cookies and sessions. We'll start with sessions.

Handling Sessions Securely

1. **Regenerating Session ID**

   A session ID is a unique identifier assigned to a user's session when they visit a website. It is typically stored as a cookie or in the URL. The session ID helps the server recognize a user and associate their requests with their specific session. Regenerating a session ID means generating a new, unique session ID and associating it with the user's session data.

CHAPTER 2   PHP CORE SECURITY

Importance from a Security Perspective

Regenerating session IDs is crucial for several security reasons:

1. **Preventing Session Fixation Attacks**
   - ession fixation is an attack where an attacker tricks a user into using a known session ID. The attacker sets a session ID (possibly obtained through social engineering) and waits for the user to authenticate with that session ID.
   - If the session ID is not regenerated upon login, the attacker can gain unauthorized access to the victim's session and sensitive information.

2. **Reducing the Window of Opportunity**
   - Even if the session ID is obtained maliciously, regenerating it limits the window of opportunity for an attacker to exploit it. When a session is regenerated, the previously known session ID becomes invalid.

3. **Mitigating Session Hijacking**
   - Regenerating session IDs makes it challenging for attackers to hijack an active session. If an attacker gains access to a user's session data but cannot predict or control the newly generated session ID, they can't effectively impersonate the user.

4. **Enhancing Session Security**
   - In many cases, session IDs are generated based on predictable patterns (e.g., incremental numbers or timestamps). By regenerating session IDs, you make it difficult for attackers to predict future session IDs.

CHAPTER 2 PHP CORE SECURITY

In PHP, you can regenerate session IDs using the "session_regenerate_id()" function. It's advisable to regenerate session IDs after a user logs in or changes their security context (e.g., from an unauthenticated state to an authenticated state). Here's an example:

```php
session_start();
session_regenerate_id(true); // The "true" parameter deletes the old session data
```

This code starts the session, regenerates the session ID, and deletes the old session data to ensure that the old session is no longer valid. It helps mitigate session fixation attacks and enhances session security.

Regenerating session IDs is a critical security practice in PHP to protect against session fixation attacks and enhance the overall security of your web application. By frequently changing session IDs, you reduce the chances of unauthorized access to user sessions.

2. Set Session Cookie Parameters

    Setting session cookie parameters is essential for security when handling sessions in PHP. These parameters define how the session cookie is transmitted and stored on the user's browser. Let's elaborate on this point and why it's important from a security perspective.

In PHP, you can set the session cookie parameters using the "session_set_cookie_params()" function. These parameters include the following:

- "lifetime": The time (in seconds) for which the session cookie is valid

- "path": The path on the server where the cookie is available

- "domain": The domain for which the cookie is valid

- "secure": A flag indicating whether the cookie should only be transmitted over HTTPS

- "httponly": A flag indicating whether the cookie should be accessible via JavaScript

- "samesite": A flag specifying the SameSite attribute for cross-site request protection (e.g., "Lax" or "Strict")

Why It's Important from a Security Perspective

1. Session Duration Control: By setting the "lifetime" parameter, you control how long a session remains valid. Shorter lifetimes are more secure, as they reduce the window of opportunity for attackers to hijack a session.

2. Path and Domain Restriction: Specifying the "path" and "domain" parameters helps restrict the session cookie's availability. This is crucial because it prevents cookies from being accessed by unauthorized parts of your website.

CHAPTER 2   PHP CORE SECURITY

3. Secure Flag: Setting the "secure" flag ensures that the session cookie is transmitted only over secure connections (HTTPS). This is vital for protecting sensitive data transmitted between the user's browser and the server.

4. HttpOnly Flag: Enabling the "httponly" flag prevents client-side JavaScript from accessing the session cookie. This is a powerful security measure to protect against XSS (cross-site scripting) attacks, where malicious scripts attempt to steal cookies.

5. SameSite Attribute: The "samesite" attribute allows you to define how the browser should handle cookies in cross-site requests. It can help prevent CSRF (cross-site request forgery) attacks. Using "Strict" as the value ensures that cookies are only sent in first-party requests, enhancing security.

Here's an example of how to set session cookie parameters in PHP:

```php
session_set_cookie_params([
    'lifetime' => 0,    // Expire when the browser
                        is closed
    'path'     => '/', // Available to the
                        entire domain
    'domain'   => 'example.com',
    'secure'   => true, // Only transmitted over HTTPS
    'httponly' => true, // Inaccessible via JavaScript
```

```
        'samesite' => 'Strict' // Cross-site request
protection
]);

session_start();
```
```

By defining these parameters, you enhance the security of your sessions and help protect your application from various common web security threats, including session hijacking, data leakage, and cross-site attacks.

3. Protect Session Data

   Session data is information stored on the server that is associated with a user's visit to a website. It can include user-specific information, such as their username, preferences, shopping cart contents, and other data that needs to persist across multiple web pages during a user's session.

   Session data often contains sensitive information and user-specific settings. Protecting session data is critical to prevent unauthorized access, data tampering, and information leakage. Here are key reasons why it's important:

   1. Confidentiality: Session data may include user identifiers, email addresses, or other personal information. Unauthorized access to this data can lead to privacy breaches and identity theft.
```

CHAPTER 2   PHP CORE SECURITY

2. Integrity: If session data is modified by an attacker, it can result in unexpected behavior, unauthorized actions, or even security vulnerabilities. Ensuring the integrity of session data is essential.

3. `Authentication and Authorization: Session data is often used to track a user's authenticated state and determine their access rights within the application. Protecting session data is crucial for maintaining secure user sessions.

4. Preventing Session Hijacking: Malicious users may attempt to steal a valid session ID to impersonate another user. By protecting session data, you reduce the risk of session hijacking.

Avoiding storing sensitive data in sessions is crucial for maintaining the security of your web application. Sensitive data should be stored in a more secure manner, such as within a database with proper encryption. Here's an example of why you should avoid storing sensitive data in sessions and how to handle it.

Why You Should Avoid Storing Sensitive Data in Sessions

1. Session Data Persistence: Session data is typically stored on the server and associated with a user's session. However, it can persist for a longer duration than the user's active session if not properly managed. Sensitive data, like passwords or credit card numbers, should not be left in server-side sessions.

CHAPTER 2   PHP CORE SECURITY

2. Security Risks: If the server's session data is compromised or if session management is not secure, sensitive data can be exposed to attackers. For example, session data could be accessed through session fixation attacks or session theft.

3. Data Leakage: There's a risk of accidental data leakage if session data is not handled correctly. Developers may inadvertently expose sensitive information in logs or debug outputs.

Example of Avoiding Storing Sensitive Data in Sessions

Let's consider a scenario where a user logs in to a web application. You should avoid storing their password in the session data. Instead, you should only store a secure identifier, such as a user ID or username, to reference the user's account:

```php
// Login process
if (user_credentials_are_valid($_POST['username'], $_POST['password'])) {
    // Don't store the password in the session
    $_SESSION['user_id'] = get_user_id_by_username($_POST['username']);
    // Other session variables like 'logged_in' can be set for authentication state
    $_SESSION['logged_in'] = true;
}
```

CHAPTER 2   PHP CORE SECURITY

In this example, the session stores the user's ID after successful authentication, not their password. The user's password should never be stored in the session. When you need to verify the user's identity, you can retrieve their password from a secure storage mechanism (e.g., a hashed password in a database) and compare it with the provided credentials.

By following this practice, you prevent the unnecessary storage of sensitive data in sessions, reducing the risk of data exposure and enhancing the overall security of your web application.

4. Destroy Sessions Appropriately

Destroying sessions appropriately is a crucial aspect of session management in PHP, primarily for security reasons. Let's elaborate on what it means and why it is essential from a security perspective.

When we talk about destroying sessions appropriately, we're referring to ending a user's session in a controlled and secure manner when it's no longer needed. This process involves cleaning up the session data, unsetting session variables, and informing the server that the session is no longer active. Properly ending sessions is essential to prevent unauthorized access and maintain the security of user data.

Why It's Important from a Security Perspective

1. Preventing Unauthorized Access: Sessions often contain sensitive user data, such as login credentials, permissions, and personal information. If a user forgets to log out or if their session remains active indefinitely, it could be exploited by an attacker who gains access to the user's device.

2. Protecting User Privacy: Users expect their data to be handled securely. Ending sessions when they are no longer needed ensures that sensitive information is not exposed to unauthorized individuals who might gain physical or digital access to the user's device.

3. Preventing Session Hijacking: Session hijacking occurs when an attacker gains access to a user's active session. Ending sessions appropriately helps minimize the window of opportunity for such attacks. When a session is destroyed, even if an attacker has the session ID, they won't be able to access the session's data.

4. Reducing Session Fixation Risk: Session fixation is a vulnerability where an attacker sets a known session ID in the user's browser. If sessions are destroyed correctly, changing the session ID upon login or after a certain period mitigates the risk of session fixation.

5. Mitigating Exposure to CSRF Attacks: By ending sessions when users log out or after inactivity, you reduce the risk of cross-site request forgery

CHAPTER 2   PHP CORE SECURITY

(CSRF) attacks. When sessions are destroyed upon logout, the user is protected from potential unauthorized actions initiated by malicious sites.

In PHP, you can use the "session_unset()" and "session_destroy()" functions to end sessions appropriately. The "session_unset()" function unsets all session variables, and "session_destroy()" terminates the session. This ensures that the session data is no longer accessible or exploitable after the session is ended.

Here's an example of how to destroy a session upon user logout:

```php
session_start(); // Start the session
session_unset();  // Unset all session variables
session_destroy(); // End the session
```

Destroying sessions appropriately is a critical security practice that helps protect user data, privacy, and the integrity of your web application. It ensures that session-related vulnerabilities and unauthorized access are minimized, contributing to a more secure online experience for users.

5. Session Timeout

   Session timeout is a security mechanism that defines the period of inactivity after which a user's session is automatically terminated. It's essential from a security perspective for several reasons:

1. Prevent Unauthorized Access

   Session timeout helps prevent unauthorized access to a user's session in cases where the user forgets to log out or closes the browser without explicitly ending the session. Without session timeouts, an attacker who gains access to an active session (e.g., via session hijacking) could continue to perform actions on behalf of the user indefinitely.

2. Mitigate Session Fixation Attacks

   Session fixation is an attack in which an attacker tricks a user into using a session ID they control. By setting a session timeout, the server can invalidate a session after a certain period of inactivity, reducing the window of opportunity for session fixation attacks.

3. Reduce Exposure to Attacks

   An active session represents a security risk if the user is no longer interacting with the application. Session timeout limits the time frame in which an attacker can potentially exploit a user's session, minimizing the exposure to attacks like session theft and privilege escalation.

4. Protect User Privacy

   In scenarios where a user accesses a web application on a shared or public computer, a session timeout ensures that their session is terminated automatically, preventing the next user from accessing the same session.

CHAPTER 2 PHP CORE SECURITY

5. Enhance User Experience

    Session timeouts can also improve the user experience by preventing the user from being locked into an active session when they've walked away or fogotten to log out. It allows them to re-authenticate when they return to the application.

Here's how you can implement session timeout in PHP:

```php
session_start();
$_SESSION['last_activity'] = time();
$session_timeout = 1800;  // 30 minutes

if (isset($_SESSION['last_activity']) && (time() - $_SESSION['last_activity'] > $session_timeout)) {
    session_unset(); // Clear the session data
    session_destroy(); // Destroy the session
}
```

In this example, the "$_SESSION['last_activity']" timestamp is updated each time a user interacts with the application. If the user remains inactive for more than 30 minutes (the defined session timeout), the session data is cleared, and the session is destroyed.

By setting an appropriate session timeout, you ensure that sessions are automatically terminated after a reasonable period of inactivity, thereby

105

CHAPTER 2 PHP CORE SECURITY

enhancing the security of your web application. It's a critical aspect of session management and contributes to overall security hygiene.

6. Use Session Variables Securely

Using session variables securely means properly handling and managing data stored in PHP sessions to prevent security vulnerabilities and data breaches. It involves ensuring that sensitive information is protected and user input is validated and sanitized to prevent common security threats.

```php
session_start();
$user_input = $_SESSION['user_input'];
// Validate and sanitize $user_input to
prevent injection attacks
```

7. Implement CSRF Protection

CSRF, which stands for cross-site request forgery, is a security vulnerability that allows an attacker to trick a user into performing actions on a web application without their consent. These actions can include changing account settings, making purchases, or performing any action that the user is authorized to do.

```php
session_start();
$token = bin2hex(random_bytes(32));
```

```
    $_SESSION['csrf_token'] = $token;
```

In the form:

```html
<input type="hidden" name="csrf_token" value="<?php echo $_SESSION['csrf_token']; ?>">
```

On form submission, validate the token.

Now, let's cover handling cookies securely:

1. Set Cookie Attributes

    1. Lifetime (Expires)

        Setting the cookie lifetime allows you to control how long the cookie remains valid. Here's an example that sets a cookie to expire in one hour:

        ```php
        setcookie('user', 'John', time() + 3600, '/', 'example.com', false, true);
        ```

        In this example, "time() + 3600" sets the expiration time to one hour from the current time. After this duration, the cookie will automatically be removed from the user's browser.

    2. Path

        The "path" attribute determines the URL path for which the cookie is valid. Here's an example specifying a path to "/secure":

CHAPTER 2   PHP CORE SECURITY

```php
setcookie('user', 'John', time() + 3600,
'/secure', 'example.com', false, true);
```

With this setting, the cookie is only accessible to pages under the "/secure" path on the "example.com" domain.

3. Domain

    The "domain" attribute defines the domain that can access the cookie. This example allows the cookie to be accessed by subdomains of "example.com":

    ```php
    setcookie('user', 'John', time() + 3600,
    '/', '.example.com', false, true);
    ```

    The leading dot (".") before the domain indicates that subdomains like "sub.example.com" can access the cookie.

4. Secure

    The "secure" attribute ensures that the cookie is transmitted only over secure (HTTPS) connections. Here's an example:

    ```php
    setcookie('user', 'John', time() + 3600,
    '/', 'example.com', true, true);
    ```

CHAPTER 2   PHP CORE SECURITY

With "true" as the fourth parameter, the cookie is sent securely. It's important for protecting sensitive data during transmission.

5. HttpOnly

    The "HttpOnly" attribute prevents client-side scripts from accessing the cookie's value. Here's how you set an HttpOnly cookie:

    ```php
    setcookie('user', 'John', time() + 3600, '/', 'example.com', true, true);
    ```

    By setting the last parameter to "true", you make the cookie HttpOnly, enhancing security by protecting it from JavaScript access.

6. SameSite

    The "SameSite" attribute controls when cookies are sent in cross-origin requests. You can set it to "Lax" or "Strict" to enhance security. Here's an example with "Strict":

    ```php
    setcookie('user', 'John', time() + 3600, '/', 'example.com', true, true, 'Strict');
    ```

    The "Strict" value ensures that cookies are not sent in cross-origin requests, making it more secure against cross-site request forgery (CSRF) attacks.

Using these cookie attributes appropriately helps you tailor the behavior and security of cookies in your PHP web application according to your specific requirements.

2. Avoid Storing Sensitive Data

    Storing sensitive data in cookies refers to the practice of placing confidential or personally identifiable information within browser cookies. Sensitive data can include items like passwords, Social Security numbers, credit card numbers, or any information that, if compromised, could lead to identity theft, fraud, or other security breaches.

    Below example is not a good security practice:

    ```php
    setcookie('password', 'hashed_password', time() + 3600, '/', 'example.com', true, true, 'Strict');
    ```

These examples provide practical implementations of secure session and cookie handling in PHP. Remember that security requirements may vary based on your application, so tailor these practices to your specific use case.

Secure File Handling and Uploads

Securing file handling and uploads in PHP is crucial to prevent various security vulnerabilities and potential exploits.

CHAPTER 2   PHP CORE SECURITY

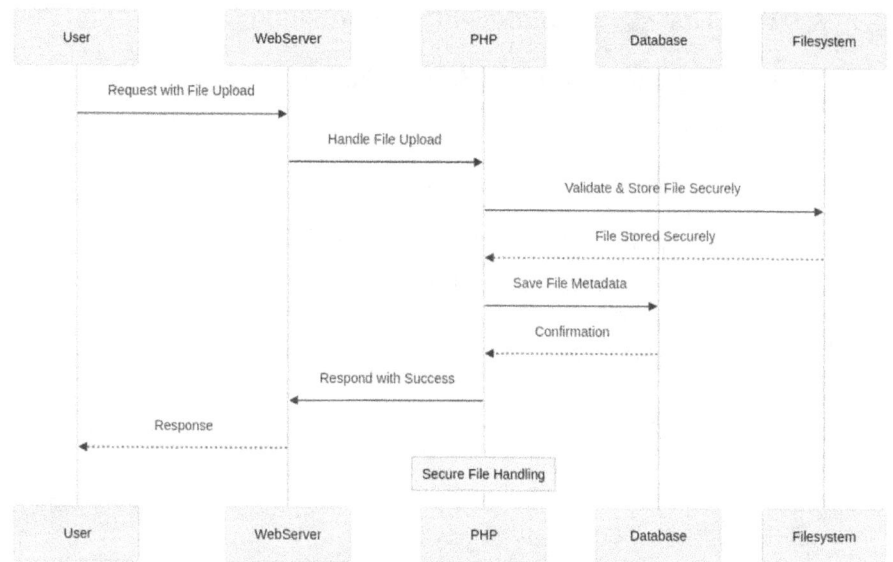

Figure 2-8. *Request-response cycle showing file upload*

In Figure 2-8:

1. The User initiates a request with a file upload to the WebServer.

2. The WebServer forwards the request to the PHP script (PHP) for file handling.

3. PHP performs secure file handling by validating and storing the file securely on the Filesystem. This process should include checks for file type, size, and ensuring the file is not executable.

4. After successfully handling the file, the Filesystem confirms that the file has been stored securely.

5. PHP saves metadata about the file in the Database, which can include details like the file's name, location, and ownership.

CHAPTER 2 PHP CORE SECURITY

6. The Database responds with a confirmation.

7. PHP responds to the WebServer with a success message.

8. The WebServer sends a response to the User.

The "Secure File Handling" section is highlighted in the diagram, representing the secure processing and storage of uploaded files.

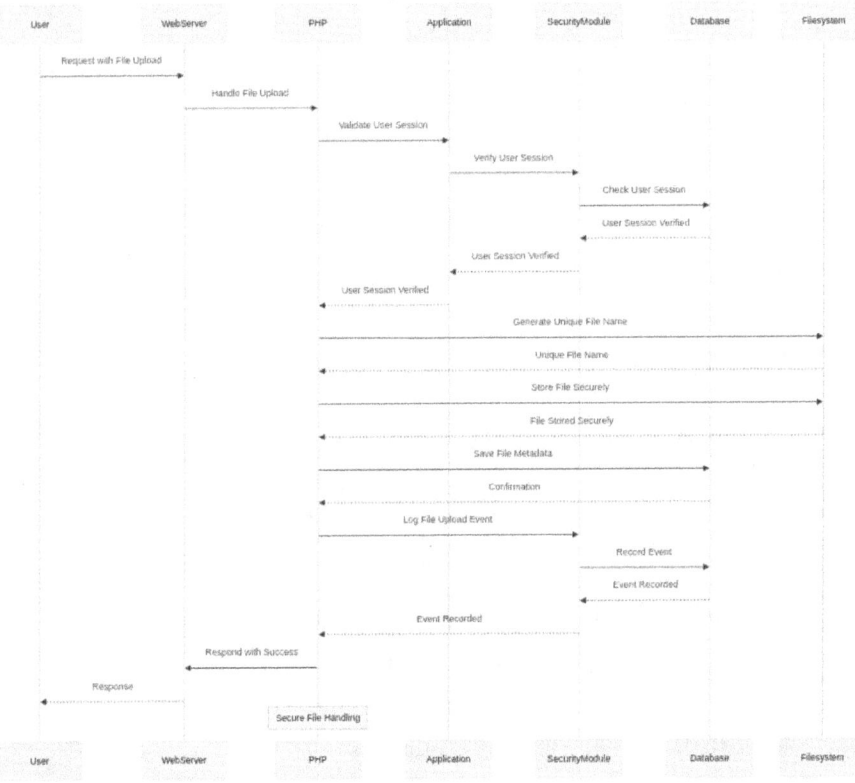

Figure 2-9. *Request-response cycle showcasing secure file handling*

CHAPTER 2 PHP CORE SECURITY

In Figure 2-9:

1. The User initiates a request with a file upload to the WebServer.
2. The WebServer forwards the request to the PHP script (PHP) for file handling.
3. PHP checks and validates the user's session with the Application. This step ensures that the user is authenticated.
4. The Application verifies the user's session with the SecurityModule.
5. The SecurityModule queries the Database to confirm the user's session.
6. Once the session is verified, the process continues.
7. PHP generates a unique file name to prevent overwriting existing files.
8. The Filesystem confirms the unique file name.
9. PHP securely stores the file on the Filesystem, including checks for file type and security measures to prevent malicious files.
10. The Database stores metadata about the uploaded file.
11. PHP logs the file upload event to the SecurityModule.
12. The SecurityModule records the event in the Database for auditing purposes.
13. The response is sent back through the WebServer to the User.

CHAPTER 2 PHP CORE SECURITY

The "Secure File Handling" section is highlighted, emphasizing the security checks, session verification, and secure storage of the uploaded file.

Below are provided a few best practices and code examples to demonstrate secure file handling and uploads in PHP.

Limit File Types

Allow only specific file types to be uploaded, and reject others. You can use the "$_FILES" array to check the file type.

```php
$allowedExtensions = ['jpg', 'jpeg', 'png', 'pdf'];
$uploadedExtension = pathinfo($_FILES['file']['name'], PATHINFO_EXTENSION);
if (!in_array($uploadedExtension, $allowedExtensions)) {
    die("Invalid file type.");
}
```

Rename Uploaded Files

Rename uploaded files to a unique name. This prevents overwriting existing files and helps avoid security issues related to predictable file names.

```php
$filename = uniqid() . '_' . $_FILES['file']['name'];
move_uploaded_file($_FILES['file']['tmp_name'], 'uploads/' . $filename);
```

Use a Secure Directory

Store uploaded files in a directory outside the web root to prevent direct access. Define the file path explicitly.

```php
$uploadDirectory = '/var/www/myapp/uploads/';
move_uploaded_file($_FILES['file']['tmp_name'],
$uploadDirectory . $filename);
```

Set Appropriate Permissions

Ensure that the upload directory has proper permissions. It should be writable by the server but not executable. Restrict directory permissions to the minimum necessary.

```shell
chmod 755 /var/www/myapp/uploads/
```

Validate File Size

Limit the maximum file size that can be uploaded to prevent server overloads and denial-of-service attacks.

```php
$maxFileSize = 10 * 1024 * 1024; // 10MB
if ($_FILES['file']['size'] > $maxFileSize) {
    die("File is too large.");
}
```

Use a Randomized Upload Path

Create a randomized directory structure for uploaded files to prevent predictable paths. This can be done using a function like "uniqid()".

```php
$randomPath = uniqid();
$uploadDirectory = '/var/www/myapp/uploads/' . $randomPath . '/';
mkdir($uploadDirectory);
move_uploaded_file($_FILES['file']['tmp_name'], $uploadDirectory . $filename);
```

Prevent Double Extensions

Some file systems may allow files to have double extensions (e.g., ".php.jpg"). To prevent this, you can check and remove double extensions:

```php
$filename = preg_replace("/\.[.]+/", ".", $filename);
```

Validate and Sanitize File Names

Validate and sanitize file names to remove potentially dangerous characters. You can use "preg_replace()" to achieve this.

```php
$filename = preg_replace("/[^\w\-.]/", '', $_FILES['file']['name']);
```

CHAPTER 2   PHP CORE SECURITY

Regularly Clean the Uploads Directory

Implement a routine to clean the uploads directory from files that are no longer needed. Old, unneeded files can pose a security risk.

Implement an Authentication and Authorization System

Ensure that only authorized users can upload files, and restrict access to the file uploads section based on user roles and permissions.

By following these practices and securing your file handling and uploads in PHP, we can significantly reduce the risk of security vulnerabilities such as file inclusion attacks, arbitrary code execution, and unauthorized access to your server.

Securing Database Operations in PHP

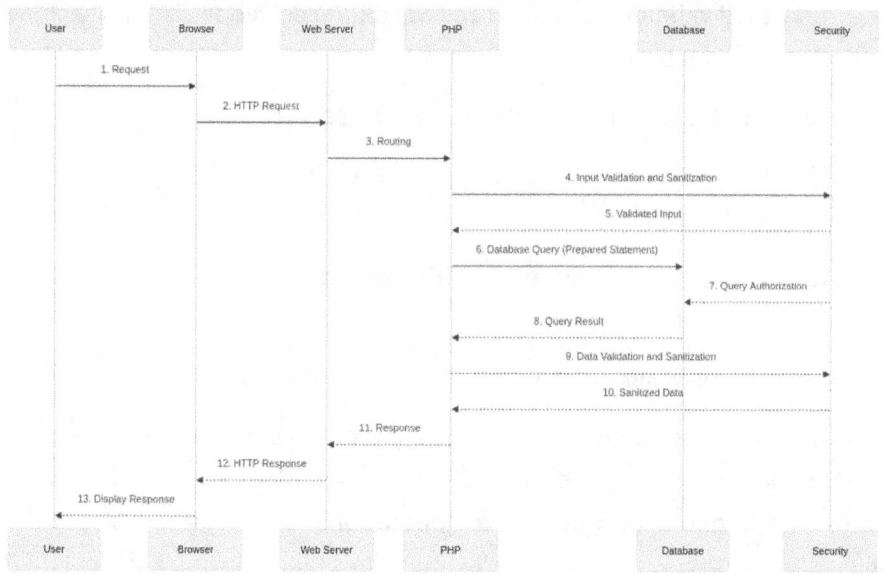

Figure 2-10. *Request-response cycle showing secure database access*

CHAPTER 2   PHP CORE SECURITY

In Figure 2-10:

1. The user initiates a request.
2. The browser sends an HTTP request to the web server.
3. The web server routes the request to the PHP application.
4. PHP performs input validation and sanitization with the help of a security layer.
5. Validated input is passed to the PHP application.
6. PHP executes a secure database query using a prepared statement.
7. Security authorizes the database query.
8. The database executes the query and sends the result back to PHP.
9. PHP validates and sanitizes the data received from the database.
10. Sanitized data is passed to the web server.
11. PHP generates a response and sends it to the web server.
12. The web server sends an HTTP response to the browser.
13. The browser displays the response to the user.

The "Database Security" aspect is represented in steps 6 and 7, where a secure database query is executed, and the security layer authorizes the query to ensure that only authorized operations are performed. These steps highlight the database security measures taken during a typical PHP request-response cycle.

CHAPTER 2 PHP CORE SECURITY

Securing database operations in PHP involves several best practices and techniques to protect against common vulnerabilities like SQL injection and unauthorized access. Below we will discuss some key practices and code examples to secure database operations in PHP.

Use Prepared Statements (Parameterized Queries)

Use prepared statements to prevent SQL injection.

```php
$pdo = new PDO('mysql:host=localhost;dbname=mydb', 'username', 'password');
$stmt = $pdo->prepare("SELECT * FROM users WHERE username = :username");
$stmt->bindParam(':username', $_POST['username']);
$stmt->execute();
```

Input Validation and Sanitization

Validate and sanitize user input. Here's an example using "filter_var":

```php
$user_email = filter_var($_POST['email'], FILTER_VALIDATE_EMAIL);
if ($user_email === false) {
    // Invalid email address
} else {
    // Proceed with the validated email
}
```

119

CHAPTER 2   PHP CORE SECURITY

Authentication and Authorization

Implement user authentication and authorization checks before executing database operations as discussed before.

Limit Database Privileges

For example, when creating a MySQL user, grant only necessary privileges. Avoid granting the "SUPER" privilege:

```sql
GRANT SELECT, INSERT, UPDATE, DELETE ON mydb.* TO 'username'@'localhost';
```

Protect Database Credentials

Store database credentials securely in a configuration file and use PHP constants and environment variables to reference them:

```php
define('DB_HOST', 'localhost');
define('DB_NAME', 'mydb');
define('DB_USER', 'username');
define('DB_PASS', 'password');
```

Validate User Input for Query Parameters

Validate and sanitize user input for query parameters to prevent unexpected behavior:

```php
$user_input = $_POST['user_input'];
if (strlen($user_input) > 100) {
    $user_input = substr($user_input, 0, 100); // Limit the
    input length
}
$user_input = htmlspecialchars($user_input, ENT_QUOTES,
'UTF-8'); // Sanitize for HTML output
```

Regularly Update and Patch

Keep your database software and PHP up to date for security patches and improvements.

Error Handling

Use custom error handling to prevent sensitive information exposure. Example using "try-catch" blocks:

```php
try {
    $pdo = new PDO('mysql:host=localhost;dbname=mydb',
    'username', 'password');
    // Database operations here
} catch (PDOException $e) {
    // Handle database errors
}
```

CHAPTER 2   PHP CORE SECURITY

Logging and Monitoring

Implement logging and monitoring for detecting and responding to suspicious activities.

Secure Your Environment

Ensure your web server, database server, and network are securely configured. Protect against common vulnerabilities like XSS and CSRF.

Data Encryption

Use TLS/SSL to encrypt data in transit, and consider encryption for data at rest.

For data at rest encryption, for example, you can use MySQL's built-in encryption functions, such as "AES_ENCRYPT" and "AES_DECRYPT", to encrypt sensitive data before storing it in the database. Here's an example of inserting and selecting encrypted data:

```sql
-- Insert encrypted data
INSERT INTO users (username, password) VALUES ('john', AES_ENCRYPT('secretpassword', 'encryption_key'));

-- Select and decrypt data
SELECT username, AES_DECRYPT(password, 'encryption_key') AS decrypted_password FROM users WHERE username = 'john';
```

Summary

In this chapter, we have delved into the crucial aspects of PHP core security, highlighting the various measures necessary to fortify your PHP applications against potential threats. By starting with the importance of choosing the right PHP version, we emphasized how staying updated with the latest releases can help mitigate vulnerabilities. We then explored secure PHP configuration practices, providing a foundation for a robust security setup.

The significance of input validation and sanitization techniques was underscored, ensuring that all data entering your application is rigorously checked and cleaned. Handling sessions and cookies securely was also addressed, emphasizing the need for proper management to prevent session hijacking and other related attacks.

We covered secure file handling and uploads, providing strategies to safeguard your system from malicious files and unauthorized access. Lastly, we discussed securing database operations in PHP, outlining best practices to protect against SQL injection and other database-related vulnerabilities.

By implementing the guidance and techniques discussed in this chapter, you can significantly enhance the security posture of your PHP applications, ensuring they are well protected against a wide range of security threats.

CHAPTER 3

Web Security for PHP Applications

Web security is no longer just an afterthought in the development of PHP applications – it's a fundamental requirement. As attackers become increasingly sophisticated, web application vulnerabilities can expose even the most secure sites to malicious activities such as data theft, unauthorized access, and reputational damage. In this chapter, we'll delve into the key principles of web application security and explore how they apply specifically to PHP applications. We'll examine three critical areas of concern: cross-site scripting (XSS), SQL injection, and cross-site request forgery (CSRF) attacks – all common vulnerabilities that can have devastating consequences if left unaddressed. By understanding these fundamental aspects of web security, developers can take proactive steps to safeguard their applications, protect user data, and maintain a strong online presence.

CHAPTER 3 WEB SECURITY FOR PHP APPLICATIONS

Principles of Web Application Security

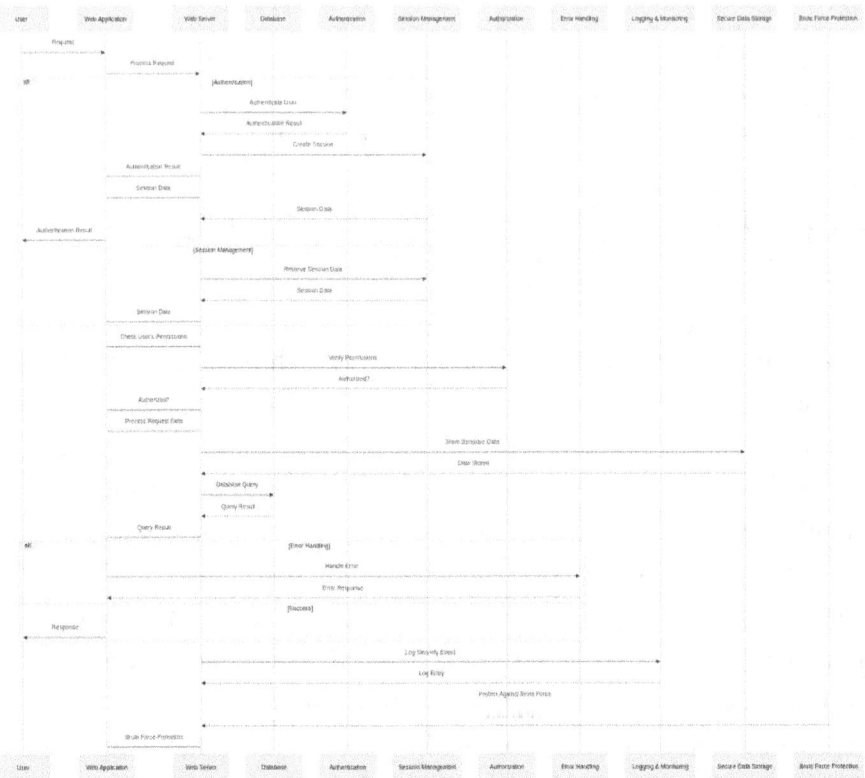

Figure 3-1. *Request-response cycle showcasing various aspects of principles of web application security*

Web application security is a critical aspect of modern web development. Adhering to principles of web application security helps protect your applications and their users from various threats and vulnerabilities. Let's discuss key principles of web application security.

CHAPTER 3   WEB SECURITY FOR PHP APPLICATIONS

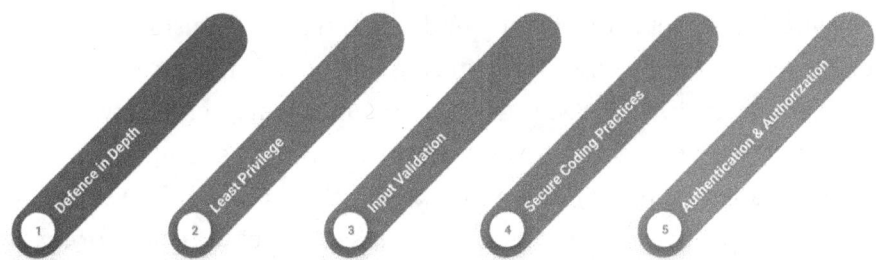

Figure 3-2. Principles of web application security

Defense in Depth

Defense in depth is a security strategy that involves deploying multiple layers of security mechanisms and controls to protect an organization's information systems and data. The primary goal of defense in depth is to provide a series of barriers or safeguards so that even if one layer is breached, there are additional layers of security to thwart attackers. This approach aims to enhance the overall security posture by reducing the likelihood of a successful attack and minimizing the potential impact.

Implementing Multiple Layers of Security Mechanisms

Network Security
Network security involves protecting the infrastructure of an organization's network. This can include firewalls, which act as barriers to block unauthorized access, and intrusion detection systems (IDS), which monitor network traffic for suspicious activity.

Example: Imagine our organization is like a castle. The castle has a high wall (firewall) to keep invaders out. Guards (intrusion detection systems) patrol the wall and look for anyone trying to sneak in.

Server Security
Server security involves protecting the physical and virtual servers that host an organization's applications and data. This can include

127

CHAPTER 3 WEB SECURITY FOR PHP APPLICATIONS

ensuring that servers are regularly updated and patched, using strong authentication methods, and monitoring for unusual activity.

Example: Inside the castle, there are secure rooms (servers) where important treasures (data) are kept. These rooms have strong locks (authentication methods), and we make sure the locks are always in good condition (updates and patches). Guards inside the castle (monitoring systems) also watch for anyone trying to tamper with the locks.

Application Security

Application security involves protecting the software applications that users interact with. This can include input validation, secure coding practices, and regular security testing to identify vulnerabilities.

Example: Within the secure rooms, there are special chests (applications) where the treasures are stored. These chests have complex locks (secure coding practices), and we make sure that only the right keys (input validation) can open them. Regularly, we check the chests to ensure they have no hidden flaws (security testing).

Using Firewalls, IDS, and Security Policies

Firewalls act as a barrier to prevent unauthorized access to the network, intrusion detection systems (IDS) monitor network traffic and alert administrators of suspicious activity, and security policies define the rules and procedures for how the organization manages and protects its information.

Let's think about our organization as a big playground.

Network Security – We put up a big fence (firewall) around the playground to keep out strangers. We have watchful guards (IDS) who patrol the fence and make sure no one is trying to climb over it.

Server Security – Inside the playground, we have special locked boxes (servers) where we keep our favorite toys (data). We make sure the locks are strong and always in good shape (updates and patches). More guards (monitoring systems) inside the playground keep an eye on these boxes to make sure no one is trying to break into them.

Application Security – Each toy box (application) has a unique lock (secure coding practices) that only opens with the right key (input validation). We regularly check these toy boxes to ensure there are no cracks or weaknesses (security testing).

Least Privilege

The principle of least privilege (PoLP) is a security concept that recommends providing individuals, processes, or systems with the minimum levels of access and permissions required to perform their tasks. The goal is to limit potential damage in case of a security breach or accidental mishap. In PHP and web application development, implementing the least privilege principle involves restricting access to resources and functionalities based on a user's or process's specific needs.

Implementing the Principle of Least Privilege

Ensuring Minimum Necessary Permissions: We should make sure that users, processes, and components only have the permissions they absolutely need to perform their tasks. This means not giving them more access than necessary. For example, imagine we have a library. Not everyone needs access to every room. If someone is just there to read, they only need access to the reading area, not the staff room or the archive.

Think about a big toy store. The cashier only needs access to the cash register, not the storage room or the manager's office. This way, if the cashier makes a mistake, it won't affect other parts of the store.

In PHP, we ensure that users and processes only have the necessary permissions by carefully setting user roles and permissions in our application's code and database.

Example:

```
<?php
// Setting permissions for a user role
$userRole = 'reader'; // This could be dynamically set based on
                      the logged-in user
```

CHAPTER 3 WEB SECURITY FOR PHP APPLICATIONS

```
// Check if the user has the required permission before
performing an action
if ($userRole == 'reader') {
    // Allow access to reading area
} else {
    // Deny access
}
```

Implementing Role-Based Access Control (RBAC): Role-Based Access Control (RBAC) is a method where access permissions are assigned based on roles within an organization. Each role has a defined set of permissions, and users are assigned roles based on their job responsibilities.

Example 1: In our library, we have different roles like Librarian, Reader, and Janitor. Each role has specific access: Librarian has access to all rooms, including the staff room and archive. Reader has access to the reading area and public catalog. Janitor has access to cleaning supplies and maintenance areas.

Example 2: In our toy store, we have different roles. Cashier can only use the cash register. Stocker can only access the storage room. Manager can go everywhere in the store. By giving each role only what they need, we keep everything organized and safe.

RBAC in PHP involves defining roles and their permissions and then assigning these roles to users.

Example:

```php
// Define roles and their permissions
$roles = [
    'librarian' => ['access_all'],
    'reader' => ['access_reading_area'],
    'janitor' => ['access_maintenance']
];
```

```
// Assign a role to a user
$userRole = 'reader'; // This could be retrieved from a
                         database based on the logged-in user

// Check if the user has permission to perform an action
if (in_array('access_reading_area', $roles[$userRole])) {
    // Allow access
} else {
    // Deny access
}
```

By implementing the principle of least privilege, we can significantly reduce the risk of unauthorized access and limit the potential damage from security breaches. This approach helps ensure that each user or process only has access to the resources they need, enhancing the overall security of our application.

Input Validation

We touched upon the concept of input validation and will briefly reiterate here. Input validation is crucial for maintaining the security and integrity of a web application. By validating and sanitizing user input, we can prevent injection attacks and other malicious activities.

Validate and sanitize user input to prevent injection attacks: Validating and sanitizing user input ensures that only correctly formatted data enters our application. This helps prevent various types of injection attacks, such as SQL injection and cross-site scripting (XSS). For example, imagine we're baking cookies. We need to make sure all the ingredients are the right kind and not spoiled. Using filter functions in PHP is like checking if the sugar is real sugar and not salt before mixing it in.

Use PHP filter functions for input validation: In PHP, we have built-in filter functions that help us validate and sanitize user input efficiently. For instance, we can use filter_var() to validate an email address. Think of our web application as a fancy tea party. We want to make sure everyone coming in is dressed properly (valid input). For example, if someone is supposed to bring a fruit (email address), we check if it's a real fruit and not a rock. And if they bring flowers (text), we make sure there are no thorns (harmful characters) that could hurt anyone.

```php
$userInput = $_POST['input_field'];
if (filter_var($userInput, FILTER_VALIDATE_EMAIL)) {
    // Valid email address
} else {
    // Invalid email address
}
```

Secure Coding Practices

Secure coding practices involve following guidelines and techniques that prioritize security during the software development process. These practices aim to minimize the risk of vulnerabilities and protect applications from various security threats. Following secure coding practices ensures that the software we develop is robust against attacks and vulnerabilities. By being mindful of security from the start, we can reduce the chances of our application being compromised. Think of building a sandcastle at the beach. We need to build it strong and sturdy so that it doesn't get washed away by the waves. Secure coding practices are like using strong, reliable materials to build our sandcastle, ensuring it stands firm against any threats.

Follow secure coding practices: We should avoid using functions that are known to be insecure and always validate user input to prevent malicious data from entering our system.

Avoid insecure functions and always validate input: Avoid using functions that are known to be insecure, such as md5() for hashing passwords. Instead, use more secure alternatives like password_hash(). Imagine we have a box where we keep our treasures (passwords). Instead of just putting them in the box, we wrap them in a special paper (hashing) that only we can unwrap. This makes sure that even if someone finds the box, they can't see our treasures.

```php
$password = $_POST['password'];
$hashedPassword = password_hash($password,
PASSWORD_BCRYPT);
```

Authentication and Authorization

Authentication is the process of verifying the identity of a user, system, or entity trying to access a resource. It answers the question, "Who are you?" Authentication mechanisms include usernames and passwords, biometrics (fingerprint, facial recognition), smart cards, tokens, and multifactor authentication (MFA). The primary goal of authentication is to ensure that only legitimate and authorized users or entities gain access to a system or resource. **Authorization** is the process of determining what actions or resources an authenticated user or entity is allowed to access. It answers the question, "What are you allowed to do?"

Authorization rules define the specific permissions and restrictions associated with a user's role or identity. These rules dictate whether a user can read, write, delete, or perform other actions on data or resources. Authorization is closely tied to access control, as it enforces restrictions on who can access what parts of a system or data.

CHAPTER 3   WEB SECURITY FOR PHP APPLICATIONS

In PHP, you can implement authentication and authorization by following certain best practices and utilizing PHP's built-in features or libraries. Below is a high-level overview of how to implement authentication and authorization.

Authentication

Authentication involves verifying the identity of a user or entity. You can use various methods to implement authentication in PHP.

Username and Password

The most common method is using a username and password for user authentication.

Here's an example of implementing username and password authentication in PHP:

```php
// User submits a login form with username and password
$username = $_POST['username'];
$password = $_POST['password'];

// Verify credentials (usually stored in a database)
if (verifyCredentials($username, $password)) {
    // Successful authentication
    // Create a session to keep the user logged in
    session_start();
    $_SESSION['user'] = $username;
} else {
    // Authentication failed
    // Display an error message
}
```

CHAPTER 3   WEB SECURITY FOR PHP APPLICATIONS

Multifactor Authentication (MFA)

Implementing MFA enhances security by requiring users to provide additional authentication factors, such as a one-time code sent to their mobile device. PHP libraries like "PHPGangsta/GoogleAuthenticator" can be used for implementing MFA.

Authorization

Authorization involves determining what actions or resources an authenticated user is allowed to access. You can implement authorization by defining user roles and permissions.

Role-Based Access Control (RBAC)

One effective way to implement authorization is through Role-Based Access Control (RBAC). RBAC involves creating different user roles, such as admin, editor, and guest, and assigning specific permissions to these roles. By defining roles, we can streamline the process of managing user permissions and ensure consistency across the application.

For instance, an admin role might have permissions to create, read, update, and delete resources, while an editor might only have permissions to create and read resources. A guest role might be limited to read-only access. When a user tries to access a resource or perform an action, the application checks the user's role and verifies if they have the required permissions.

Implementing RBAC not only simplifies permission management but also enhances security by ensuring that users cannot access or modify resources beyond their authorization. This approach minimizes the risk of unauthorized actions and helps maintain the integrity and confidentiality of the application's data.

```php
function canEditContent($userRole) {
    // Define permissions
    $permissions = [
        'admin' => ['edit', 'delete'],
        'editor' => ['edit'],
        'guest' => []
    ];

    // Check if the user's role has the 'edit' permission
    return in_array('edit', $permissions[$userRole]);
}

$userRole = getUserRole(); // Retrieve the user's role
if (canEditContent($userRole)) {
    // User is authorized to edit content
} else {
    // Authorization denied
}
```

Database-Driven Authorization

To enhance RBAC, we can implement database-driven authorization. In this approach, user roles and permissions are stored in a database, allowing for dynamic retrieval and validation of permissions based on the user's role and the requested action or resource. For instance, an admin role might have permissions to create, read, update, and delete resources, while an editor might only have permissions to create and read resources. A guest role might be limited to read-only access. When a user tries to access a resource or perform an action, the application queries the database to check the user's role and verifies if they have the required permissions.

This method offers flexibility and scalability, as it allows administrators to easily update roles and permissions without modifying the application code. It also ensures that permission checks are consistently applied across the application, reducing the risk of unauthorized access. Implementing database-driven RBAC not only simplifies permission management but also enhances security by ensuring that users cannot access or modify resources beyond their authorization. This approach minimizes the risk of unauthorized actions and helps maintain the integrity and confidentiality of the application's data.

Secure Session Management

Secure session management is a critical component of web application security that involves maintaining user sessions and storing user roles safely. By properly managing sessions, we can ensure that user identities and permissions are handled securely throughout their interaction with the application. Secure session management involves creating and maintaining sessions for authenticated users and ensuring that user roles and permissions are stored securely. This helps protect user data and maintain the integrity of the application.

For example, imagine our web application as a secure library. When a user (visitor) logs in, they receive a special card (session) that tells the library staff who they are and what sections they can access (user roles). The library keeps a record of all these cards in a secure database. Each time the user tries to enter a section of the library, the staff checks the card (session) to verify if it grants them access to that section. If a visitor does not have a card or tries to access a section they are not allowed to, they are guided back to the entrance (login page) to authenticate themselves properly.

Here's a simple PHP example that demonstrates secure session management by starting a session, checking if a user is authenticated, and retrieving their role:

```php
session_start();

if (isset($_SESSION['user'])) {
    $userRole = getUserRole($_SESSION['user']);
} else {
    // Redirect to the login page if not authenticated
}
```

Custom Middleware or Access Control Lists (ACL)

In addition to secure session management, implementing custom middleware or Access Control Lists (ACLs) can be crucial for enforcing authorization rules in your web application. These techniques are particularly useful for managing complex authorization logic and ensuring that users can only access resources they are permitted to.

Middleware is a layer that sits between the HTTP request and the application logic, allowing you to intercept and handle requests before they reach the application. By creating custom middleware, you can enforce authorization rules consistently across your application. Think of middleware as a security guard at the entrance of different rooms in a building. The guard checks if you have the right key (permissions) to enter the room. If you don't have the key, the guard redirects you to a different room (login page).

ACLs are used to define which users or groups of users have access to specific resources within an application. An ACL is essentially a table that maps users or roles to their permissions for various resources. Think

CHAPTER 3 WEB SECURITY FOR PHP APPLICATIONS

of an ACL as a chart that shows which kids can play with which toys. For example, the chart says that only the big kids (admins) can use the scissors (delete documents), while everyone can use the crayons (read documents).

Example:

Imagine you have an application with different resources like documents, projects, and settings. An ACL would specify which users can read, write, or delete each resource.

```
// Define ACL
$acl = [
    'admin' => [
        'documents' => ['read', 'write', 'delete'],
        'projects' => ['read', 'write', 'delete'],
        'settings' => ['read', 'write'],
    ],
    'editor' => [
        'documents' => ['read', 'write'],
        'projects' => ['read', 'write'],
    ],
    'guest' => [
        'documents' => ['read'],
        'projects' => ['read'],
    ],
];

// Check if the user has permission to perform an action
function hasPermission($role, $resource, $action)
{
    global $acl;
    return in_array($action, $acl[$role][$resource]);
}
```

139

```
// Example usage
$role = 'editor';
$resource = 'documents';
$action = 'write';

if (hasPermission($role, $resource, $action)) {
    // Perform the action
} else {
    // Deny access
}
```

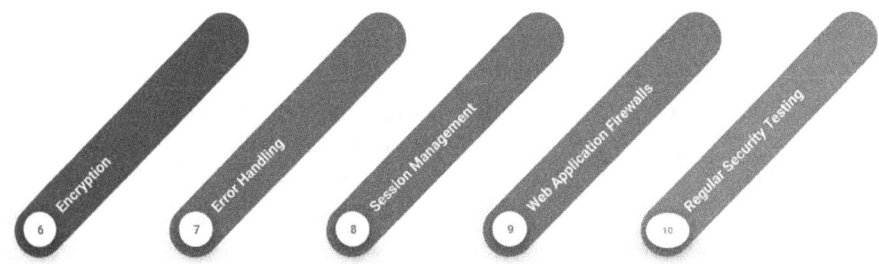

Figure 3-3. Principles of web application security

Encryption

Encryption is the process of converting plain text data into a scrambled, unreadable format (ciphertext) using algorithms and keys. The primary purpose of encryption is to protect the confidentiality and privacy of sensitive information.

It plays a crucial role in security for several reasons:

1. Confidentiality: Encryption ensures that only authorized parties can access and read the data. Even if an attacker gains access to the encrypted data, they cannot make sense of it without the decryption key.

2. Data Protection: It safeguards sensitive data, such as personal information, financial records, trade secrets, and intellectual property, from unauthorized access and theft.

3. Privacy: Encryption is essential for protecting the privacy of individuals and organizations. It prevents eavesdropping and unauthorized surveillance of communication channels, both online and offline.

4. Compliance: Many data protection regulations, such as the General Data Protection Regulation (GDPR) and the Health Insurance Portability and Accountability Act (HIPAA), mandate the use of encryption to protect personal and sensitive data. Compliance with these regulations is essential for legal and ethical reasons.

5. Data Integrity: While the primary goal of encryption is confidentiality, it can also be used to verify the integrity of data. By comparing encrypted data with a hash or digital signature, it's possible to detect if the data has been tampered with during transmission.

6. Secure Communication: Encryption is crucial for secure communication over the Internet, as it protects data transmitted over networks from interception and eavesdropping. Technologies like SSL/TLS encrypt data between web browsers and servers, ensuring secure online transactions and protecting sensitive information during online activities.

CHAPTER 3   WEB SECURITY FOR PHP APPLICATIONS

7. Protecting Passwords: Storing passwords in a hashed and salted format is a form of encryption. Hashing passwords makes it difficult for attackers to reverse-engineer and recover the original passwords.

8. Secure File Storage: Encrypting files and data at rest ensures that even if physical access to a storage device is gained, the data remains protected. Full-disk encryption is commonly used to secure data on laptops and mobile devices.

9. Secure E-commerce: Encryption is vital in e-commerce for securing online transactions, including credit card payments. Without encryption, sensitive payment data could be intercepted and misused.

10. Mitigating Insider Threats: Encryption can help protect data from internal threats, such as employees or contractors with access to sensitive information. Even with access to the data, they cannot read it without proper authorization and decryption keys.

Encrypt Sensitive Data in Transit and at Rest Using TLS/SSL

Encryption is a critical component of data security, ensuring that sensitive information is protected both while it is being transmitted (in transit) and when it is stored (at rest). Here are some key practices and examples of how to achieve this using TLS/SSL for data in transit and PHP's openssl functions for data at rest.

CHAPTER 3 WEB SECURITY FOR PHP APPLICATIONS

To protect data as it travels across the network, use Transport Layer Security (TLS) or Secure Sockets Layer (SSL). These protocols encrypt the data before it is transmitted, preventing eavesdroppers from intercepting sensitive information. Imagine sending a secret message to your friend through a mail carrier. Using TLS/SSL is like putting your message in a locked box before handing it to the carrier, so no one can read it on the way.

Example:

Use HTTPS: Ensure that your web server is configured to use HTTPS, which employs TLS/SSL to encrypt data between the client and the server.

Configure Your Web Server: Install an SSL certificate on your web server (e.g., Apache, Nginx). Update your server configuration to enforce HTTPS connections.

Encrypt Data Using PHP's "openssl" Functions

To protect data stored on your server, use encryption algorithms provided by PHP's openssl functions. This ensures that even if someone gains unauthorized access to your storage, the data remains unreadable without the proper decryption key. Think of the encrypted data as a toy box (data) that you lock with a super-strong padlock (encryption). The IV is like a unique sticker you put on each box to make sure every box is different, even if they hold the same toys.

```php
$encryptedData = openssl_encrypt($data, 'AES-256-CBC', $encryptionKey, 0, $iv);
```

CHAPTER 3   WEB SECURITY FOR PHP APPLICATIONS

Parameters Breakdown

- Data ($data): This is the plain text data that you want to encrypt. It can be any string that you need to keep secure.

- Cipher Method ('AES-256-CBC'): This specifies the encryption method to use. 'AES-256-CBC' means the function will use the AES (Advanced Encryption Standard) algorithm with a 256-bit key in CBC (Cipher Block Chaining) mode. This is a strong encryption method commonly used for securing sensitive data.

- Encryption Key ($encryptionKey): This is the secret key used for encryption. It must be kept confidential, as anyone with this key can decrypt the data. The key length should match the requirements of the cipher method (e.g., 256 bits for AES-256).

- Options (0): This parameter can be used to specify additional options for the encryption process. 0 means no special options are set. Typically, you use 0 or OPENSSL_RAW_DATA to get the raw binary output of the encrypted data.

- Initialization Vector ($iv): The Initialization Vector (IV) is a random value used to ensure that the same plain text encrypted with the same key will produce different cipher text. The length of the IV should match the block size of the cipher method (e.g., 16 bytes for AES-256-CBC).

CHAPTER 3 WEB SECURITY FOR PHP APPLICATIONS

Error Handling

Error handling is the practice of managing and responding to errors, exceptions, and unexpected conditions in software applications. Effective error handling is crucial for both security and the overall reliability of an application. It encompasses various practices and mechanisms to detect, report, and manage errors, ensuring that the application remains robust and secure.

Avoid Displaying Detailed Error Messages to Users: One important aspect of error handling is to avoid displaying detailed error messages to users. Detailed error messages can reveal sensitive information about the application's internal workings, such as database structures, server configurations, or file paths. This information can be exploited by attackers to find vulnerabilities and launch attacks. Instead, show users generic error messages that inform them that something went wrong without disclosing technical details.

Implement Custom Error Handling and Logging: Implementing custom error handling and logging is another critical component of effective error management. Custom error handlers can catch exceptions and errors, allowing the application to handle them gracefully. This can include redirecting users to a custom error page, logging the error for further investigation, and notifying administrators of critical issues.

```php
error_reporting(0); // Disable error reporting
```

Session Management

Session management is a critical aspect of web application development that involves creating, maintaining, and handling user sessions. A session is a temporary interaction between a user and a web application. During a session, the application can recognize and remember the user's identity and state, allowing for a personalized and continuous user experience. Session management is important for user authentication, authorization, and preserving user data between multiple requests. However, if not implemented correctly, it can pose security risks.

Implement Secure Session Management Practices: To ensure the security and reliability of session management, it's essential to follow best practices. This includes using secure methods to handle session data, protecting session IDs from being intercepted or guessed, and ensuring sessions are properly terminated when no longer needed.

Using PHP's Built-In session_start() and $_SESSION Superglobal: In PHP, session management can be easily implemented using the built-in session_start() function and the $_SESSION superglobal. Here's a basic example:

```php
session_start();
if (isset($_SESSION['user_id'])) {
    // User is authenticated
}
```

Web Application Firewalls (WAFs)

A web application firewall (WAF) is a security solution designed to protect web applications from a wide range of online threats, vulnerabilities, and attacks. Acting as a protective barrier between a web application and potential malicious users, a WAF helps filter, monitor, and block incoming traffic that could pose security risks. Implementing a WAF is crucial for enhancing the security posture of web applications, ensuring that they remain robust against various types of cyber threats.

Consider Using WAFs to Filter and Block Malicious Traffic: When considering web application security, it's essential to integrate a WAF into your security strategy. A WAF examines incoming traffic and identifies potentially malicious activities, such as SQL injection, cross-site scripting (XSS), and other common attack vectors. By filtering and blocking malicious traffic, a WAF helps prevent these attacks from reaching your web application.

Third-Party WAF Integration with PHP Applications: One popular third-party WAF is ModSecurity, which can be integrated with PHP applications to provide an additional layer of security. ModSecurity is an open source WAF that offers comprehensive protection against various threats. It can be configured to monitor HTTP traffic, detect suspicious patterns, and take actions such as blocking or logging potentially harmful requests.

Regular Security Testing

Regular security testing is an essential part of maintaining a robust web application security strategy. By continuously evaluating and testing the security of your application, you can identify and address vulnerabilities before they can be exploited by malicious actors. This proactive approach helps ensure the integrity, confidentiality, and availability of your web application.

Performing security testing involves various activities aimed at identifying and mitigating security weaknesses in your application. Two key types of security testing are vulnerability scanning and penetration testing. Vulnerability scanning involves using automated tools to scan your web application for known vulnerabilities. These scanners can quickly identify common security issues such as outdated software, misconfigurations, and missing security patches. On the other hand, penetration testing, also known as ethical hacking, involves simulating real-world attacks on your application to identify vulnerabilities that might be exploited by attackers. Pen testers use a combination of automated tools and manual techniques to find security flaws that may not be detected by vulnerability scanners.

To effectively perform these tests, you can leverage security testing tools like OWASP ZAP and Nessus. OWASP ZAP (Zed Attack Proxy) is an open source web application security scanner that helps you find security vulnerabilities by simulating various attack vectors. It can be used for both automated and manual security testing, providing features like spidering, scanning, and fuzzing. For instance, you can start by downloading and installing OWASP ZAP, configuring it to intercept and analyze traffic between your browser and the web application, and then using its spidering feature to crawl your application and identify all accessible pages. Running the automated scanner will check for common vulnerabilities, and reviewing the scan results will help you address any identified security issues.

Nessus is another powerful tool widely used for vulnerability scanning. It can identify security issues in networks, systems, and applications, providing detailed reports on vulnerabilities and suggesting remediation steps. To use Nessus, you can download and install it, configure it to scan your web application by specifying the target URL or IP address, and then run the scan to identify vulnerabilities. Reviewing the detailed scan reports will guide you in taking corrective actions based on the findings.

Think of your web application as a castle with many rooms and hidden passages. Regular security testing is like having a team of inspectors who check every room and passage to ensure there are no hidden traps or weak spots where bad guys could sneak in. Vulnerability scanning is like using a special map to quickly find known weak spots in the castle walls that need fixing. Penetration testing is like hiring friendly knights to try and break into the castle, helping you find weaknesses that the map might have missed.

CHAPTER 3 WEB SECURITY FOR PHP APPLICATIONS

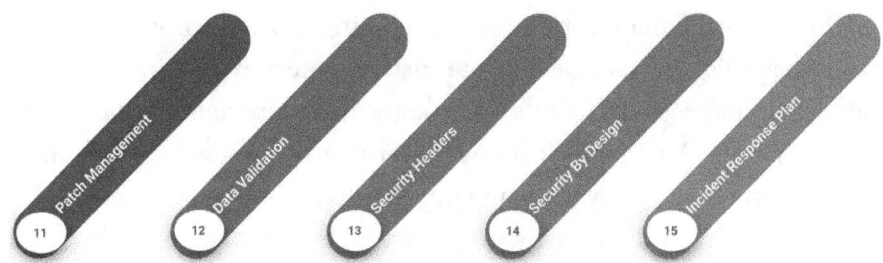

Figure 3-4. *Principles of web application security*

Patch Management

Patch management is a critical component of a robust security strategy for web applications and IT infrastructure. It involves the identification, testing, and application of software updates, patches, and security fixes to address vulnerabilities and keep systems up to date. Ensuring that all software components are up to date with security patches is essential for maintaining the integrity and security of your web applications and IT environment.

Keeping all software components up to date with security patches is a fundamental practice. This includes not just the web application itself but also the underlying server operating system, web server software, database systems, and any third-party libraries or frameworks that your application relies on. By regularly applying security patches, you can protect your systems from known vulnerabilities that could be exploited by attackers.

One key area of focus in patch management should be regularly updating PHP and its libraries. PHP, being a widely used server-side scripting language, is frequently targeted by attackers. Ensuring that your PHP installation is always up to date with the latest security patches helps mitigate the risk of security vulnerabilities. Additionally, keeping the PHP libraries and extensions used by your application updated is equally important. Outdated libraries can introduce security flaws that might compromise your application.

CHAPTER 3   WEB SECURITY FOR PHP APPLICATIONS

Think of patch management as maintaining a fortress. Imagine your web application as a castle that must be protected from invaders. The castle's defenses include its walls (software components), guards (security patches), and fortifications (libraries and frameworks). Regular maintenance is necessary to ensure the walls are strong, the guards are alert, and the fortifications are sturdy. If a weakness is discovered in the castle's defenses, such as a crack in the wall or a sleeping guard, it's crucial to fix it immediately to prevent enemies from exploiting these vulnerabilities and breaching the castle.

Data Validation

Data validation is a critical aspect of web application security and data integrity. It involves the inspection and verification of data to ensure it meets specified criteria, adheres to expected formats, and is free from malicious or unintended content. By validating and sanitizing data from external sources and user inputs, you can prevent a wide range of security vulnerabilities and ensure that your application operates reliably and securely.

Validate and Sanitize Data from External Sources and User Inputs: Validating and sanitizing data is essential for protecting your web application from threats such as SQL injection, cross-site scripting (XSS), and other injection attacks. When data is received from external sources, such as user inputs, APIs, or third-party services, it should be thoroughly checked to ensure it conforms to expected formats and does not contain harmful content. This process involves both validation, which checks if the data meets specific criteria, and sanitization, which removes or neutralizes potentially harmful content.

For example, if your application accepts user input for a username, you would validate that the username contains only allowed characters (e.g., letters and numbers) and is of an acceptable length. Sanitization might involve escaping any special characters to prevent XSS attacks.

CHAPTER 3   WEB SECURITY FOR PHP APPLICATIONS

Use Validation Libraries Like Symfony's Validator Component: Using validation libraries can streamline the process of data validation and ensure that it is implemented correctly and consistently throughout your application. One such library is Symfony's Validator component, which provides a robust and flexible way to validate data based on a set of rules.

Security Headers

Security headers are HTTP response headers that web servers use to enhance the security of web applications and protect them from various types of attacks. They are an integral part of web security and play a crucial role in mitigating common security risks. By configuring security headers appropriately, you can significantly improve the protection of your web applications against threats like cross-site scripting (XSS), clickjacking, and other common vulnerabilities.

Setting appropriate security headers in your web server or application is a crucial step in securing your web application. These headers instruct the browser on how to handle the content and interactions from your site, ensuring that potential attack vectors are minimized. For instance, headers can dictate that your application should only be accessed over HTTPS, prevent the site from being embedded in iframes, and restrict the sources from which scripts can be loaded.

One important security header to implement is the Content Security Policy (CSP). CSP helps prevent cross-site scripting (XSS) attacks by specifying which dynamic resources are allowed to load. By defining a CSP, you create a whitelist of trusted content sources, effectively blocking the execution of malicious scripts that could compromise your application. For example, a CSP can specify that scripts can only be loaded from your own domain and disallow inline scripts, thus reducing the risk of XSS.

```php
header("Content-Security-Policy: default-src 'self'");
```

CHAPTER 3   WEB SECURITY FOR PHP APPLICATIONS

Security by Design

Security by Design is a proactive approach to integrating security considerations into every phase of the software development lifecycle, from initial design and architecture to deployment and maintenance. It emphasizes making security an inherent part of the development process rather than a retroactive or bolt-on measure. This approach ensures that security is embedded into the foundation of the application, reducing vulnerabilities and enhancing overall robustness.

Incorporating security considerations from the initial design phase is crucial. When you start a new project, think about security from the get-go. This means considering how data will be protected, how user authentication and authorization will be managed, and what measures will be in place to guard against common threats like SQL injection and cross-site scripting (XSS). By addressing these issues early, you can design the architecture to support strong security practices, making it easier to implement and maintain security measures throughout the development process.

One effective practice within Security by Design is threat modeling. Threat modeling involves identifying potential security threats to your application and devising strategies to mitigate them. This process helps you understand where your application might be vulnerable and allows you to take steps to protect those areas. For example, you might create data flow diagrams to visualize how data moves through your system and identify points where it could be intercepted or tampered with. Then, you can implement security controls such as encryption or access controls to protect those points.

Think of Security by Design like building a house with security in mind from the start. If you're constructing a house, you wouldn't wait until after it's built to think about security. Instead, you would plan for secure doors and windows, install a robust lock system, and perhaps even incorporate a security system into the design. This way, the house is secure from the moment it's built, and you don't have to make costly or complicated adjustments later on.

Using threat modeling to identify and mitigate potential risks is like planning for possible security scenarios for your house. You might consider how someone could try to break in, whether through a door, a window, or even by hacking into your security system. By anticipating these threats, you can take proactive measures to protect against them, such as installing shatterproof windows, reinforcing doors, or using a more secure security system.

Incident Response Plan

An incident response plan (IRP) is an essential part of any organization's security strategy, designed to address and manage security incidents and breaches efficiently and effectively. Having an IRP in place ensures that your organization can quickly respond to security threats, minimizing potential damage and facilitating faster recovery. The process involves preparing for potential threats, establishing clear roles and responsibilities, and creating procedures to follow during an incident.

Developing an incident response plan starts with preparation. You need to identify the types of incidents that could affect your organization, such as data breaches, malware infections, or denial-of-service attacks. It's crucial to form a response team with specific roles and responsibilities, ensuring everyone knows what to do when an incident occurs. Establishing communication plans is also important so that all stakeholders are informed and coordinated during an incident.

Identification is the next step, where you implement monitoring tools and processes to detect potential security incidents. It's important to define what constitutes an incident and prioritize them based on their severity and impact. Once an incident is identified, containment strategies are needed to prevent further damage. This could involve isolating affected systems, disabling compromised accounts, or blocking malicious traffic.

Eradication involves finding the root cause of the incident and removing it from the affected systems. This might include deleting malware, closing vulnerabilities, or applying necessary patches. After the threat is eradicated, recovery is about restoring affected systems to normal operation. This means restoring data from backups, reconfiguring systems, and ensuring everything is secure and functional again.

An essential part of the IRP is the lessons learned phase. After resolving the incident, it's important to review the response process to identify what went well and what could be improved. This review helps update the IRP and enhances future responses.

Defining roles and responsibilities within the IRP is crucial for effective incident management. For example, an Incident Response Coordinator leads the response efforts, coordinating with team members and communicating with stakeholders. IT Support handles technical aspects of containment, eradication, and recovery. Security Analysts analyze the incident to determine its cause and impact, providing guidance on remediation steps. Communications Officers manage internal and external communications, keeping everyone informed about the incident status. Legal Counsel offers guidance on legal and regulatory implications to ensure compliance.

Think of your web application as a house. An incident response plan is like having a detailed emergency plan for when something goes wrong, like a fire or a break-in. Everyone in the house knows exactly what to do: some people grab the fire extinguishers, others call the fire department, and someone makes sure everyone is safe. By having a plan, you can quickly and efficiently handle the emergency, minimize the damage, and get things back to normal as soon as possible.

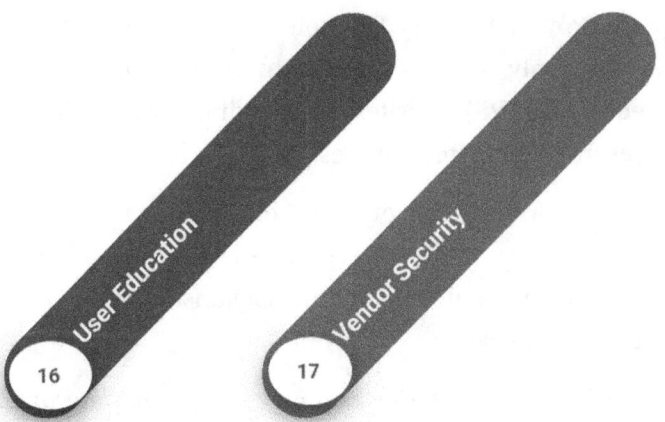

Figure 3-5. *Principles of web application security*

User Education

User education is a crucial element of web application security and an integral part of building a secure cyber environment. Educating users about security best practices empowers them to make safer choices and helps protect both their personal information and your organization's data.

Educate Users About Security Best Practices: Users are often the first line of defense against security threats. By educating them about security best practices, we can significantly reduce the risk of security incidents caused by human error or ignorance.

Key Areas to Focus On

1. Password Security: Encourage users to create strong, unique passwords for each of their accounts. A strong password typically includes a combination of letters, numbers, and special characters.

2. Recognizing Phishing Attempts: Teach users how to identify phishing emails and websites. This includes checking the sender's email address, looking for signs of urgency or threats, and avoiding clicking on suspicious links.

CHAPTER 3   WEB SECURITY FOR PHP APPLICATIONS

3. Safe Browsing Habits: Promote safe browsing habits, such as only entering personal information on secure (HTTPS) websites and avoiding downloading files from untrusted sources.

4. Regular Updates: Encourage users to keep their software and devices updated with the latest security patches to protect against known vulnerabilities.

Provide Guidance on Creating Strong Passwords and Recognizing Phishing Attempts: Creating strong passwords is essential for maintaining security in web applications. We should recommend that users create passwords that are at least 12 characters long and include a mix of upper- and lowercase letters, numbers, and special characters. This combination significantly increases the complexity and security of passwords, making them harder for attackers to crack. Additionally, users should avoid using easily guessable words or phrases such as "password123" or "admin," which are commonly exploited by hackers. Instead, encourage the use of more complex and unique combinations.

To manage the complexity and ensure the uniqueness of passwords, suggest the use of password managers. These tools can generate and securely store strong, unique passwords for each account, relieving users from the burden of remembering multiple passwords. For example, a strong password might look like this: 5!bR5^%5@2f9Q#xP. By using a password manager, users can enhance their security without the hassle of memorizing complex passwords.

Recognizing phishing attempts is equally important in safeguarding user information. Encourage users to always check the sender's email address to ensure it's legitimate. This simple step can help identify fraudulent emails that may appear to come from trusted sources. Teach users to look for red flags, such as urgent language, requests for personal information, and suspicious links, which are common indicators of phishing attempts. Additionally, advise users to hover over links to see the actual URL before clicking. This practice helps users verify the destination of the link and be cautious of shortened or unfamiliar URLs.

Vendor Security

Vendor security is a crucial aspect of an organization's overall security strategy, especially in today's interconnected and digital business landscape. Vendor security focuses on assessing and managing the security risks associated with third-party vendors, suppliers, and service providers that have access to an organization's data or infrastructure.

Assess and Trust Your Vendors' Security Measures: When working with third-party vendors, it's essential to evaluate their security practices to ensure they meet your organization's standards. This involves conducting thorough assessments of their security protocols, compliance with industry standards, and their overall security posture.

Key Steps

1. Conduct Security Audits: Perform regular security audits of your vendors to evaluate their security measures. This can include reviewing their security policies, incident response plans, and compliance with industry standards such as ISO 27001 or SOC 2.

2. Request Security Certifications: Ask vendors for security certifications and audit reports that demonstrate their commitment to security. Certifications like ISO 27001, SOC 2, and GDPR compliance are indicators of robust security practices.

3. Security Questionnaires: Use detailed security questionnaires to gather information about vendors' security practices. This can help identify potential security gaps and areas of concern.

Ensure Third-Party Libraries and Services Follow Security Best Practices: When integrating third-party libraries and services into your application, it's crucial to ensure they follow security best practices. This helps mitigate the risk of vulnerabilities being introduced through external code.

Key Steps

1. Use Reputable Sources: Only use libraries and services from reputable sources with a strong track record of security. Check for active maintenance, updates, and community support.

2. Regularly Update Libraries: Keep third-party libraries and services up to date. Regularly check for and apply updates and patches to address known vulnerabilities.

3. Review and Test Code: Conduct code reviews and security testing on third-party libraries before integrating them into your application. This helps identify and mitigate potential security issues.

4. Monitor for Vulnerabilities: Use tools and services that monitor for vulnerabilities in third-party libraries and notify you of any security risks. Implement a process for quickly addressing these vulnerabilities.

CHAPTER 3   WEB SECURITY FOR PHP APPLICATIONS

In a web application security context, various attack vectors can target vulnerabilities and weaknesses in PHP-based applications. These attack vectors can have significant security implications if not properly addressed. In the next few sections, we will consider some common attack vectors in PHP web applications:

1. SQL Injection: Attackers inject malicious SQL code into user input fields to manipulate the database. This can lead to unauthorized data access, data modification, or even data deletion.

2. Cross-Site Scripting (XSS): Attackers inject malicious scripts (usually JavaScript) into web pages viewed by other users. These scripts can steal sensitive information, hijack user sessions, or perform other malicious actions.

3. Cross-Site Request Forgery (CSRF): Attackers trick users into performing actions on a website without their knowledge or consent. This can lead to actions like changing account settings or making unauthorized transactions.

4. Remote File Inclusion (RFI) and Local File Inclusion (LFI): Attackers attempt to include external or local files by manipulating input data. RFI can lead to executing arbitrary code from remote servers, while LFI can access and display sensitive server files.

5. Command Injection: Attackers exploit vulnerabilities to execute system commands on the server. This can lead to remote code execution and server compromise.

CHAPTER 3   WEB SECURITY FOR PHP APPLICATIONS

6. Session Hijacking: Attackers steal session identifiers to impersonate legitimate users. This can result in unauthorized access to user accounts and sensitive data.

7. Directory Traversal: Attackers manipulate input to navigate to directories they should not access, potentially exposing sensitive files.

8. Brute-Force Attacks: Attackers repeatedly attempt to log in to a user's account by trying various username/password combinations, aiming to gain unauthorized access.

9. Insecure Deserialization: Attackers manipulate serialized data to execute code on the server. This can lead to remote code execution and other vulnerabilities.

10. Security Misconfigurations: Poorly configured servers, databases, and application settings can expose sensitive information or create security holes.

11. Insecure File Uploads: If an application allows file uploads without proper validation, attackers can upload malicious files that can compromise the server.

12. XML External Entity (XXE) Attacks: Attackers exploit XML parser vulnerabilities to read files on the server, gain information about the system, or launch attacks like denial of service.

CHAPTER 3   WEB SECURITY FOR PHP APPLICATIONS

13. Insecure Session Management: Weaknesses in session handling can lead to session fixation, session hijacking, or session data leakage.

14. Clickjacking: Attackers trick users into clicking on something different from what they perceive, often through hidden or transparent iframes.

15. Business Logic Flaws: Attackers can exploit flaws in an application's logic to perform actions they are not authorized to perform.

16. Data Exposure: Data leaks can expose sensitive information, such as user data or proprietary company information.

To mitigate these attack vectors in PHP web applications, it's crucial to follow best practices in coding, validate and sanitize user input, implement security mechanisms like input validation, use prepared statements for database queries, maintain proper access controls, and regularly update and patch software to address vulnerabilities. Additionally, consider employing web application firewalls (WAFs) and security testing to identify and fix potential vulnerabilities.

Protecting Against Cross-Site Scripting (XSS) Attacks

Cross-site scripting (XSS) is a common and critical web security vulnerability that occurs when a web application includes untrusted data in a web page, which is then executed by the user's web browser. This vulnerability allows an attacker to inject malicious scripts into web pages viewed by other users. XSS has significant security implications, including the following:

1. Data Theft: Attackers can steal sensitive data, such as cookies, session tokens, and personal information, from unsuspecting users by injecting malicious scripts that capture this information and send it to the attacker.

2. Session Hijacking: XSS can be used to hijack user sessions. By stealing session cookies or tokens, an attacker can impersonate a legitimate user and perform actions on their behalf, potentially compromising the user's account.

3. Malware Distribution: Attackers can use XSS to distribute malware to unsuspecting users. Malicious scripts can initiate downloads or execute code that infects a user's system with malware.

4. Defacement: XSS can be used to deface websites, replacing legitimate content with malicious or offensive content, causing reputational damage to the site owner.

5. Phishing: Attackers often use XSS to create convincing phishing pages that steal login credentials and other sensitive information from users who believe they are interacting with a legitimate website.

6. Intranet Attacks: In a corporate setting, attackers can use XSS to target internal applications and gain unauthorized access to corporate resources and sensitive data.

CHAPTER 3   WEB SECURITY FOR PHP APPLICATIONS

7. Reputation Damage: Security incidents involving XSS can damage an organization's reputation and erode user trust, especially if sensitive information is compromised.

8. Regulatory Violations: Data breaches resulting from XSS can lead to legal and regulatory consequences, including financial penalties and compliance violations.

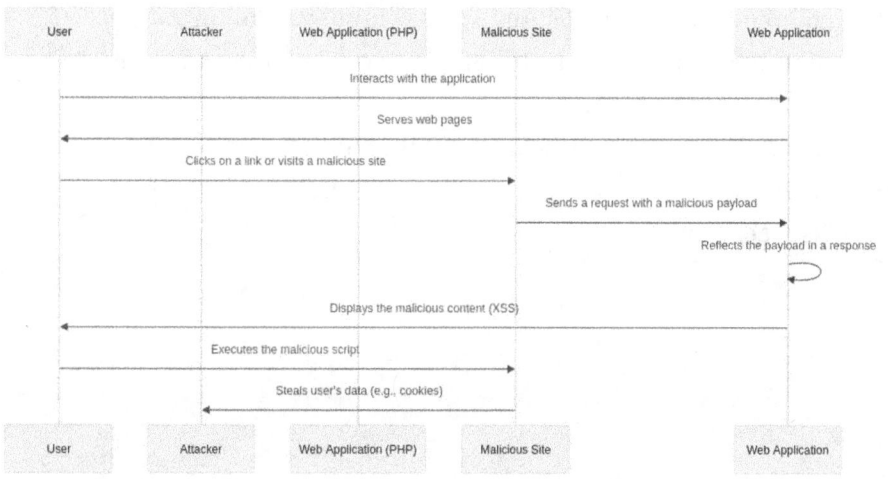

Figure 3-6. *Role of XSS in request-response lifecycle*

In Figure 3-6:

1. The user interacts with the PHP web application.

2. The user is tricked into visiting a malicious site (controlled by the attacker) or clicking on a link that leads to the malicious site.

3. The malicious site sends a request to the PHP web application with a payload that contains an XSS script.

CHAPTER 3 WEB SECURITY FOR PHP APPLICATIONS

4. The PHP application reflects the payload in its response, rendering the malicious content (XSS) on the user's browser.

5. The user's browser executes the malicious script, which can steal sensitive data, such as cookies, and sends it to the attacker's server.

This sequence illustrates how an XSS attack can lead to data theft in the context of a PHP web application. Preventing XSS attacks requires implementing security measures, such as input validation, output encoding, and content security policies, to protect users and their data from such vulnerabilities.

Protecting against cross-site scripting (XSS) attacks in PHP involves implementing a range of security techniques. Below we will discuss a few practical techniques.

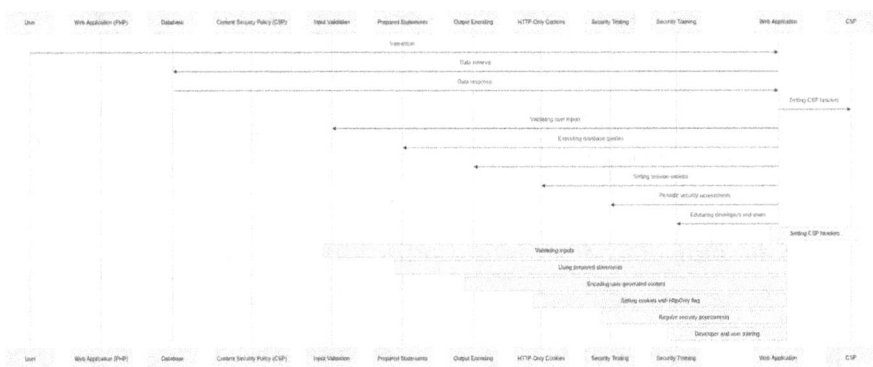

Figure 3-7. Role of XSS in request-response lifecycle

Output Encoding

Output encoding involves sanitizing and escaping user-generated content before displaying it in web pages. This prevents the browser from interpreting the content as executable scripts. PHP provides functions for this purpose, such as "htmlspecialchars()" and "htmlentities()".

```php
$userInput = '<script>alert("XSS attack");</script>';
$safeOutput = htmlspecialchars($userInput, ENT_QUOTES, 'UTF-8');
echo $safeOutput;
```

Content Security Policy (CSP)

CSP is a security feature that allows you to specify which sources of content are allowed to be loaded and executed on your web page. You can set CSP directives in your PHP application's HTTP headers to prevent inline scripts and unauthorized script sources.

Example of setting a CSP header in PHP:

```php
header("Content-Security-Policy: script-src 'self' 'unsafe-inline'");
```

Input Validation

Validate and sanitize user inputs to ensure that they adhere to expected formats. Use PHP's built-in functions, regular expressions, or custom validation functions to check input against predefined rules.

Example of input validation with PHP's "filter_var()":

```php
$email = $_POST['email'];
if (filter_var($email, FILTER_VALIDATE_EMAIL)) {
    // Valid email
} else {
    // Invalid email
}
```

Use Prepared Statements (Database Queries)

When interacting with databases, use prepared statements or parameterized queries to prevent SQL injection, which is a form of XSS. This ensures that user input is treated as data and not executable code.

Example using PDO for prepared statements:

```php
$pdo = new PDO("mysql:host=localhost;dbname=mydb", $username, $password);
$stmt = $pdo->prepare("SELECT * FROM users WHERE username = :username");
$stmt->execute(['username' => $userInput]);
```

Avoid Dynamic JavaScript Generation

Avoid generating JavaScript dynamically by concatenating user input with script code. Instead, use JSON for data interchange and avoid rendering user-generated data as JavaScript.

Example using JSON for data exchange:

```php
$userData = ['name' => 'John', 'age' => 30];
echo json_encode($userData);
```

HTTP-Only Cookies

When setting cookies, use the "HttpOnly" flag to prevent client-side JavaScript from accessing cookie values. This helps protect user session data.

Example of setting an HTTP-only cookie:

```php
setcookie("sessionCookie", "value", time() + 3600, '/',
'', false, true);
```

The last parameter for HttpOnly specifies that the cookie is accessible only through the HTTP protocol, making it inaccessible to JavaScript running in the browser. Setting this to true helps mitigate the risk of cross-site scripting (XSS) attacks.

Use Security Libraries

Consider using security libraries and frameworks that include built-in protection against XSS attacks. For example, using PHP frameworks like Symfony or Laravel can provide additional security layers.

Regular Security Testing

Regularly test your PHP application for security vulnerabilities, including XSS, using security scanning tools and penetration testing.

Security Training

Train your development team and users on secure coding practices and awareness of common security threats, including XSS.

Implementing these techniques and combining them with strong security practices will significantly reduce the risk of XSS attacks in your PHP applications, protecting both your application and your users from potential harm.

Mitigating Cross-Site Request Forgery (CSRF) Attack

Let's dive into the topic of cross-site request forgery (CSRF), a type of security vulnerability that can have significant implications for web applications. CSRF occurs when an attacker tricks a user into performing actions on a web application without their consent. This often involves embedding malicious code or links in web pages or emails that the victim is likely to interact with. The consequences of CSRF attacks can be quite severe, affecting both users and organizations.

Unauthorized Actions

One major risk of CSRF attacks is that they can lead to unauthorized actions on a web application. For example, imagine an attacker tricking a user into changing their account settings or initiating financial transactions without their knowledge. This could be as simple as clicking on a seemingly harmless link that actually executes an unwanted action.

Data Manipulation

Another danger is data manipulation. Attackers can use CSRF to alter or delete a user's data within a web application. This might result in data loss, corruption, or unauthorized changes to sensitive information. Think of it like someone sneaking into your room and rearranging or destroying your belongings while you're unaware.

Financial Loss

For applications involving financial transactions, CSRF attacks can lead to direct financial loss. An attacker might initiate fund transfers, purchase items, or change payment methods without the victim's consent. It's like someone using your credit card to make purchases without your permission.

Data Exposure

CSRF can also be used to expose sensitive data. An attacker might trick a user into revealing their private information or accessing data they should not have access to. Imagine being tricked into sending your confidential documents to someone pretending to be a trusted person.

Authentication Bypass

One particularly troubling aspect of CSRF is its potential to bypass authentication. Attackers can trick users into changing their passwords or email addresses, effectively taking over their accounts. It's like someone convincing you to give them the keys to your house and then locking you out.

Session Hijacking

CSRF can be combined with other attacks to hijack a user's session, gaining unauthorized access to an authenticated session. It's as if someone intercepts your conversation and pretends to be you to gain access to your private discussions.

Reputation Damage

Organizations can suffer significant reputation damage due to successful CSRF attacks. Users might lose trust and confidence in the services provided, perceiving the organization as insecure and unreliable. It's akin to a restaurant losing customers because of a food poisoning incident.

Legal and Compliance Issues

Finally, CSRF attacks can lead to legal and compliance issues. If such attacks result in data breaches or regulatory violations, organizations might face legal consequences and financial penalties. It's like getting fined for not following safety regulations that resulted in an accident.

To mitigate the security implications of CSRF attacks, web applications should implement security measures such as using anti-CSRF tokens, implementing same-site cookie attributes, and ensuring that all state-changing requests (e.g., actions that modify data or settings) require user authentication and explicit user consent. By taking these measures, web applications can significantly reduce the risk of CSRF vulnerabilities and their associated security consequences.

CHAPTER 3 WEB SECURITY FOR PHP APPLICATIONS

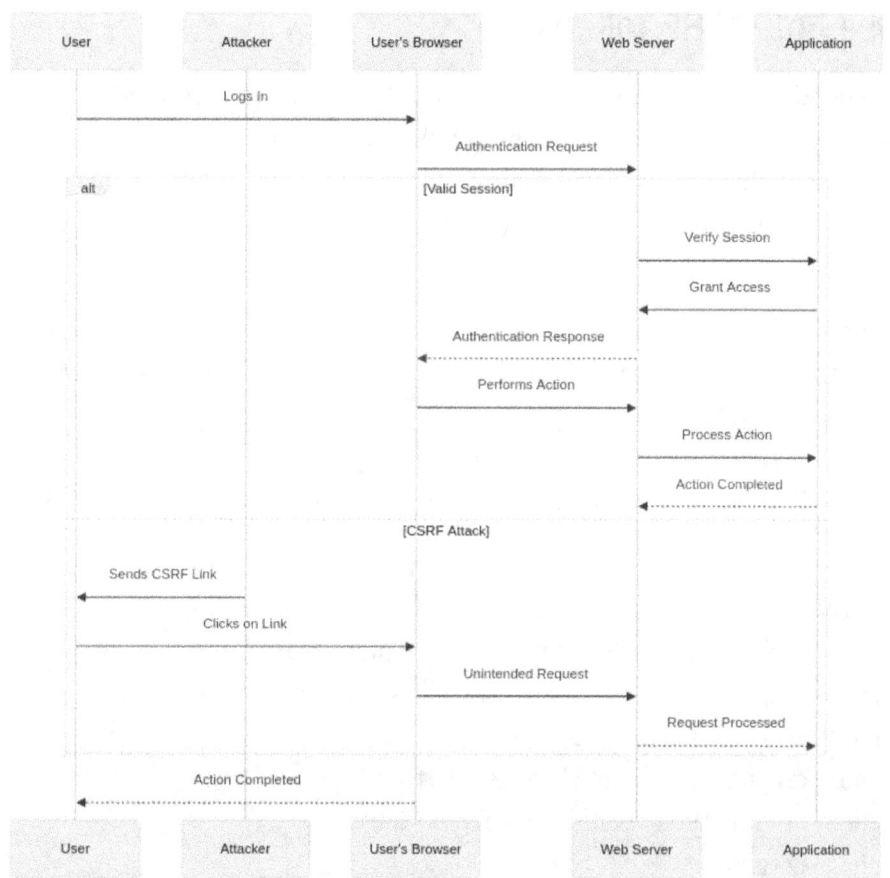

Figure 3-8. *Request-response cycle showcasing CSRF usage*

Protecting against CSRF (cross-site request forgery) attacks in PHP is essential to ensure the security of your web application. CSRF attacks occur when an attacker tricks a user into unknowingly making an unwanted request to a different site while authenticated. To prevent CSRF attacks, we can use the following techniques in PHP.

CHAPTER 3   WEB SECURITY FOR PHP APPLICATIONS

Use Anti-CSRF Tokens

We need to include a unique token in our forms, which is verified on form submission. This token should be generated for each user session and must be included with each request.

Code sample:

```php
<?php
// Generate a CSRF token and store it in the user's session
session_start();
if (!isset($_SESSION['csrf_token'])) {
    $_SESSION['csrf_token'] = bin2hex(random_bytes(32));
}

// Include the token in the form
echo '<form action="process.php" method="post">';
echo '<input type="hidden" name="csrf_token" value="' . $_SESSION['csrf_token'] . '">';
echo '<input type="text" name="data">';
echo '<input type="submit" value="Submit">';
echo '</form>';
?>
```

Check Referer Header

We need to verify that the HTTP Referer header matches our domain to ensure the request is coming from an expected source. Note that this method isn't foolproof, as some clients may not send this header.

Code sample:

```php
<?php
$referer = $_SERVER['HTTP_REFERER'];
if (parse_url($referer, PHP_URL_HOST) != 'yourdomain.com') {
    // Request does not come from your domain, handle
        accordingly
    exit('Invalid request');
}
?>
```

Verify Origin Header (Same-Site Cookies)

Using the Same-Site attribute for cookies ensures they are only sent with requests originating from our domain. This helps protect against CSRF attacks by preventing the browser from sending cookies to cross-origin requests.

Code sample (in PHP.ini or .htaccess):

```php
// Set SameSite attribute for cookies
ini_set('session.cookie_samesite', 'Lax');
```

Use POST Requests for Sensitive Operations

Whenever possible, restrict sensitive operations to HTTP POST requests. This makes it more difficult for attackers to create malicious links or forms for performing actions on behalf of the user.

Code sample (HTML form):

```html
<form action="process.php" method="post">
    <!-- Form fields -->
    <input type="submit" value="Submit">
</form>
```

Check and Validate User Session

Always validate the user's session on the server to ensure that the request is coming from an authenticated user. Ensure that sensitive operations are protected by user authentication.

Code sample:

```php
session_start();
if (!isset($_SESSION['user_id'])) {
    // User is not authenticated, handle accordingly
    exit('Authentication required');
}
```

Summary

Protecting against CSRF attacks is crucial for ensuring the integrity and security of web applications. By implementing robust defenses, such as token-based verification and secure cookie management, developers can prevent attackers from exploiting user sessions.

To safeguard against CSRF threats, we need to ensure that tokens have limited lifetimes, are generated securely, and are validated on each request. Regularly update your application's security framework to stay ahead of evolving threats.

By prioritizing CSRF protection, we can enhance the overall security posture of your web application and provide a safer experience for users. Remember to educate users about the risks associated with CSRF attacks and encourage them to report any suspicious activity.

CHAPTER 4

Framework Security

In the ever-evolving landscape of web development, the significance of robust security measures cannot be overstated. As developers harness the power and flexibility of PHP frameworks to expedite application development, an inherent responsibility arises to fortify these frameworks against potential vulnerabilities. Framework security in PHP is a multidimensional concept encompassing practices, tools, and protocols designed to safeguard web applications built on frameworks like Laravel, Symfony, or CodeIgniter.

The security of a PHP framework is crucial not only for the protection of sensitive user data but also to shield against various cyber threats such as SQL injection, cross-site scripting (XSS), cross-site request forgery (CSRF), and other malicious exploits. With cyberattacks becoming more sophisticated, ensuring the robustness of your PHP framework is paramount for maintaining the integrity and trustworthiness of web applications.

This chapter delves into the key principles, best practices, and tools that developers can employ to use the security features of PHP frameworks. From input validation and secure coding practices to utilizing built-in security features offered by frameworks, we explore the arsenal of measures available to mitigate risks and fortify the foundations of PHP-based web applications. As we navigate through this chapter, the goal is to empower developers with the knowledge and tools needed to construct resilient, secure, and reliable web applications within the PHP framework ecosystem.

CHAPTER 4   FRAMEWORK SECURITY

Introduction to Laravel Security Features

Laravel, a popular PHP framework, incorporates a range of security features to help developers build robust and secure web applications. It can be visited at `https://laravel.com/`. Let's discuss some key Laravel security features in various contexts of PHP security, along with code examples.

Cross-Site Request Forgery (CSRF) Protection

Laravel includes built-in CSRF protection to guard against cross-site request forgery attacks. The "csrf" middleware automatically generates and verifies CSRF tokens.

```php
<?php
// Blade template example
<form method="POST" action="/profile">
    @csrf
    <!-- Form fields go here -->
</form>
```

CHAPTER 4 FRAMEWORK SECURITY

Detailed Explanation

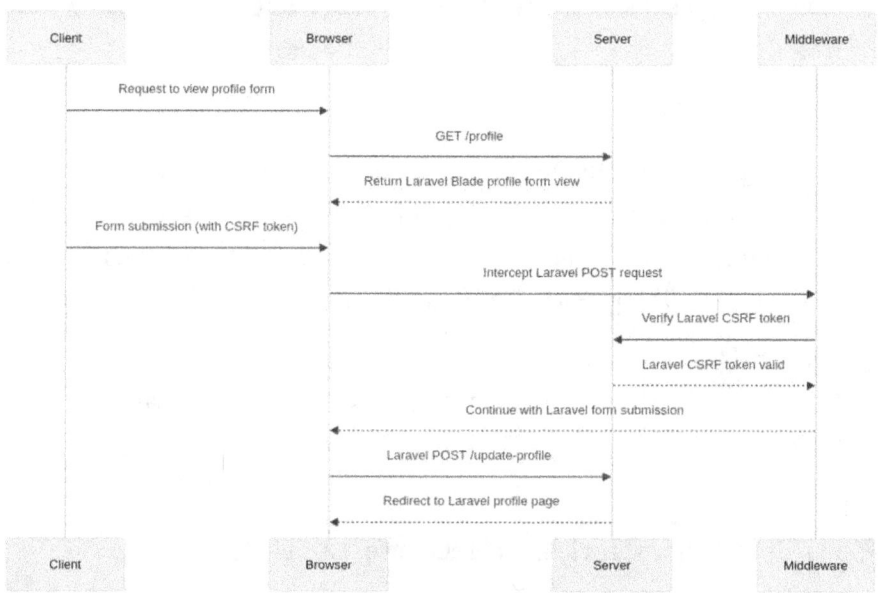

Figure 4-1. *Laravel usage of CSRF token workflow*

Front End (Blade Template)

Suppose you have a simple form in a Blade template that allows users to update their profile information.

```blade
<!-- resources/views/profile.blade.php -->
@if(session()->has('success'))
<div>
{{ session()->get('success') }}
</div>
@endif

<form method="POST" action="{{ route('updateProfile') }}">
    @csrf
```

CHAPTER 4 FRAMEWORK SECURITY

```html
<!-- other form fields -->
<button type="submit">Update Profile</button>
</form>
```

In this example:

- "@csrf": This Blade directive generates a hidden input field containing the CSRF token. This token is essential for Laravel to verify that the form submission originates from your application and not from a malicious site.

Back End (Controller)

Now, let's look at the corresponding back-end code in a Laravel controller.

```php
<?php
// app/Http/Controllers/ProfileController.php

namespace App\Http\Controllers;

use Illuminate\Http\Request;

class ProfileController extends Controller
{
    public function showForm()
    {
        return view('profile');
    }

    public function updateProfile(Request $request)
    {
        // Validation and processing logic here
        // ...
```

```
        return redirect()->route('profile')->with('success',
        'Profile updated successfully!');
    }
}
```

In this example:

- The "showForm" method displays the form view.
- The "updateProfile" method handles the form submission. Notice that there's no explicit code for CSRF validation; Laravel's built-in middleware takes care of this.

Middleware (VerifyCsrfToken)

Laravel includes middleware, such as "VerifyCsrfToken", to automatically validate CSRF tokens for all incoming POST, PUT, and DELETE requests.

```
<?php
// app/Http/Middleware/VerifyCsrfToken.php

namespace App\Http\Middleware;

use Illuminate\Foundation\Http\Middleware\VerifyCsrfToken as Middleware;

class VerifyCsrfToken extends Middleware
{
    protected $addHttpCookie = true;

    protected $except = [
        // Add routes that should be excluded from CSRF
           protection here
    ];
}
```

By default, Laravel automatically applies this middleware globally for web routes.

Explanation

Front End

In the front-end part of a Laravel application, forms are typically created using Blade templates. Within these templates, it is common practice to include the @csrf directive. This directive generates a hidden input field containing a CSRF (cross-site request forgery) token. The CSRF token is a unique, secret value that is used to verify the authenticity of the form submission. This verification helps to ensure that the form submission is coming from a legitimate source and not from a malicious actor attempting to exploit the application.

Back End

On the back end, the controller methods manage the display and processing of the forms. Specifically, methods like showForm are responsible for rendering the form to the user, while methods like updateProfile handle the submission of the form data. Laravel provides built-in CSRF protection through the web middleware group. This means that any routes assigned to this middleware group automatically have CSRF protection applied, ensuring that any form submissions to these routes are validated using the CSRF token.

Middleware

The VerifyCsrfToken middleware, located in app/Http/Middleware/VerifyCsrfToken.php, is responsible for checking the CSRF token on incoming POST, PUT, and DELETE requests. This middleware ensures that the token provided in the form matches the token stored in the user's session. If the tokens do not match, the request is rejected. Additionally, this middleware can be customized to exclude certain routes from CSRF protection if there are specific endpoints that should not be subject to this validation.

CHAPTER 4 FRAMEWORK SECURITY

Cross-Site Scripting (XSS) Protection

Laravel's Blade templating engine automatically escapes output, providing protection against XSS attacks. However, developers should still be cautious and use proper escaping when needed.

```
<?php
// Blade template example
{{ $userInput }}
```

Detailed Explanation

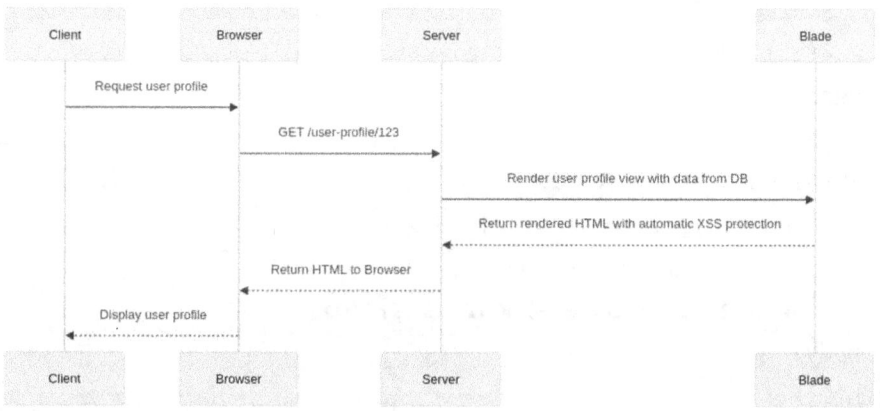

Figure 4-2. *Laravel XSS usage flow*

Let's go through an example of how Laravel helps protect against cross-site scripting (XSS) by automatically escaping output in Blade templates. We'll cover both the front end and back end, including a detailed explanation.

Front End (Blade Template)

CHAPTER 4   FRAMEWORK SECURITY

Suppose you have a Blade template to display user data in a safe manner:

blade
```
<!-- resources/views/user_profile.blade.php -->
<!DOCTYPE html>
<html lang="en">
<head>
    <meta charset="UTF-8">
    <meta name="viewport" content="width=device-width, initial-scale=1.0">
    <title>User Profile</title>
</head>
<body>
    <h1>User Profile</h1>
    <p>Name: {{ $user->name }}</p>
    <p>Email: {{ $user->email }}</p>
    <p>Address: {{ $user->address }}</p>
</body>
</html>
```

In this example, notice that we use Blade syntax ("{{ }}") to output user data. Laravel automatically escapes the output, ensuring that any potentially harmful content is treated as plain text and not as HTML or JavaScript.

Back End (Controller)

Now, let's look at the corresponding back-end code in a Laravel controller.

```
<?php
// app/Http/Controllers/UserController.php

namespace App\Http\Controllers;
```

CHAPTER 4   FRAMEWORK SECURITY

```
use Illuminate\Http\Request;
use App\Models\User;

class UserController extends Controller
{
    public function showProfile($userId)
    {
        $user = User::find($userId);

        return view('user_profile', ['user' => $user]);
    }
}
```

In this example, the "showProfile" method retrieves a user from the database and passes it to the "user_profile" view.

Explanation

Front End

In the front-end section of a Laravel application, the user_profile.blade.php Blade template is used to display user information. The template accesses and outputs user data using expressions like {{ $user->name }}, {{ $user->email }}, and {{ $user->address }}. The Blade templating engine in Laravel automatically escapes these outputs, converting any HTML or JavaScript characters into a plain text format. This built-in escaping mechanism is crucial for preventing cross-site scripting (XSS) attacks. As a result, even if the user data contains potentially harmful HTML or JavaScript code, it will be rendered harmlessly as plain text.

Back End

On the back end, the UserController plays a vital role in managing user data. It retrieves user information from the database based on a provided user ID ($userId). Once the user data is fetched, it is passed to the user_profile view. This process ensures that the correct user data is available for display in the Blade template. By separating data retrieval and presentation logic, Laravel promotes a clean and organized code structure, making the application more maintainable and secure.

CHAPTER 4 FRAMEWORK SECURITY

By utilizing Blade templating and Laravel's automatic output escaping, we can mitigate the risk of XSS attacks. It's important to always use the Blade syntax ("{{ }}") for outputting user-generated content and avoid using raw output ("{!! !!}") unless absolutely necessary and with proper validation.

Remember that while automatic output escaping helps prevent many XSS attacks, we should also be aware of other security best practices, such as validating and sanitizing user input and using other security mechanisms provided by Laravel.

SQL Injection Protection

Laravel's Eloquent ORM uses parameterized queries, preventing SQL injection attacks. Developers are encouraged to use Eloquent or the query builder for database interactions.

```php
<?php
// Using Eloquent
$users = User::where('name', '=', $input)->get();
```

Detailed Explanation

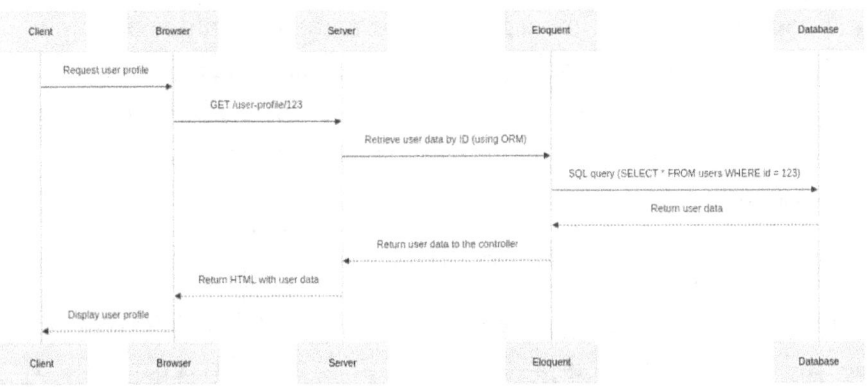

Figure 4-3. SQL injection protection in Laravel

CHAPTER 4　FRAMEWORK SECURITY

Let's go through an example of how Laravel protects against SQL injection by using Eloquent, the built-in ORM (Object-Relational Mapping) tool. This example will cover both the front end and back end, including detailed explanation.

Front End (Blade Template)

Suppose you have a Blade template to display user data:

```blade
<!-- resources/views/user_profile.blade.php -->

<!DOCTYPE html>
<html lang="en">
<head>
    <meta charset="UTF-8">
    <meta name="viewport" content="width=device-width, initial-scale=1.0">
    <title>User Profile</title>
</head>
<body>
    <h1>User Profile</h1>
    <p>Name: {{ $user->name }}</p>
    <p>Email: {{ $user->email }}</p>
    <p>Address: {{ $user->address }}</p>
</body>
</html>
```

Back End (Controller)

Now, let's look at the corresponding back-end code in a Laravel controller.

```php
// app/Http/Controllers/UserController.php

namespace App\Http\Controllers;
```

CHAPTER 4 FRAMEWORK SECURITY

```php
use Illuminate\Http\Request;
use App\Models\User;

class UserController extends Controller
{
    public function showProfile($userId)
    {
        // Using Eloquent to retrieve user data by ID
        $user = User::find($userId);

        return view('user_profile', ['user' => $user]);
    }
}
```

Explanation

Front End (Blade Template)

In the front-end of a Laravel application, the user_profile.blade.php Blade template is used to display user information. This template utilizes Blade's double curly braces ({{ }}) syntax to output user data, such as {{ $user->name }}, {{ $user->email }}, and {{ $user->address }}. Blade's templating engine automatically escapes this output, converting special characters into HTML entities. This escaping mechanism is designed to prevent cross-site scripting (XSS) attacks by ensuring that any potentially harmful code embedded in user data is rendered as plain text.

Back End (Controller)

On the back end, the UserController contains methods responsible for handling user data. Specifically, the showProfile method retrieves user information from the database using Eloquent, Laravel's ORM (Object-Relational Mapping) tool. The method typically uses Eloquent's find method to fetch a user based on their ID. Eloquent handles parameter binding automatically, treating the $userId parameter as a placeholder and ensuring it is safely incorporated into the SQL query. This approach provides protection against SQL injection attacks, as Eloquent ensures that the input is securely processed and executed.

This example showcases how Eloquent, by default, protects against SQL injection. It uses parameterized queries, ensuring that user input is properly sanitized and preventing malicious SQL injection attempts.

Laravel's use of Eloquent ORM provides a high level of protection against SQL injection vulnerabilities by automatically handling parameter binding and sanitizing user input. We can leverage this feature to write secure database queries without the need for explicit sanitization.

Authentication and Authorization

Laravel simplifies user authentication and authorization, providing guards and policies for controlling access to resources. It includes features like password hashing and protection against timing attacks.

```php
<?php
// Authentication
if (Auth::attempt(['email' => $email, 'password' => $password])) {
    // Authentication passed
}

// Authorization
if (Gate::allows('update-post', $post)) {
    // User is authorized to update the post
}
```

CHAPTER 4   FRAMEWORK SECURITY

Detailed Explanation

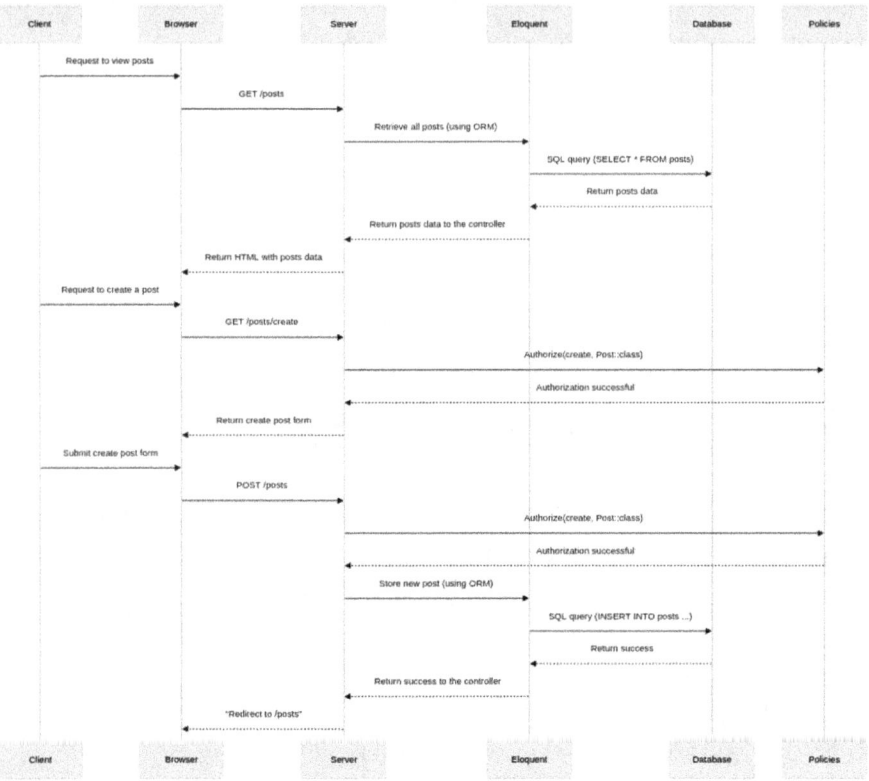

Figure 4-4. *Authentication and authorization flow in Laravel*

Let's go through an example of how Laravel handles authentication and authorization. This will include setting up user authentication, creating controllers with authorization checks, and utilizing Laravel's built-in features for secure user management.

Step 1: Set Up Authentication

Laravel Breeze is a package that provides a simple and lightweight way to set up authentication in Laravel applications. Let's follow below steps to set it up:

Step 1: Install Laravel Breeze

To start, you need to install Laravel Breeze using Composer, which is the dependency manager for PHP, by running the below command, we are telling composer to download and install the Breeze package as a development dependency in your Laravel project. This package contains all the necessary files and configurations to quickly scaffold authentication functionality:

```bash
composer require laravel/breeze --dev
```

Step 2: Install Breeze's Authentication Scaffolding

Once Breeze is installed, we need to set up the authentication scaffolding by running

```bash
php artisan breeze:install
```

This command generates the necessary authentication views, routes, controllers, and other files required for a basic authentication system. These files are placed in the appropriate directories within your Laravel project, providing a foundation for user login, registration, password reset, and email verification.

Step 3: Run Migrations

Laravel uses migrations to manage the database schema. To create the required database tables for authentication, run

```bash
php artisan migrate
```

This command executes the migration files, which create the tables for users, password resets, and any other required entities in your database. Migrations ensure that your database schema is consistent and version-controlled.

CHAPTER 4 FRAMEWORK SECURITY

Step 4: Install NPM Dependencies and Compile Assets

Laravel Breeze includes front-end assets that need to be compiled. First, install the necessary Node.js dependencies by running

```bash
npm install
```

This command downloads and installs all the required packages listed in the package.json file. After installing the dependencies, compile the front-end assets with

```bash
npm run dev
```

This command uses tools like Webpack to compile and bundle your JavaScript and CSS files. It prepares the front-end assets for development, enabling you to see the changes immediately as you work on the application.

Step 2: Create a Resource Controller

Next, create a resource controller for managing a resource (e.g., posts) with CRUD operations.

```bash
php artisan make:controller PostController --resource
```

This command generates a controller ("PostController") with methods for index, create, store, show, edit, update, and destroy.

Step 3: Define Routes

In the "routes/web.php" file, define routes for authentication and the resource controller.

```
<?php
use App\Http\Controllers\PostController;
use Illuminate\Support\Facades\Route;
```

```
// Authentication Routes
require __DIR__.'/auth.php';

// Resource Routes
Route::resource('posts', PostController::class);
```

Step 4: Implement Authorization in the Controller

Edit the "PostController" to include authorization checks. For example, only authenticated users should be able to create, update, and delete posts.

```
<?php
// app/Http/Controllers/PostController.php

namespace App\Http\Controllers;

use App\Models\Post;
use Illuminate\Http\Request;

class PostController extends Controller
{
    public function index()
    {
        $posts = Post::all();
        return view('posts.index', compact('posts'));
    }

    // Other methods...

    public function create()
    {
        $this->authorize('create', Post::class);
        return view('posts.create');
    }
```

```php
public function store(Request $request)
{
    $this->authorize('create', Post::class);
    // Validation and store logic
    // ...

    return redirect()->route('posts.index');
}

// Other methods...
}
```

Step 5: Implement Authorization in Views

In your Blade views, you can use the "@can" directive to conditionally show or hide content based on the user's authorization.

```php
<!-- resources/views/posts/index.blade.php -->

@if(Auth::check())
    <a href="{{ route('posts.create') }}">Create Post</a>
@endif

@foreach($posts as $post)
    <p>{{ $post->title }}</p>
    <!-- Show edit and delete links only for authorized
    users -->
    @can('update', $post)
        <a href="{{ route('posts.edit', $post->id) }}">Edit</a>
    @endcan

    @can('delete', $post)
        <form action="{{ route('posts.destroy', $post->id) }}"
        method="POST">
            @csrf
            @method('DELETE')
```

```
            <button type="submit">Delete</button>
        </form>
    @endcan
@endforeach
```

Step 6: Define Policies

In Laravel, you can use policies to encapsulate authorization logic. Create a policy for the "Post" model.

bash
```
php artisan make:policy PostPolicy
```

Define the authorization logic in the "PostPolicy" class.

```
<?php
// app/Policies/PostPolicy.php

namespace App\Policies;

use App\Models\User;
use App\Models\Post;

class PostPolicy
{
    public function update(User $user, Post $post)
    {
        return $user->id === $post->user_id;
    }

    public function delete(User $user, Post $post)
    {
        return $user->id === $post->user_id;
    }
}
```

CHAPTER 4   FRAMEWORK SECURITY

Step 7: Register Policies

In the "AuthServiceProvider", register the "PostPolicy" with the corresponding model.

```php
<?php
// app/Providers/AuthServiceProvider.php

namespace App\Providers;

use App\Models\Post;
use App\Policies\PostPolicy;
use Illuminate\Foundation\Support\Providers\AuthServiceProvider
 as ServiceProvider;

class AuthServiceProvider extends ServiceProvider
{
    protected $policies = [
        Post::class => PostPolicy::class,
    ];

    public function boot()
    {
        $this->registerPolicies();
    }
}
```

Step 8: Authorize in the Controller

Refactor the "PostController" to use the "authorize" method instead of manual checks.

```php
<?php
// app/Http/Controllers/PostController.php

namespace App\Http\Controllers;

use App\Models\Post;
use Illuminate\Http\Request;
```

196

```php
class PostController extends Controller
{
    public function index()
    {
        $posts = Post::all();
        return view('posts.index', compact('posts'));
    }

    // Other methods...

    public function create()
    {
        $this->authorize('create', Post::class);
        return view('posts.create');
    }

    public function store(Request $request)
    {
        $this->authorize('create', Post::class);
        // Validation and store logic
        // ...

        return redirect()->route('posts.index');
    }

    // Other methods...
}
```

Explanation

Authentication

Laravel Breeze simplifies the setup of authentication by scaffolding the necessary views, controllers, and routes. Unlike the deprecated make:auth command, Breeze offers a modern and minimal approach to authentication. The authentication routes, once Breeze is installed, are defined in the routes/web.php file, allowing users to register, log in, and manage passwords with ease.

Authorization in the Controller

Authorization in Laravel controllers ensures that only authenticated users can perform certain actions. In the PostController, methods such as create and store check if the user is authenticated using the authorize method. This method verifies if the user has the necessary permissions based on defined policies. If the user is not authenticated, they are redirected to the login page, ensuring secure access control.

Authorization in Views

In Blade views, Laravel provides the @can directive to conditionally display content based on user permissions. This directive checks the authorization policies associated with the user and determines if specific content, such as links to edit or delete a post, should be shown. This feature ensures that only authorized users can see and interact with certain parts of the user interface.

Policies

Laravel's policies encapsulate authorization logic for specific models, such as Post. These policies are created using the make:policy command. Policies define methods that correspond to various actions a user can perform on a model, such as updating or deleting a post. By centralizing authorization logic, policies make it easier to manage and maintain secure access control..

Register Policies

Policies must be registered in the AuthServiceProvider to be recognized by Laravel. In the AuthServiceProvider, policies are mapped to their respective models. This registration ensures that Laravel uses the correct policy for authorization checks, linking models like Post to their corresponding PostPolicy.

Authorize in the Controller Using Policies

The PostController leverages the authorize method to enforce authorization checks based on policies. When a user attempts to perform an action, such as creating or updating a post, the controller calls the relevant policy method to verify if the user has the necessary permissions. This approach provides a consistent and secure way to handle authorization across the application.

This end-to-end example demonstrates how Laravel handles user authentication and authorization, leveraging Eloquent ORM for user management and policies for fine-grained authorization control. It helps ensure that only authenticated users can perform specific actions and that authorization logic is centralized and easily maintainable.

Session Security

Laravel secures user sessions by encrypting the session data. It also provides options for using secure, HTTP-only cookies. Session security in Laravel is a crucial aspect of web application development. Laravel provides a robust and secure session management system out of the box.

```
<?php
// Storing data in the session
session(['key' => 'value']);
```

CHAPTER 4 FRAMEWORK SECURITY

Detailed Explanation

Figure 4-5. *Session security in Laravel*

Let's review a detailed example of how to implement and secure sessions in a Laravel application.

CHAPTER 4 FRAMEWORK SECURITY

Step 1: Session Configuration

Laravel's session configuration is stored in the "config/session.php" file. You can customize various aspects of the session behavior here. Ensure that your configuration is set up securely. Laravel uses the "cookie" driver by default, storing session data in encrypted cookies.

```php
<?php
// config/session.php

'driver' => env('SESSION_DRIVER', 'cookie'),
...
'secure' => env('SESSION_SECURE_COOKIE', true),
...
```

Step 2: Controller and Routes

Create a controller with routes to demonstrate session usage. In this example, we'll create a simple controller named "SessionController" with methods for starting, reading, and destroying sessions.

```bash
php artisan make:controller SessionController
```

```php
<?php
// app/Http/Controllers/SessionController.php

namespace App\Http\Controllers;

use Illuminate\Http\Request;

class SessionController extends Controller
{
    public function startSession(Request $request)
    {
        $request->session()->put('key', 'value');
        return 'Session started.';
    }
```

CHAPTER 4   FRAMEWORK SECURITY

```php
    public function readSession(Request $request)
    {
        $value = $request->session()->get('key', 'default');
        return 'Session value: ' . $value;
    }

    public function destroySession(Request $request)
    {
        $request->session()->forget('key');
        return 'Session destroyed.';
    }
}
```

Register the routes in "web.php":

```php
<?php
// routes/web.php

Route::get('/start-session', 'SessionController@startSession');
Route::get('/read-session', 'SessionController@readSession');
Route::get('/destroy-session', 'SessionController@destroySession');
```

Step 3: Middleware

Laravel includes a "web" middleware group, which includes the "EncryptCookies" middleware. This middleware encrypts cookies, providing additional security for session data.

```php
<?php
// app/Http/Kernel.php

protected $middlewareGroups = [
    'web' => [
        ...
        \Illuminate\Cookie\Middleware\EncryptCookies::class,
```

```
        ...
    ],
    ...
];
```

Step 4: CSRF Protection

Laravel includes CSRF protection by default. The "csrf" middleware checks that each incoming POST, PUT, and DELETE request includes a CSRF token. Ensure that your forms include the "@csrf" Blade directive.

```blade
<!-- Example Blade form -->
<form method="POST" action="/example">
    @csrf
    <!-- Your form fields go here -->
    <button type="submit">Submit</button>
</form>
```

Step 5: Session Encryption

Laravel automatically encrypts session data for security. Ensure that the "encrypt" configuration option is set to "true" in the "config/session.php" file.

```php
<?php
// config/session.php

'encrypt' => true,
```

Step 6: Session Flash Data

Session flash data allows you to store temporary data that is available during the next HTTP request. This is commonly used for status messages.

```php
<?php
// Controller method
public function storeData(Request $request)
```

```
{
    $request->session()->flash('status', 'Data stored
    successfully!');
    return redirect('/');
}
// Blade view
@if (session('status'))
    <div class="alert alert-success">
        {{ session('status') }}
    </div>
@endif
```

Explanation

Session Configuration

In Laravel, the config/session.php file is the central place for configuring various session settings. This file allows you to define parameters such as the session driver, lifetime, expiration behavior, and more, tailoring session management to suit the specific needs of your application.

Controller and Routes

The SessionController is responsible for demonstrating the basic operations of session management, including starting a session, reading session data, and destroying a session. The routes that map to these controller actions are defined in the web.php file, establishing the necessary endpoints for session interactions within your application.

Middleware

The EncryptCookies middleware, which is included in the web middleware group, ensures that all cookies are encrypted. This middleware adds a layer of security by protecting cookie data from being easily read or tampered with, thus enhancing the overall security of session data.

CHAPTER 4   FRAMEWORK SECURITY

CSRF Protection

Laravel includes cross-site request forgery (CSRF) protection by default. This protection is implemented to secure your application against CSRF attacks by verifying that the requests received by your application are legitimate and intended. CSRF tokens are automatically generated and verified, making this process seamless and robust.

Session Encryption

To further secure session data, Laravel encrypts all session data before storing it. This means that even if an attacker gains access to the session storage, the data will be unreadable without the proper encryption key, thus maintaining the confidentiality and integrity of the session information.

Session Flash Data

Laravel provides a feature called session flash data, which allows for the temporary storage of data between requests. Flash data is useful for storing transient messages or data that only needs to be available for the next request, such as success or error messages after form submissions. This data is automatically removed after it has been read, ensuring that it does not persist longer than necessary.

This example demonstrates the basics of session security in Laravel, including configuration, middleware, CSRF protection, encryption, and flash data. Always ensure that your session management aligns with security best practices.

File Upload Security

When handling file uploads, Laravel includes features like file validation and disk storage configuration to enhance security.

```
<?php
// File validation in a controller
$request->validate([
```

CHAPTER 4   FRAMEWORK SECURITY

```
    'file' => 'required|file|max:10240', // Max 10MB
]);

// Storing the uploaded file
$path = $request->file('file')->store('uploads');
```

Detailed Explanation

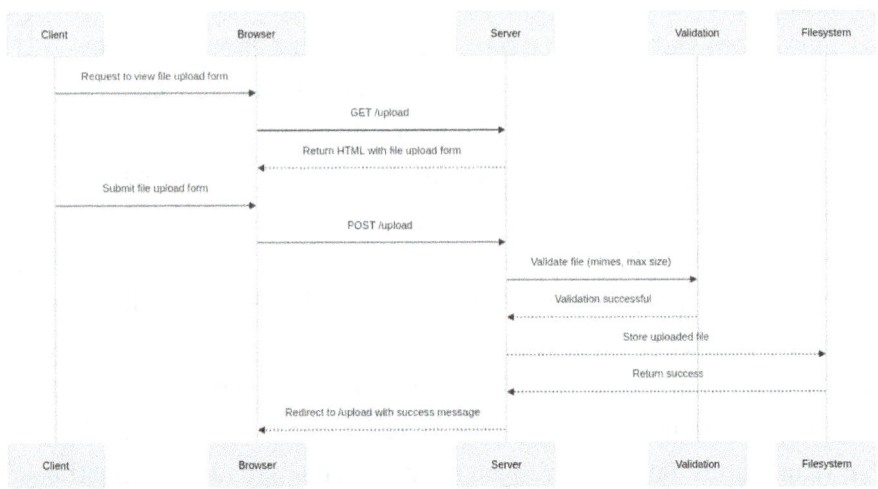

Figure 4-6. Securing file upload in Laravel

File upload security is crucial to prevent potential vulnerabilities. Laravel provides features to handle file uploads securely. Let's check a detailed example of how to implement secure file uploads in Laravel, including explanations.

Step 1: Create a Form for File Upload

Create a Blade view with a form for uploading files.

```blade
<!-- resources/views/upload.blade.php -->

<!DOCTYPE html>
<html lang="en">
```

206

```html
<head>
    <meta charset="UTF-8">
    <meta name="viewport" content="width=device-width, initial-scale=1.0">
    <title>File Upload</title>
</head>
<body>
    <h1>File Upload</h1>

    <form action="{{ route('upload') }}" method="post" enctype="multipart/form-data">
        @csrf
        <input type="file" name="file" accept=".pdf, .doc, .docx">
        <button type="submit">Upload</button>
    </form>
</body>
</html>
```

Step 2: Create a Controller to Handle File Upload

Create a controller that handles file upload requests.

```bash
php artisan make:controller FileController
```

```php
<?php
// app/Http/Controllers/FileController.php

namespace App\Http\Controllers;

use Illuminate\Http\Request;

class FileController extends Controller
{
    public function showUploadForm()
```

CHAPTER 4   FRAMEWORK SECURITY

```
    {
        return view('upload');
    }

    public function upload(Request $request)
    {
        $request->validate([
            'file' => 'required|mimes:pdf,doc,docx|max:2048',
        ]);

        $file = $request->file('file');
        $filename = time() . '_' . $file-
        >getClientOriginalName();

        $file->storeAs('uploads', $filename, 'public');

        return redirect()->route('upload')->with('success',
        'File uploaded successfully!');
    }
}
```

Explanation

HTML Form

To handle file uploads securely in Laravel, start with an HTML form that includes an input field of type "file". This form must also have the enctype="multipart/form-data" attribute, which is essential for allowing file uploads through the form. This ensures that the file data is properly encoded and transmitted to the server.

Controller Methods

In the controller, two methods manage the file upload process. The showUploadForm method is responsible for displaying the file upload form to the user. The upload method handles the actual file upload process once the form is submitted. These methods work together to provide a seamless user experience for file uploads.

CHAPTER 4   FRAMEWORK SECURITY

Validation Rules

To ensure that only appropriate files are uploaded, the validate method is used to enforce strict validation rules on the file upload request. The rule 'file' => 'required|mimes:pdf,doc,docx|max:2048' ensures that the uploaded file is mandatory, restricts the file types to PDF, DOC, and DOCX, and limits the file size to a maximum of 2MB. This validation is crucial for preventing the upload of potentially harmful files and managing server storage efficiently.

File Storage

Once validated, the uploaded file is stored in the storage/app/public/uploads directory. To ensure each file name is unique and avoid overwriting, the file name is prefixed with the current timestamp before storage. This approach not only helps in organizing the files but also prevents naming conflicts.

Step 3: Define Routes

Let's define the routes in "routes/web.php":

```php
<?php
// routes/web.php

use App\Http\Controllers\FileController;

Route::get('/upload', [FileController::class, 'showUploadForm'])->name('upload');
Route::post('/upload', [FileController::class, 'upload']);
```

Step 4: Configure Storage

Make sure your storage link is created:

```bash
php artisan storage:link
```

CHAPTER 4　FRAMEWORK SECURITY

Step 5: Update .env for Filesystem
Ensure your ".env" file is configured correctly:

env
```
FILESYSTEM_DRIVER=public
```

Step 6: Display Success Messages
Update the Blade view to display success messages:

blade
```
<!-- resources/views/upload.blade.php -->

<!-- ... -->

<body>
    <h1>File Upload</h1>

    @if(session('success'))
        <p style="color: green;">{{ session('success') }}</p>
    @endif

    <form action="{{ route('upload') }}" method="post"
    enctype="multipart/form-data">
        @csrf
        <input type="file" name="file" accept=".pdf,
        .doc, .docx">
        <button type="submit">Upload</button>
    </form>
</body>
</html>
```

This example outlines a secure method for implementing file uploads in Laravel, focusing on key aspects to ensure safety and efficiency.

HTML Form

The HTML form is set up with the enctype="multipart/form-data" attribute, which is essential for enabling file uploads. This attribute ensures that the file data is correctly encoded and sent to the server.

Controller Methods

Two controller methods manage the file upload process: one for displaying the file upload form and another for handling the actual upload. The first method shows the form to the user, while the second processes the uploaded file once the form is submitted.

Validation Rules

To maintain security and integrity, the file upload request is validated using specific rules. These rules check that the file type is allowed (e.g., PDF, DOC, DOCX) and that the file size does not exceed a certain limit (e.g., 2MB). This step is crucial for preventing malicious files from being uploaded.

File Storage

Uploaded files are stored in the public/uploads directory. To ensure uniqueness and avoid overwriting existing files, the file name is prefixed with a timestamp. This organizational method helps manage files effectively and prevents naming conflicts.

Routes Configuration

Routes are set up to manage the display of the file upload form and the processing of file uploads. These routes ensure that the correct controller methods are called in response to user actions, providing a seamless experience.

File System Configuration

The file system is configured to use the public disk for storing uploaded files. This configuration allows files to be publicly accessible while ensuring they are stored securely and can be managed easily through Laravel's file system features.

CHAPTER 4 FRAMEWORK SECURITY

Middleware for Additional Protection

Laravel allows developers to create custom middleware for additional security checks, logging, or any other requirements.

```
<?php
// Custom middleware
public function handle($request, Closure $next)
{
    // Perform security checks

    return $next($request);
}
```

Detailed Explanation

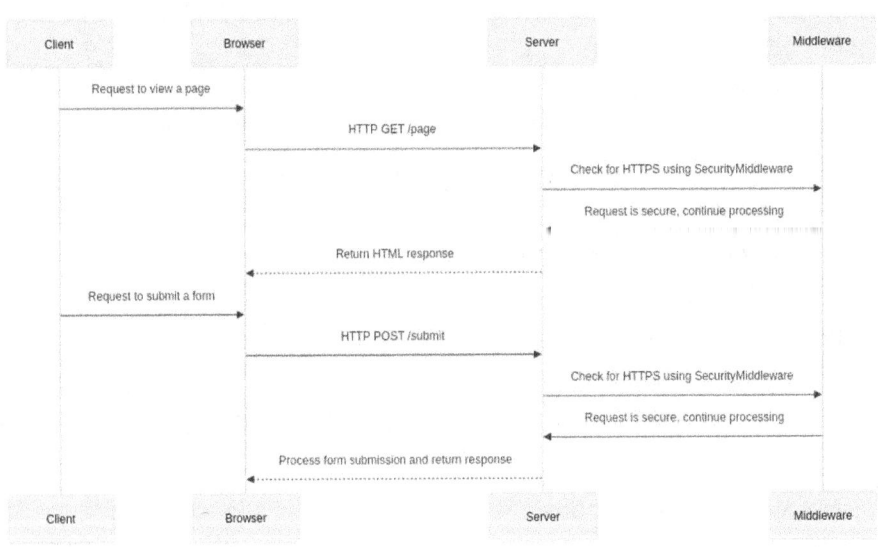

Figure 4-7. *Middleware protection using Laravel*

Middleware in Laravel provides a convenient way to filter HTTP requests that enter your application. Middleware can be used for various purposes, including adding an extra layer of security to your application. Let's create a simple middleware to illustrate how you can add additional protection to your Laravel application.

Step 1: Create a Middleware

Run the following Artisan command to create a new middleware:

```bash
php artisan make:middleware SecurityMiddleware
```

This will generate a new middleware class in the "app/Http/Middleware" directory.

Step 2: Implement the Middleware Logic

Open the generated "SecurityMiddleware" class ("app/Http/Middleware/SecurityMiddleware.php") and implement the desired security checks. In this example, we'll add a basic check to ensure that the request is using HTTPS.

```php
<?php
// app/Http/Middleware/SecurityMiddleware.php

namespace App\Http\Middleware;

use Closure;

class SecurityMiddleware
{
    public function handle($request, Closure $next)
    {
        // Check if the request is secure (HTTPS)
        if (!$request->secure()) {
            return redirect()->secure($request->getRequestUri());
        }
```

```
        return $next($request);
    }
}
```

Step 3: Register the Middleware

Add your middleware to the "$routeMiddleware" array in the "app/Http/Kernel.php" file highlighted in bold.

```
<?php
// app/Http/Kernel.php

namespace App\Http;

use Illuminate\Foundation\Http\Kernel as HttpKernel;

class Kernel extends HttpKernel
{
    protected $middleware = [
        // ...
    ];

    protected $middlewareGroups = [
        'web' => [
            // ...
            \App\Http\Middleware\SecurityMiddleware::class,
        ],
        'api' => [
            // ...
        ],
    ];
    // ...
}
```

Step 4: Apply the Middleware to Routes

You can apply the middleware globally to all web routes or selectively to specific routes or route groups.

Applying globally:

```php
<?php
// app/Http/Kernel.php

protected $middlewareGroups = [
    'web' => [
        // ...
        \App\Http\Middleware\SecurityMiddleware::class,
    ],
];
```

Applying selectively:

```php
<?php
// routes/web.php

Route::middleware(['web', 'security'])->group(function () {
    // Your routes here
});
```

Explanation

SecurityMiddleware Logic

In Laravel, middleware is used to filter and modify HTTP requests entering your application. The handle method within a middleware class is executed for each incoming request. In this example, the middleware checks if the request is secure, meaning it uses HTTPS. If the request is not secure, the middleware redirects the user to the secure version of the URL. This ensures that all communications between the client and server are encrypted, protecting sensitive data from being intercepted.

CHAPTER 4 FRAMEWORK SECURITY

Middleware Registration

To activate the middleware, it must be registered in the app/Http/Kernel.php file under the appropriate middleware group. In this case, the middleware is added to the web middleware group, which applies to all web routes by default. This central registration ensures that the security checks are consistently applied across the application.

Middleware Application

The middleware can be applied in different scopes. It can be applied globally to all web routes by including it in the web middleware group. Alternatively, it can be applied selectively to specific routes or route groups. This flexibility allows you to enforce HTTPS on certain parts of your application while leaving others accessible over HTTP, if necessary.

This example illustrates a straightforward security middleware that enforces HTTPS for web routes. In a real-world scenario, you may need to implement more advanced security measures tailored to your application's requirements. These could include input validation to prevent SQL injection, setting content security policies to guard against XSS attacks, and implementing anti-CSRF protection to secure form submissions. By using middleware effectively, you can enhance the security posture of your Laravel application significantly.

Middleware is a powerful tool in Laravel for adding layers of security to your application, and it allows you to intercept and inspect requests at different stages of the HTTP request lifecycle.

HTTPS and Secure Configuration

Configuring Laravel to use HTTPS and securing sensitive configuration settings are essential for overall application security.

```
<?php
// Configuring secure settings in .env file
APP_ENV=production
APP_DEBUG=false
```

Detailed Explanation

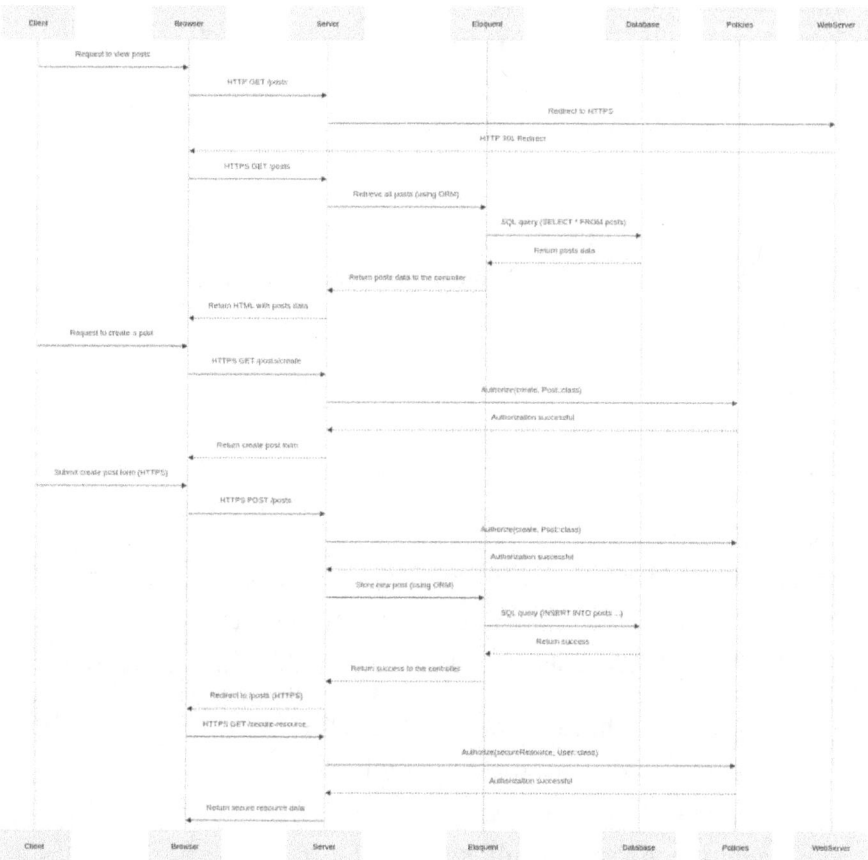

Figure 4-8. *HTTPS and secure configuration in Laravel*

Securing your Laravel application with HTTPS involves configuring your web server to use SSL/TLS and enforcing secure configurations in your Laravel application. Let's follow a step-by-step guide along with code snippets to enable HTTPS in Laravel.

Step 1: Obtain an SSL Certificate

First, you need an SSL certificate for your domain. You can obtain one from a Certificate Authority (CA) like Let's Encrypt, or you can purchase one. Let's Encrypt provides free SSL certificates.

CHAPTER 4   FRAMEWORK SECURITY

Step 2: Configure Web Server (Apache or Nginx)

Apache Configuration

For Apache, you need to configure the VirtualHost to use SSL. Edit your Apache configuration file or create a new one for your Laravel project.

```apache
<VirtualHost *:80>
    ServerName your-domain.com
    Redirect permanent / https://your-domain.com/
</VirtualHost>

<VirtualHost *:443>
    ServerName your-domain.com
    DocumentRoot /path/to/your/laravel/public

    SSLEngine on
    SSLCertificateFile /path/to/your/ssl_certificate.crt
    SSLCertificateKeyFile /path/to/your/private_key.key
    SSLCertificateChainFile /path/to/your/chain_file.pem

    <Directory /path/to/your/laravel/public>
        Options Indexes FollowSymLinks
        AllowOverride All
        Require all granted
    </Directory>
</VirtualHost>
```

Nginx Configuration

For Nginx, configure your server block to use SSL.

```nginx
server {
    listen 80;
```

```
    server_name your-domain.com;
    return 301 https://$host$request_uri;
}
server {
    listen 443 ssl;
    server_name your-domain.com;
    root /path/to/your/laravel/public;

    ssl_certificate /path/to/your/ssl_certificate.crt;
    ssl_certificate_key /path/to/your/private_key.key;
    ssl_trusted_certificate /path/to/your/chain_file.pem;

    # Other SSL/TLS configurations

    location / {
        try_files $uri $uri/ /index.php?$query_string;
    }

    # Additional Nginx configurations...
}
```

Step 3: Configure Laravel for HTTPS

In your Laravel application, you need to configure it to work seamlessly with HTTPS. Update your ".env" file with the following settings:

```env
APP_URL=https://your-domain.com
```

Step 4: Enable HTTPS in Laravel Middleware

Create a middleware to force HTTPS. Run the following command to generate a new middleware:

```bash
php artisan make:middleware ForceHttps
```

CHAPTER 4 FRAMEWORK SECURITY

Edit the generated "ForceHttps" middleware:

```php
<?php
// app/Http/Middleware/ForceHttps.php

namespace App\Http\Middleware;

use Closure;

class ForceHttps
{
    public function handle($request, Closure $next)
    {
        if (!$request->secure() && env('APP_ENV') ===
        'production') {
            return redirect()->secure($request-
            >getRequestUri());
        }

        return $next($request);
    }
}
```

Register the middleware in the "App\Http\Kernel" class:

```php
<?php
// app/Http/Kernel.php

protected $middleware = [
    // Other middleware...
    \App\Http\Middleware\ForceHttps::class,
];
```

This middleware checks if the request is not secure (not using HTTPS) and redirects to the secure version in a production environment.

CHAPTER 4 FRAMEWORK SECURITY

Step 5: Update Service Providers

In "config/app.php", make sure the "url" configuration is set to use HTTPS:

```php
<?php
'url' => env('APP_URL', 'https://your-domain.com'),
```

Step 6: HSTS (HTTP Strict Transport Security)

To enhance security, you can enable HTTP Strict Transport Security (HSTS) in your Laravel application. Add the following middleware to your "$middleware" array in "App\Http\Kernel":

```php
<?php
// app/Http/Kernel.php

protected $middleware = [
    // Other middleware...
    \App\Http\Middleware\ForceHttps::class,
    \Illuminate\Http\Middleware\FrameGuard::class,
    \App\Http\Middleware\AddHstsHeader::class,
];
```

Create a new middleware for HSTS:

```bash
php artisan make:middleware AddHstsHeader
```

Edit the generated "AddHstsHeader" middleware:

```php
<?php
// app/Http/Middleware/AddHstsHeader.php

namespace App\Http\Middleware;

use Closure;
```

CHAPTER 4   FRAMEWORK SECURITY

```
class AddHstsHeader
{
    public function handle($request, Closure $next)
    {
        $response = $next($request);

        // Add HSTS header
        $response->headers->add(['Strict-Transport-Security' =>
        'max-age=31536000; includeSubDomains']);

        return $response;
    }
}
```

Explanation

Obtain an SSL Certificate

The first step in securing your Laravel application with HTTPS is to acquire an SSL certificate for your domain. This can be done through a Certificate Authority (CA) like Let's Encrypt. An SSL certificate encrypts the data transferred between your server and clients, ensuring privacy and data integrity.

Configure Web Server

Once you have the SSL certificate, update your web server configuration to use SSL. For Apache, this involves specifying the paths to your SSL certificate files in the configuration file. For Nginx, similar adjustments are made in the server block. These configurations tell the server to use the SSL certificate for encrypted communications.

Configure Laravel for HTTPS

Next, set the APP_URL in your Laravel .env file to use the HTTPS protocol. This configuration ensures that all URL generation within your Laravel application defaults to HTTPS, providing a consistent secure link structure across your site.

CHAPTER 4 FRAMEWORK SECURITY

Enable HTTPS in Laravel Middleware

To enforce HTTPS, create a middleware that forces all requests to use HTTPS. Register this middleware in the middleware stack to ensure that every request is redirected to the secure HTTPS version of your site. This step is crucial to prevent any unsecured access.

Update Service Providers

Ensure that the URL configuration in config/app.php is set to use HTTPS. This adjustment ensures that all URLs generated by Laravel's URL generator are secure, reinforcing the HTTPS protocol across all parts of your application.

HSTS (HTTP Strict Transport Security)

Optionally, you can implement HTTP Strict Transport Security (HSTS) by adding middleware that sets the Strict-Transport-Security header. HSTS instructs browsers to always use HTTPS for your domain, even if the user attempts to access it via HTTP. This additional layer of security helps to protect your site from protocol downgrade attacks and cookie hijacking.

By following these steps, we secure our Laravel application with HTTPS, ensuring encrypted communication between clients and your server. The provided code snippets and explanations cover essential aspects of configuring Laravel for HTTPS and enhancing security measures.

These are just a few examples of how Laravel addresses security concerns in different contexts. It's crucial for developers to stay informed about best practices and regularly update their applications and dependencies to benefit from the latest security enhancements.

CHAPTER 4   FRAMEWORK SECURITY

Secure Configuration and Deployment in Laravel

Secure configuration and deployment in Laravel are crucial aspects of building and maintaining a secure web application. Properly securing your Laravel application involves several key practices, from protecting sensitive information to enforcing HTTPS for secure communication.

Protecting Sensitive Information

In Laravel, secure configuration is essential for protecting sensitive information such as API keys, database credentials, and other environment-specific settings. Laravel uses the .env file, which allows for centralized and secure management of these configuration variables. During deployment, it is critical to ensure that sensitive information is not exposed in configuration files or logs. Secure deployment practices, such as using environment variables and secrets management tools, help prevent unintended exposure of credentials or other sensitive data throughout the deployment process.

Preventing Security Vulnerabilities

Configuring Laravel with best security practices helps prevent common vulnerabilities. This includes setting proper session, cookie, and encryption configurations. For example, ensuring that cookies are set with the Secure and HttpOnly flags and configuring encryption keys properly contribute to a more secure application. Regularly deploying security updates and patches is crucial to address vulnerabilities in Laravel or its dependencies. Automated deployment pipelines and tools can help ensure consistent and secure deployments, making it easier to apply updates without manual intervention.

Enforcing HTTPS for Secure Communication

Configuring Laravel to use HTTPS ensures encrypted communication between the client and the server. This protects user data, login credentials, and other sensitive information from interception. To enforce HTTPS, you need to configure your web server (such as Apache or Nginx) to support HTTPS and update your Laravel configuration to use the HTTPS protocol. This includes setting the APP_URL in the .env file to https:// and possibly creating middleware to redirect all HTTP traffic to HTTPS. Enforcing HTTPS is a critical security measure, especially in production environments.

Implementing HTTP Strict Transport Security (HSTS)

Enabling HSTS in the web server configuration ensures that browsers communicate with the server over secure connections only. This prevents protocol downgrade attacks and ensures a more secure browsing experience for users. During deployment, setting up HSTS headers in your web server configuration helps protect against man-in-the-middle attacks. This involves adding the Strict-Transport-Security header to your responses, which instructs browsers to only interact with your site over HTTPS for a specified period.

Maintaining Production-Ready Environments

Configuring Laravel for production environments involves optimizing settings for performance, security, and stability. This includes disabling debug mode, ensuring proper error reporting, and optimizing cache and session settings. Proper configuration ensures that error messages do not expose sensitive information. Deployment practices should focus on maintaining a consistent and secure production environment. Regularly testing and validating deployments in staging environments before production deployment is crucial to catch potential issues and ensure a smooth transition.

Enhancing Overall Application Security

Adhering to secure configuration practices helps build a foundation for overall application security. Laravel's built-in security features, when properly configured, help protect the application against common web application vulnerabilities such as SQL injection, XSS, and CSRF attacks. Secure deployment practices extend beyond the deployment process to include monitoring and incident response. Implementing continuous security practices, such as regular security audits, vulnerability scanning, and monitoring, ensures that security remains a priority throughout the application's lifecycle.

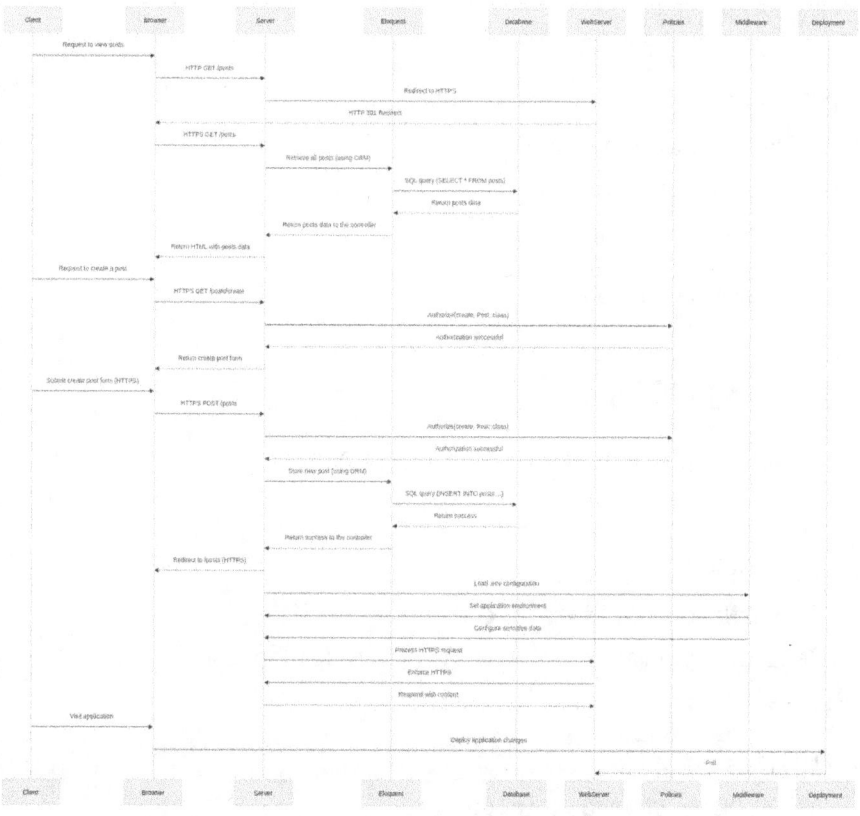

Figure 4-9. *Secure configuration in Laravel workflow*

Secure Configuration

".env" File:

Ensure sensitive information is securely stored. Avoid storing critical information directly in the ".env" file.

dotenv
APP_ENV=production
APP_KEY=your_generated_key

CHAPTER 4 FRAMEWORK SECURITY

```
DB_CONNECTION=mysql
DB_HOST=127.0.0.1
DB_PORT=3306
DB_DATABASE=your_database
DB_USERNAME=your_username
DB_PASSWORD=your_password

# Other configurations...
```

HTTPS and HSTS

Web Server Configuration (Apache Example):

```apache
<VirtualHost *:80>
    ServerName your-domain.com
    Redirect permanent / https://your-domain.com/
</VirtualHost>

<VirtualHost *:443>
    ServerName your-domain.com
    DocumentRoot /path/to/your/laravel/public

    SSLEngine on
    SSLCertificateFile /path/to/your/ssl_certificate.crt
    SSLCertificateKeyFile /path/to/your/private_key.key
    SSLCertificateChainFile /path/to/your/chain_file.pem

    <Directory /path/to/your/laravel/public>
        Options Indexes FollowSymLinks
        AllowOverride All
        Require all granted
    </Directory>
```

```
    Header always set Strict-Transport-Security "max-
    age=31536000; includeSubDomains"
</VirtualHost>
```

Middleware for HTTPS Redirection:

```
<?php
// app/Http/Middleware/ForceHttps.php

namespace App\Http\Middleware;

use Closure;
use Illuminate\Support\Facades\App;

class ForceHttps
{
    public function handle($request, Closure $next)
    {
        if (!$request->secure() &&
        App::environment('production')) {
            return redirect()->secure($request-
            >getRequestUri());
        }

        return $next($request);
    }
}
```

Middleware for HSTS Header:

```
<?php
// app/Http/Middleware/AddHstsHeader.php

namespace App\Http\Middleware;

use Closure;
```

Chapter 4 Framework Security

```php
class AddHstsHeader
{
    public function handle($request, Closure $next)
    {
        $response = $next($request);

        // Add HSTS header
        $response->headers->add(['Strict-Transport-Security' =>
        'max-age=31536000; includeSubDomains']);

        return $response;
    }
}
```

Middleware Registration in Kernel:

```php
<?php
// app/Http/Kernel.php

protected $middleware = [
    // Other middleware...
    \App\Http\Middleware\ForceHttps::class,
    \App\Http\Middleware\AddHstsHeader::class,
];
```

Deployment Best Practices

Set Laravel to Production Mode:
In the ".env" file:

```dotenv
APP_ENV=production
```

Optimize for Production:

```bash
php artisan optimize
```

Composer Autoloader Optimization:

```bash
composer dump-autoload --optimize
```

Secure File Permissions:

```bash
chmod -R 755 storage bootstrap/cache
```

Secure configuration and deployment practices are integral to building and maintaining a secure Laravel application. They help protect sensitive information, prevent security vulnerabilities, enforce secure communication, and contribute to an overall robust security posture. Regularly reviewing and updating configurations, deploying security patches, and following best practices are essential for a secure and reliable Laravel application.

CHAPTER 4   FRAMEWORK SECURITY

Protecting Routes, Middleware, and Controllers

Figure 4-10. Routes, middleware, and controllers in Laravel

Protecting routes, middleware, and controllers in Laravel is essential for ensuring the security and integrity of your web application. These components play a crucial role in controlling access, filtering requests, and implementing security measures. Let's check a few reasons why safeguarding them is important in a security context.

1. Access Control and Authorization

Laravel's routing system allows you to define routes that map to specific controllers or closures. Controlling access to these routes is vital for enforcing proper authorization. Middleware can be employed to check user roles, permissions, or any custom logic before allowing or denying access to a particular route. This helps prevent unauthorized users from accessing sensitive parts of your application.

2. Input Validation and Sanitization

Middleware, which operates between the request and the controller, is a powerful tool for input validation and sanitization. By filtering and validating incoming data through middleware, you can protect your application from common security threats like SQL injection, XSS (cross-site scripting), and CSRF (cross-site request forgery). Proper validation ensures that the data reaching your controllers is safe and adheres to the expected format, reducing the risk of malicious input.

3. Defense Against Attacks and Security Policies

Controllers handle the core logic of your application. Protecting controllers involves implementing security policies to safeguard against various attacks. Laravel provides features like route model binding, dependency injection, and resource controllers, which, when used securely, contribute to the prevention of attacks such as parameter tampering and injection attacks. Middleware, on the other hand, allows you to apply security-related policies at a broader level, affecting multiple routes and controllers.

4. Logging and Monitoring

Laravel's middleware and controllers can be leveraged for logging and monitoring activities within your application. By implementing logging mechanisms in middleware and controllers, you can capture information about user actions, failed access attempts, or any suspicious behavior. This logging data is invaluable for security audits, forensic analysis, and proactive identification of potential security threats.

Protecting routes, middleware, and controllers in Laravel involves a combination of authentication, authorization, and other security measures. Let's review an end-to-end example with detailed code snippets, highlighting best security practices.

Step 1: Set Up Authentication

First, ensure that you have user authentication set up. Laravel provides an easy way to scaffold authentication with the "make:auth" command:

```bash
php artisan make:auth
```

This command generates the necessary views, controllers, and routes for user registration and login.

Step 2: Create Middleware for Authorization

Create a middleware to handle authorization. For this example, let's create a middleware called "CheckRole" that checks if the user has a specific role.

```bash
php artisan make:middleware CheckRole
```

CHAPTER 4   FRAMEWORK SECURITY

Edit the generated "CheckRole" middleware:

```php
<?php
// app/Http/Middleware/CheckRole.php

namespace App\Http\Middleware;

use Closure;

class CheckRole
{
    public function handle($request, Closure $next, $role)
    {
        if (!$request->user() || !$request->user()->
        hasRole($role)) {
            abort(403, 'Unauthorized action.');
        }

        return $next($request);
    }
}
```

Step 3: Define User Roles

In your "User" model, define a method to check if a user has a specific role:

```php
<?php
// app/Models/User.php

namespace App\Models;

use Illuminate\Foundation\Auth\User as Authenticatable;

class User extends Authenticatable
{
    // ...
```

CHAPTER 4 FRAMEWORK SECURITY

```php
    public function hasRole($role)
    {
        return $this->role === $role;
    }
}
```

Step 4: Register Middleware in Kernel

Register the "CheckRole" middleware in the "$routeMiddleware" array in the "App\Http\Kernel" class:

```php
<?php
// app/Http/Kernel.php

protected $routeMiddleware = [
    // Other middleware...
    'checkRole' => \App\Http\Middleware\CheckRole::class,
];
```

Step 5: Apply Middleware to Routes

Apply the "CheckRole" middleware to the routes you want to protect:

```php
<?php
// routes/web.php

Route::middleware(['auth', 'checkRole:admin'])->group(function () {
    // Your protected routes go here
});
```

Step 6: Secure Controller Actions

In your controller, use the "authorize" method to perform authorization checks:

```php
<?php
// app/Http/Controllers/ExampleController.php
```

CHAPTER 4 FRAMEWORK SECURITY

```php
namespace App\Http\Controllers;

use Illuminate\Http\Request;

class ExampleController extends Controller
{
    public function adminAction(Request $request)
    {
        $this->authorize('adminAction', $request->user());

        // Your controller logic for admin action
    }
}
```

Step 7: Define Policies

Create a policy to encapsulate your authorization logic:

bash
```
php artisan make:policy ExamplePolicy
```

Edit the generated "ExamplePolicy":

```php
<?php
// app/Policies/ExamplePolicy.php

namespace App\Policies;

use App\Models\User;

class ExamplePolicy
{
    public function adminAction(User $user)
    {
        return $user->hasRole('admin');
    }
}
```

Step 8: Register Policies

In the "AuthServiceProvider", register the "ExamplePolicy" with the corresponding model:

```php
<?php
// app/Providers/AuthServiceProvider.php

namespace App\Providers;

use App\Models\User;
use App\Policies\ExamplePolicy;
use Illuminate\Foundation\Support\Providers\AuthServiceProvider as ServiceProvider;

class AuthServiceProvider extends ServiceProvider
{
    protected $policies = [
        User::class => ExamplePolicy::class,
    ];

    public function boot()
    {
        $this->registerPolicies();
    }
}
```

Security Best Practices

Implementing security best practices in Laravel is essential to ensure your application is robust and protected against unauthorized access and other security threats. Here are some key practices to follow.

Role-Based Access Control (RBAC)

To manage user access effectively, implement Role-Based Access Control (RBAC). Instead of assigning direct permissions to each user, assign roles that encapsulate a set of permissions. This approach simplifies management and enhances security by ensuring users have the appropriate level of access based on their roles. When checking for permissions, always verify roles rather than individual permissions.

Middleware

Utilize middleware for route-specific authorization in your Laravel application. Middleware acts as a gatekeeper, intercepting requests and performing necessary checks before they reach the controller. This ensures that only authorized users can access certain routes and resources, providing an additional layer of security.

Policies

For more detailed and fine-grained authorization logic, use policies. Policies encapsulate the authorization logic related to specific models or actions within your application. By defining policies, you can centralize your authorization logic, making it easier to manage and maintain.

Authorization in Controllers

Within your controllers, use the authorize method to perform authorization checks based on your defined policies. This method ensures that the user has the necessary permissions to perform the action they are attempting. By integrating authorization checks directly into your controllers, you can maintain a clear and consistent security approach throughout your application.

CHAPTER 4   FRAMEWORK SECURITY

Middleware Parameters

Enhance the flexibility and reusability of your middleware by passing parameters to them. Middleware parameters allow you to customize the behavior of middleware for different routes or conditions, making your security measures more adaptable and efficient.

Error Handling

Implement proper error handling to provide meaningful responses when authorization fails. Instead of exposing sensitive information or returning generic errors, tailor your responses to inform the user appropriately while maintaining security. Proper error handling helps improve the user experience and aids in debugging security issues.

Route Grouping

Leverage route grouping with middleware to apply authorization checks to multiple routes at once. By grouping related routes and assigning middleware to the group, you can ensure consistent security measures across multiple endpoints. This approach simplifies the application of authorization logic and helps maintain organized and manageable route definitions.

Protecting routes, middleware, and controllers in Laravel is integral to building a secure web application. These components serve as the first line of defense against unauthorized access, input manipulation, and other security vulnerabilities. Leveraging Laravel's robust features and implementing secure coding practices in these areas helps fortify your application and ensures a safer online environment for both users and data.

CHAPTER 4   FRAMEWORK SECURITY

Securing Laravel Database Operations

Securing database operations in Laravel involves various measures, such as using Eloquent ORM, employing parameterized queries, validating user input, and implementing authorization checks. Let's follow below guide with detailed code examples and best security practices.

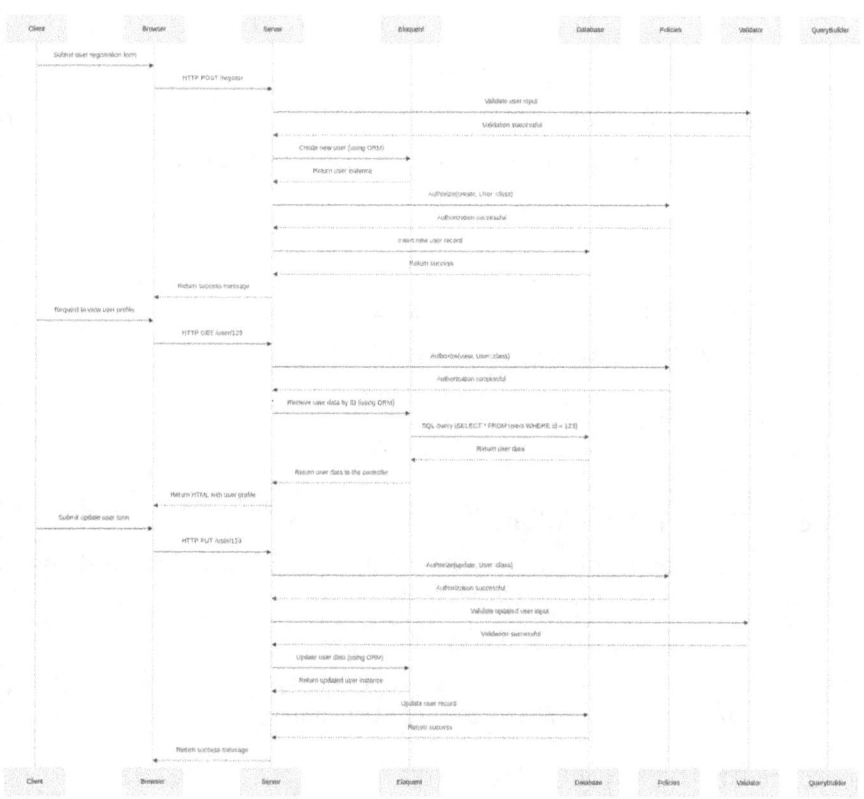

Figure 4-11. *Securing database operations in Laravel*

Step 1: Use Eloquent ORM
Model Definition

Define a model for the entity you are interacting with in the database, ensuring you use Eloquent ORM.

241

CHAPTER 4   FRAMEWORK SECURITY

```php
<?php
// app/Models/User.php

namespace App\Models;

use Illuminate\Database\Eloquent\Model;

class User extends Model
{
    $validatedData = $request->validate([
        'name' => 'required|string|max:255',
        'email' => 'required|email|unique:users|max:255',
        'password' => 'required|string|min:8',
    ]);

    // Create user using validated data
    $user = User::create($validatedData);

    // Additional logic...
}
```

Step 2: Perform Validation

Always validate user input to prevent SQL injection attacks and ensure data integrity.

```php
<?php
// app/Http/Controllers/UserController.php

namespace App\Http\Controllers;

use Illuminate\Http\Request;
use App\Models\User;

class UserController extends Controller
{
    public function store(Request $request)
```

```php
{
    $validatedData = $request->validate([
        'name' => 'required|string|max:255',
        'email' => 'required|email|unique:users|max:255',
        'password' => 'required|string|min:8',
    ]);

    // Create user using validated data
    $user = User::create($validatedData);

    // Additional logic...
    }
}
```

Step 3: Use Parameterized Queries

Laravel's Eloquent ORM automatically uses parameterized queries, helping prevent SQL injection.

```php
<?php
// app/Http/Controllers/UserController.php

namespace App\Http\Controllers;

use Illuminate\Http\Request;
use App\Models\User;

class UserController extends Controller
{
    public function findUser($id)
    {
        // Eloquent automatically uses parameterized query
        $user = User::find($id);

        // Additional logic...
    }
}
```

CHAPTER 4   FRAMEWORK SECURITY

Step 4: Implement Authorization

Leverage Laravel's built-in authorization features to control access to database operations.

Policy Definition

Create a policy to define authorization rules.

```bash
php artisan make:policy UserPolicy
```

```php
<?php
// app/Policies/UserPolicy.php

namespace App\Policies;

use App\Models\User;
use Illuminate\Auth\Access\HandlesAuthorization;

class UserPolicy
{
    use HandlesAuthorization;

    public function update(User $user, User $targetUser)
    {
        return $user->id === $targetUser->id;
    }

    // Additional authorization logic...
}
```

Authorization in Controller

Apply the policy in the controller to check if the authenticated user has the necessary permissions.

```php
<?php
// app/Http/Controllers/UserController.php

namespace App\Http\Controllers;
```

```
use Illuminate\Http\Request;
use App\Models\User;

class UserController extends Controller
{
    public function update(Request $request, User $user)
    {
        $this->authorize('update', $user);

        // Update user data...
    }
}
```

Step 5: Use Laravel Query Builder Safely

If you need to use raw SQL queries, use Laravel's Query Builder with bindings to prevent SQL injection.

```
<?php
// app/Http/Controllers/UserController.php

namespace App\Http\Controllers;

use Illuminate\Support\Facades\DB;

class UserController extends Controller
{
    public function customQuery($searchTerm)
    {
        $results = DB::select('SELECT * FROM users WHERE name = ?', [$searchTerm]);

        // Process results...
    }
}
```

Step 6: Hide Error Details in Production

Configure Laravel to hide error details in production environments to prevent exposing sensitive information.

```php
<?php
// config/app.php

'env' => env('APP_ENV', 'production'),
```

Step 7: Secure Database Credentials

Ensure that your database credentials are securely stored and not exposed in your application code. Use environment variables to store sensitive information.

Summary

This chapter delves into the critical aspects of securing a Laravel application, emphasizing the importance of robust security measures tailored to Laravel, a popular PHP framework. The chapter outlines various techniques and best practices to safeguard Laravel applications against potential vulnerabilities.

Introduction to Laravel Security Features

The chapter begins with an overview of Laravel's built-in security features, such as CSRF protection, XSS protection, and SQL injection prevention through Eloquent ORM. These features are fundamental in protecting web applications from common security threats.

Secure Configuration and Deployment in Laravel

Securing configuration and deployment involves protecting sensitive information, enforcing HTTPS, and implementing HTTP Strict Transport Security (HSTS). The use of environment variables for storing configuration settings and regular deployment of security updates are

CHAPTER 4 FRAMEWORK SECURITY

highlighted as best practices. Additionally, middleware is configured to ensure all traffic is secure, and production settings are optimized for performance and security.

Protecting Routes, Middleware, and Controllers

This section emphasizes the role of routes, middleware, and controllers in securing a Laravel application. Implementing Role-Based Access Control (RBAC) and using middleware for route-specific authorization checks ensure only authorized users can access certain parts of the application. Policies encapsulate authorization logic, making it easier to manage and maintain secure access control. Error handling and route grouping further enhance the security and usability of the application.

Securing Laravel Database Operations

To secure database operations, the chapter advocates for the use of Laravel's Eloquent ORM, which inherently uses parameterized queries to prevent SQL injection. Validation of user input, safe usage of the query builder, and proper handling of database credentials through environment variables are essential practices. Additionally, the chapter discusses the importance of implementing authorization checks using policies and controllers to ensure that only authorized users can perform specific database operations.

CHAPTER 5

Security Standards and Best Practices

In the rapidly evolving landscape of web application development, ensuring robust security is paramount. This chapter delves into the critical security standards and best practices essential for PHP application development. This chapter will explore the OWASP Top Ten, highlighting the most prevalent web application security risks, and provide guidance on implementing secure coding practices and conducting thorough code reviews. It will cover secure authentication and authorization mechanisms to safeguard user data and ensure proper access control. Additionally, the chapter will discuss methods for security testing and vulnerability assessments to identify and mitigate potential threats. Finally, it will address secure deployment and DevOps considerations, emphasizing the importance of integrating security throughout the development lifecycle. By adhering to these standards and best practices, developers can significantly enhance the security of their PHP applications, protecting both the application and its users from malicious attacks.

When it comes to security in PHP, several key standards and best practices should be followed to mitigate potential risks and protect web applications from various vulnerabilities. Input validation stands out as a foundational security measure. Ensuring that user inputs are thoroughly validated and sanitized before being processed helps prevent common attacks such as SQL injection and cross-site scripting (XSS). PHP offers functions like "filter_var()" and "htmlspecialchars()" that aid in input validation and output encoding.

Secure configuration settings play a vital role in minimizing the attack surface. PHP configurations should be fine-tuned to disable unnecessary features and functions. For example, the "allow_url_fopen" setting should be turned off to prevent remote file inclusion vulnerabilities. Regularly updating PHP to the latest stable version is essential, as each release often includes security patches and improvements to address emerging threats.

Secure coding practices involve implementing the principle of least privilege. This means granting users and processes only the minimum access rights necessary for their tasks. Strong user authentication and authorization mechanisms should be in place, ensuring that sensitive operations are performed only by authenticated and authorized users. Passwords must be securely hashed using robust algorithms, and sensitive data should be encrypted during both transmission and storage. The adoption of secure communication protocols, like HTTPS, is crucial to protect against data interception and tampering.

Continuous monitoring and proactive measures are crucial for maintaining a secure PHP application. Regular security audits, code reviews, and the use of automated tools for vulnerability scanning contribute to identifying and addressing potential security issues. Staying informed about the latest security threats and patches through active participation in the PHP community and adhering to established security best practices are key components of a robust security strategy for PHP applications.

CHAPTER 5 SECURITY STANDARDS AND BEST PRACTICES

OWASP Top Ten: Key Web Application Security Risks

The OWASP (Open Web Application Security Project) Top Ten is a widely recognized document outlining the most critical web application security risks. Let's discuss some key thoughts on OWASP Top Ten and how to handle these risks in PHP using the Laravel framework.

Injection (SQL, NoSQL, OS)

Injection vulnerabilities occur when untrusted data is sent to an interpreter as part of a command or query, leading to unauthorized access or remote code execution.

Solution in Laravel: We can use parameterized queries with Laravel's Eloquent ORM or the Query Builder to prevent SQL injection.

```
<?php
// Example using Laravel Eloquent ORM
$users = User::where('username', $input)->get();
```

Cross-Site Scripting (XSS)

XSS vulnerabilities involve injecting malicious scripts into web pages, enabling attackers to steal user data or manipulate content.

Solution in Laravel: We can utilize Laravel's Blade templating engine, which automatically escapes output by default, preventing XSS attacks.

```
<?php
// Example using Blade templates
<p>{{ $userInput }}</p>
```

CHAPTER 5   SECURITY STANDARDS AND BEST PRACTICES

Broken Authentication

Weaknesses in authentication mechanisms can lead to unauthorized access, compromised user accounts, or session hijacking.

Solution in Laravel: We can leverage Laravel's built-in authentication system, including secure password hashing and session management.

```php
<?php
// Example of user authentication in Laravel
if (Auth::attempt(['email' => $email, 'password' => $password])) {
    // Authentication successful
}
```

Insecure Direct Object References (IDOR)

IDOR occurs when an attacker gains unauthorized access to objects or data by manipulating input parameters.

Solution in Laravel: We can implement proper authorization checks and use Laravel's policies and gates for fine-grained access control.

```php
<?php
// Example using Laravel policies
if (Gate::allows('view-post', $post)) {
    // User is authorized to view the post
}
```

Security Misconfigurations

Security misconfigurations occur when systems are not securely configured, exposing sensitive information or providing unauthorized access.

CHAPTER 5　SECURITY STANDARDS AND BEST PRACTICES

Solution in Laravel: We can regularly review and audit Laravel configuration files, using environment variables for sensitive settings.

```
<?php
// Example of using environment variables in Laravel configuration
'mysql' => [
    'host' => env('DB_HOST', 'default-host'),
    // ...
],
```

Sensitive Data Exposure

This risk involves exposing sensitive information, leading to potential data breaches.

Solution in Laravel: We can encrypt sensitive data using Laravel's encryption features and avoid storing sensitive information in client-side storage.

```
<?php
// Example of encrypting data in Laravel
$encrypted = encrypt($sensitiveData);
```

Missing Function-Level Access Control

Inadequate access controls at the function level can lead to unauthorized users performing sensitive actions.

CHAPTER 5   SECURITY STANDARDS AND BEST PRACTICES

Solution in Laravel: We can implement proper access controls in your application logic using Laravel middleware and policies.

```php
<?php
// Example using Laravel middleware for access control
Route::middleware(['admin'])->group(function () {
    // Admin-only routes
});
```

Cross-Site Request Forgery (CSRF)

CSRF attacks trick users into unintentionally performing actions on a site where they are authenticated.

Solution in Laravel: Laravel includes built-in CSRF protection. We can ensure the CSRF token is included in forms.

```php
<?php
// Example of Laravel CSRF protection in Blade templates
<form method="POST" action="/profile">
    @csrf
    <!-- Form contents -->
</form>
```

Using Components with Known Vulnerabilities

This issue arises when outdated or vulnerable third-party components are integrated into an application.

Solution in Laravel: We can regularly update Laravel and its dependencies, monitoring security advisories for Laravel and third-party packages.

```bash
# Update Laravel dependencies
composer update
```

Unvalidated Redirects and Forwards

Unvalidated redirects and forwards may allow attackers to redirect users to malicious sites.

Solution in Laravel: We need to avoid using user input to construct redirect URLs and use Laravel's named routes to generate URLs securely.

```php
<?php
// Example of using named routes in Laravel
return redirect()->route('dashboard');
```

These code examples showcase how Laravel's features and best practices can be applied to address the OWASP Top Ten security risks. It's important to integrate these practices into the development lifecycle and stay updated on security considerations in both Laravel and web application security as a whole.

Secure Coding Practices and Code Reviews

Secure coding practices and code reviews are crucial for ensuring the security and robustness of our software applications. When we write secure code, we take a proactive approach to identify and mitigate vulnerabilities during the development phase, which helps reduce the risk of security breaches once our software is in production. Code reviews complement this process by involving our peers or security experts who can provide valuable insights, identify potential issues, and enforce coding standards. Let's explore some key reasons why secure coding practices and code reviews are essential for us.

Firstly, by focusing on risk mitigation, we can identify and address security vulnerabilities early in the development process. This proactive approach helps us reduce the risk of exploitation by malicious actors, ensuring that our applications are secure from the start.

Secondly, adhering to secure coding practices helps us meet compliance requirements with industry regulations and standards, such as GDPR, HIPAA, or PCI DSS. This adherence ensures that our applications are not only secure but also legally compliant, protecting us from potential regulatory issues.

Thirdly, when we follow secure coding practices, we contribute to the maintainability and readability of our code. This makes it easier for us and our fellow developers to understand and modify the code without introducing security risks, promoting a more collaborative and efficient development environment.

Fourthly, addressing security issues during development is more cost-effective for us. By fixing security problems early on, we save resources and avoid the higher costs associated with addressing these issues post-deployment. This approach allows us to allocate our budget more effectively and avoid unnecessary expenses.

Lastly, by developing secure applications, we build trust among our users and stakeholders, preserving the reputation of our organization and its products. Secure applications demonstrate our commitment to protecting user data and maintaining high standards of security, which is crucial for our success and reputation.

Secure Coding Practices in PHP

Implementing secure coding practices in PHP is essential for developing robust and secure web applications. By following these best practices, we can protect our applications from common vulnerabilities and ensure the safety of our users' data.

Input Validation and Sanitization

Input validation and sanitization are fundamental practices. We need to validate and sanitize all user inputs to prevent injection attacks. For

CHAPTER 5 SECURITY STANDARDS AND BEST PRACTICES

example, we can use the filter_input function to sanitize input fields like usernames:

```php
<?php
  $username = filter_input(INPUT_POST, 'username',
  FILTER_SANITIZE_STRING);
```

By doing so, we ensure that any data entering our application is clean and secure, mitigating the risk of malicious code being executed.

Password Handling

Handling passwords securely is another crucial aspect. We should always store passwords using strong hashing algorithms, such as bcrypt. The password_hash function in PHP allows us to hash passwords securely, making it difficult for attackers to decipher them even if they gain access to our database:

```php
<?php
  $hashedPassword = password_hash($password,
  PASSWORD_BCRYPT);
```

Session Management

Session management also plays a vital role in securing our applications. By implementing secure session management techniques, we can prevent session hijacking. This involves starting sessions securely with session_start and ensuring session data is protected throughout the user's interaction with our application:

```php
<?php
  session_start();
```

CHAPTER 5   SECURITY STANDARDS AND BEST PRACTICES

Error Handling

Proper error handling is essential to prevent the leakage of sensitive information in production. Instead of displaying detailed error messages to users, we should use custom error handlers to log errors. This way, we can maintain logs for debugging purposes without exposing critical information to potential attackers:

```php
<?php
// Set a custom error handler
set_error_handler("customErrorHandler");

function customErrorHandler($errno, $errstr, $errfile, $errline) {
    // Log errors instead of displaying them to users
    error_log("Error: $errstr in $errfile on line $errline");
}
```

File Upload Security

If our application allows file uploads, we must ensure that these uploads are secure. This involves validating file types, storing files in secure locations, and generating unique file names. For example, we can check the MIME type of uploaded files to ensure they meet our security requirements before processing and storing them:

```php
<?php
// Example of file upload validation in PHP
$allowedTypes = ['image/jpeg', 'image/png'];
```

```
if (in_array($_FILES['file']['type'], $allowedTypes)) {
    // Process and store the file securely
} else {
    // Handle invalid file type
}
```

Cross-Site Request Forgery (CSRF) Tokens

To protect against cross-site request forgery (CSRF) attacks, we should include CSRF tokens in forms and refresh them for each form submission. Generating a new token using random_bytes and storing it in the session helps prevent unauthorized actions on behalf of the user:

```
<?php
// Generate and refresh CSRF token
$token = bin2hex(random_bytes(32));
$_SESSION['csrf_token'] = $token;
```

Data Validation and Sanitization

Data validation and sanitization go hand in hand with input validation. By using PHP filter functions, we can validate and sanitize inputs like email addresses, ensuring they meet our application's requirements before processing:

```
<?php
// Example of using PHP filter functions for input
    validation
$email = filter_var($_POST['email'], FILTER_
VALIDATE_EMAIL);
```

Secure Password Recovery

For secure password recovery, we should implement mechanisms that prevent unauthorized access to user accounts. Using time-limited reset tokens, which expire after a set period, adds an extra layer of security to the password recovery process:

```php
<?php
// Example of generating a time-limited reset token
$resetToken = bin2hex(random_bytes(32));
$resetExpiration = time() + 3600; // Token expires in 1 hour
```

Content Security Policy (CSP)

Implementing a Content Security Policy (CSP) helps mitigate the risk of cross-site scripting (XSS) attacks. By setting CSP headers, we can specify which content sources are allowed, thereby restricting the execution of potentially harmful scripts. For instance, we can configure CSP headers to allow scripts only from trusted sources:

```php
<?php
// Example of setting CSP headers in PHP
header("Content-Security-Policy: default-src 'self'; script-src 'self' https://example.com");
```

Database Connection Security

Securing database connections is another critical practice. We should use strong credentials and limit database user privileges to the minimum necessary. Establishing secure connections, such as using mysqli with appropriate error handling, ensures that our application communicates with the database securely:

CHAPTER 5   SECURITY STANDARDS AND BEST PRACTICES

```php
<?php
// Example of connecting to a MySQL database securely
$conn = new mysqli($servername, $username, $password, $dbname);

if ($conn->connect_error) {
    die("Connection failed: " . $conn->connect_error);
}
```

Session Security

Session security can be further enhanced by using secure session settings and regenerating session IDs after login. This helps prevent session fixation attacks and ensures that session data remains secure throughout the user's session:

```php
<?php
// Example of using secure session settings
ini_set('session.cookie_secure', 1);
ini_set('session.cookie_httponly', 1);
```

SSL/TLS Usage

Using SSL/TLS to encrypt data in transit is essential. We should always enforce HTTPS for our web applications to protect data exchanged between the client and server. Redirecting HTTP requests to HTTPS ensures that all communication is encrypted, safeguarding sensitive information from potential eavesdroppers:

```php
<?php
// Example of enforcing HTTPS in PHP
if ($_SERVER['HTTPS'] !== 'on') {
```

```
        header("Location: https://" . $_SERVER['HTTP_HOST'] .
        $_SERVER['REQUEST_URI']);
        exit();
    }
```

Adopting these additional secure coding practices enhances the overall security posture of PHP applications, providing a robust defense against common web application vulnerabilities.

Secure Coding Practices in Laravel

Implementing secure coding practices in Laravel is essential for developing robust and secure web applications. By following these best practices, we can protect our applications from common vulnerabilities and ensure the safety of our users' data.

Middleware for Authentication and Authorization

Middleware for authentication and authorization is a key aspect. We can use Laravel middleware to handle authentication and authorization checks efficiently. Middleware allows us to apply specific checks across multiple routes, ensuring that only authenticated and authorized users can access certain parts of our application:

```
<?php
Route::middleware(['auth', 'admin'])->group(function () {
    // Admin-only routes
});
```

CHAPTER 5   SECURITY STANDARDS AND BEST PRACTICES

Use Laravel's Authentication System

Leveraging Laravel's built-in authentication system with the Breeze package is highly beneficial. Breeze provides a comprehensive authentication setup, including secure password hashing, session management, and features like multifactor authentication. By using Breeze, we can quickly scaffold the authentication components securely, reducing the risk of implementing custom and potentially insecure authentication mechanisms:

bash

```
# Install Breeze package
composer require laravel/breeze --dev

# Install Breeze scaffolding
php artisan breeze:install

# Run migrations
php artisan migrate

# Install frontend assets
npm install && npm run dev
```

Validation with Requests

For input validation, using Form Requests allows us to centralize validation logic and keep our controllers clean. Form Requests are dedicated classes where we define validation rules, ensuring that our input validation is consistent and reusable across the application:

```
<?php
// Example of validation in a Form Request
public function rules()
{
```

```
        return [
            'email' => 'required|email',
            'password' => 'required|min:8',
        ];
    }
```

Authorization with Policies and Gates

Authorization can be handled effectively with policies and gates, providing fine-grained access control. By generating policies with php artisan make:policy MyModelPolicy, we can define complex authorization logic and apply it to our models, ensuring that users have the appropriate permissions to perform actions:

```
<?php
// Example of using a Laravel policy
if (Gate::allows('update-post', $post)) {
    // User is authorized to update the post
}
```

Use Eloquent ORM Safely

Using Laravel's Eloquent ORM for database interactions helps protect against SQL injection. Eloquent provides a fluent and expressive interface for querying the database, automatically escaping inputs and preventing injection attacks. We should avoid direct user input in queries and rely on Eloquent methods for filtering and ordering:

```
<?php
// Example of using Eloquent ORM
$user = User::where('email', $email)->first();
```

CHAPTER 5　SECURITY STANDARDS AND BEST PRACTICES

Cross-Site Request Forgery (CSRF) Protection

Laravel includes built-in cross-site request forgery (CSRF) protection, which we should utilize by ensuring the CSRF token is included in forms. This protection helps prevent malicious forms from being submitted on behalf of authenticated users:

```php
<?php
// Example of Laravel CSRF protection in Blade templates
<form method="POST" action="/profile">
    @csrf
    <!-- Form contents -->
</form>
```

Secure Session Management

Secure session management is crucial for preventing session fixation attacks. We should implement secure session settings and regenerate session IDs after login. This can be configured in the config/session.php file, ensuring our session data is protected:

```php
<?php
// Example of using secure session settings
'secure' => env('SESSION_SECURE_COOKIE', true),
'same_site' => 'lax',
```

CHAPTER 5   SECURITY STANDARDS AND BEST PRACTICES

Content Security Policy (CSP)

Implementing Content Security Policy (CSP) headers helps mitigate the risk of cross-site scripting (XSS) attacks by specifying which content sources are allowed. Setting CSP headers restricts the execution of potentially harmful scripts:

```php
<?php
// Example of setting CSP headers in Laravel
header("Content-Security-Policy: default-src 'self'; script-src 'self' https://example.com");
```

Use Dependency Injection

Using dependency injection over global functions or facades improves testability and reduces the risk of injection attacks. By injecting dependencies through the constructor or method parameters, we create more modular and testable code:

```php
<?php
// Example of dependency injection in a controller
public function __construct(MyService $service)
{
    $this->service = $service;
}
```

Database Migrations and Seeders

Laravel's migrations and seeders provide a secure way to version control our database schema and seed initial data. Migrations allow us to define schema changes, while seeders populate the database with initial data:

CHAPTER 5   SECURITY STANDARDS AND BEST PRACTICES

```php
<?php
// Example of a Laravel migration file
public function up()
{
    Schema::create('users', function (Blueprint $table) {
        $table->id();
        $table->string('name');
        // ... other columns
        $table->timestamps();
    });
}
```

Use HTTPS

Always using HTTPS to encrypt data in transit is essential. We can enforce HTTPS by configuring our web server to redirect HTTP traffic to HTTPS and ensuring Laravel enforces this in production environments:

```php
<?php
// Example of enforcing HTTPS in Laravel
if (App::environment('production')) {
    URL::forceScheme('https');
}
```

Adhering to these secure coding practices in Laravel helps us create applications that are more resilient to common web vulnerabilities.

Code Reviews

Code reviews play a crucial role in enhancing the security of software applications. One significant advantage is the early identification of security vulnerabilities. By reviewing code early in the development process, teams can detect and fix security issues before they become

CHAPTER 5   SECURITY STANDARDS AND BEST PRACTICES

deeply embedded in the software. This proactive approach is not only more cost-effective but also helps maintain the integrity of the application throughout its lifecycle.

Moreover, code reviews facilitate knowledge sharing and training among team members. Senior developers can mentor junior developers by sharing best practices and security guidelines during the review process. This collaborative environment fosters a security-aware development team, ensuring that all members are up to date with the latest security protocols and techniques.

Adherence to security standards is another critical benefit of code reviews. These reviews ensure that developers follow established security standards and coding guidelines, maintaining a consistent and secure code base across the entire application. This consistency is vital for creating a reliable and safe software product.

In addition, code reviews help prevent common security pitfalls. By meticulously examining the code, reviewers can catch issues such as input validation problems, insecure coding patterns, and inadequate error handling. This proactive approach prevents security vulnerabilities from being introduced into the code base in the first place.

Validation of security controls is another essential aspect of code reviews. Reviewers can verify that security features like authentication, authorization, and encryption are correctly implemented and functioning as intended. This validation ensures that the application's security mechanisms provide the necessary protection against threats.

During code reviews, developers can also engage in threat modeling and risk assessment. These discussions help identify potential security threats and assess risks within the code base. By pinpointing high-risk areas, teams can prioritize security measures and allocate resources more effectively.

Code reviews promote a culture of continuous improvement within development teams. By learning from past mistakes and applying lessons learned, teams can continuously enhance their understanding of security best practices. This ongoing learning process helps improve the overall security posture of the software over time.

CHAPTER 5 SECURITY STANDARDS AND BEST PRACTICES

Furthermore, code reviews help ensure compliance with regulatory requirements. Many industries have specific standards and regulations related to software security. Regular code reviews ensure that the code base adheres to these regulations, reducing the risk of legal and financial repercussions.

The early detection of security issues is another key benefit of regular code reviews. By identifying security problems early in the development process, teams can address them promptly, reducing the likelihood of vulnerabilities making their way into the production environment.

Code reviews help build a security-aware culture within the development team. When security considerations become an integral part of the development process, the overall security posture of the software improves. This cultural shift toward prioritizing security helps create more resilient and secure applications.

Peer Reviews

Peer reviews are an essential practice in software development, involving colleagues in the code review process to identify issues and provide diverse perspectives. Regular peer reviews focus on various aspects such as code readability, adherence to coding standards, and security considerations. By incorporating multiple viewpoints, we can spot potential problems that might be overlooked by a single developer, thus enhancing the overall quality and security of the code.

Static Code Analysis

In addition to peer reviews, integrating static code analysis tools into the development workflow can significantly improve code security. Tools like PHPStan, Psalm, or PHP_CodeSniffer automatically analyze the code to identify potential security vulnerabilities. These tools provide immediate feedback on code issues, enabling developers to address security concerns early in the development process.

Security Linters and Scanners

Security linters and scanners play a crucial role in detecting common security issues. Utilizing specialized tools such as OWASP Dependency-Check helps identify vulnerabilities in third-party dependencies. This proactive approach ensures that external libraries and frameworks used in the project do not introduce security risks, maintaining the integrity of the application.

Checklist-Based Reviews

Checklist-based reviews are another effective method for ensuring comprehensive security coverage. By developing and adhering to a security checklist during code reviews, we can systematically verify that all critical security aspects are addressed. Items such as input validation, authentication and authorization checks, data encryption, and error handling should be included in the checklist to ensure thorough examination of the code's security posture.

Automated Testing

Automated testing, particularly security-focused automated tests, is vital for validating the effectiveness of security controls. Including security-specific test cases, such as penetration testing or security unit tests, in the automated testing suite helps identify and mitigate vulnerabilities continuously. This automated approach ensures that security checks are consistently applied throughout the development lifecycle, catching potential issues before they reach production.

By integrating these secure coding practices and code review strategies into the development process, we can create more resilient and secure PHP and Laravel applications. These practices contribute to building a culture of security awareness within development teams, ultimately leading to more robust and reliable software products.

CHAPTER 5   SECURITY STANDARDS AND BEST PRACTICES

Security-Related Packages in Laravel

Custom Composer packages in Laravel play a crucial role in enhancing security, scalability, and maintainability of your applications. These packages allow you to encapsulate and share reusable pieces of code, reducing duplication across projects and facilitating modular development. In the context of security, custom Composer packages can offer solutions for common security concerns, such as authentication, authorization, and input validation. Let's discuss some important custom Composer packages related to security in Laravel, along with examples of how to use them.

Laravel Bouncer (for Authorization)

Laravel Bouncer is a powerful package for handling complex authorization logic. It allows you to define and manage roles and abilities with ease.

Usage:

- Install the package using Composer:

    ```bash
    composer require silber/bouncer
    ```

- Set up and migrate the Bouncer tables:

    ```bash
    php artisan bouncer:install
    ```

- Define abilities and roles in your code:

    ```
    <?php
    // Example of defining an ability
    Bouncer::allow('admin')->to('edit-users');
    ```

CHAPTER 5   SECURITY STANDARDS AND BEST PRACTICES

- Check for authorization in your application:

```php
<?php
// Example of checking authorization
if (Bouncer::can('edit-users')) {
    // User is authorized to edit users
}
```

Laravel Sanctum (for API Authentication)

Laravel Sanctum provides a simple and convenient way to authenticate APIs using token-based authentication.

Usage:

- Install the package using Composer:

    bash
    ```
    composer require laravel/sanctum
    ```

- Publish and run migrations:

    bash
    ```
    php artisan vendor:publish --provider="Laravel\Sanctum\SanctumServiceProvider"
    php artisan migrate
    ```

- Add Sanctum's middleware to your API routes:

    ```php
    <?php
    // Example of using Sanctum middleware in routes
    Route::middleware('auth:sanctum')->get('/user', function () {
        return Auth::user();
    });
    ```

- Issue API tokens:

```php
<?php
// Example of issuing API tokens
$token = $user->createToken('token-name')->plainTextToken;
```

Laravel Debugbar (for Debugging and Profiling)

Laravel Debugbar is a development package that provides insights into your application's performance and allows you to debug and profile requests.

Usage:

- Install the package using Composer:

    ```bash
    composer require barryvdh/laravel-debugbar --dev
    ```

- Add the service provider to your "config/app.php":

    ```php
    <?php
    // Example of adding the Debugbar service provider
    'providers' => [
        // ...
        Barryvdh\Debugbar\ServiceProvider::class,
    ],
    ```

- Optionally, publish the configuration file:

    ```bash
    php artisan vendor:publish --provider="Barryvdh\Debugbar\ServiceProvider"
    ```

CHAPTER 5   SECURITY STANDARDS AND BEST PRACTICES

- Access the debug bar in your application:

```php
<?php
// Example of accessing the debug bar
$debugbar = app('debugbar');
```

Laravel Scout (for Full-Text Search)

Laravel Scout is a powerful package for adding full-text search functionality to your application.

Usage:

- Install the package using Composer:

```bash
composer require laravel/scout
```

- Publish the configuration file:

```bash
php artisan vendor:publish --provider="Laravel\Scout\ScoutServiceProvider"
```

- Implement search functionality in your models:

```php
<?php
// Example of using Laravel Scout in a model
use Laravel\Scout\Searchable;

class Post extends Model
{
    use Searchable;
}
```

CHAPTER 5   SECURITY STANDARDS AND BEST PRACTICES

- Index your data:

    ```bash
    php artisan scout:import "App\Post"
    ```

- Perform searches:

    ```php
    <?php
    // Example of searching with Laravel Scout
    $results = Post::search('laravel')->get();
    ```

Laravel Telescope (for Monitoring and Debugging)

Laravel Telescope provides insight into the requests coming into your application, exceptions, log entries, database queries, and more.

Usage:

- Install the package using Composer:

    ```bash
    composer require laravel/telescope --dev
    ```

- Publish the assets and migrate the database:

    ```bash
    php artisan telescope:install
    php artisan migrate
    ```

- Add the service provider to your "config/app.php":

    ```php
    <?php
    // Example of adding the Telescope service provider
    'providers' => [
    ```

```
    // ...
    Laravel\Telescope\TelescopeServiceProvider::
    class,
],
```

- Access the Telescope dashboard in your application:

```
<?php
// Example of accessing the Telescope dashboard
Route::get('/telescope', function () {
    return view('telescope');
});
```

Laravel Nova (for Admin Panel)

Laravel Nova is a beautifully designed administration panel for Laravel applications, offering a convenient way to manage your application's data.

Usage:

- Install the package using Composer:

  ```bash
  composer require laravel/nova
  ```

- Publish the assets and run migrations:

  ```bash
  php artisan nova:install
  php artisan migrate
  ```

- Access the Nova dashboard in your application:

  ```
  <?php
  // Example of accessing the Nova dashboard
  Route::get('/nova', function () {
      return view('nova');
  });
  ```

CHAPTER 5   SECURITY STANDARDS AND BEST PRACTICES

Spatie Laravel Activitylog (for Activity Logging)

This package provides a simple way to log activity within your Laravel application, helping to track changes and monitor user actions.

Usage:

- Install the package using Composer:

    ```bash
    composer require spatie/laravel-activitylog
    ```

- Publish the migration and run it:

    ```bash
    php artisan vendor:publish --provider="Spatie\Activitylog\ActivitylogServiceProvider" --tag="migrations"
    php artisan migrate
    ```

- Log activity within your application:

    ```php
    <?php
    // Example of logging activity
    activity()->log('User performed some action.');
    ```

Intervention Image (for Image Handling)

Intervention Image is a powerful image handling library for Laravel, providing features like image resizing, cropping, and manipulation.

Usage:

- Install the package using Composer:

    ```bash
    composer require intervention/image
    ```

CHAPTER 5   SECURITY STANDARDS AND BEST PRACTICES

- Use the package in your Laravel application:

```php
<?php
// Example of resizing an image
$img = Image::make('path/to/image.jpg')->
resize(300, 200)->save('path/to/resized_image.jpg');
```

Laravel Dusk (for Browser Testing)

Laravel Dusk is an expressive, easy-to-use browser testing and automation tool for Laravel applications.

Usage:

- Install the package using Composer:

```bash
composer require --dev laravel/dusk
```

- Set up Dusk and create a sample test:

```bash
php artisan dusk:install
php artisan dusk
```

- Write browser tests:

```php
<?php
// Example of a Dusk browser test
$this->browse(function ($browser) {
    $browser->visit('/')
            ->assertSee('Welcome to Laravel');
});
```

CHAPTER 5 SECURITY STANDARDS AND BEST PRACTICES

Laravel Medialibrary (for Media Management)

- Importance: This package simplifies media management, allowing you to associate files with Eloquent models and easily handle file uploads and transformations.

Usage:

- Install the package using Composer:

    ```bash
    composer require spatie/laravel-medialibrary
    ```

- Publish the configuration file and run migrations:

    ```bash
    php artisan vendor:publish --provider="Spatie\MediaLibrary\MediaLibraryServiceProvider" --tag="migrations"
    php artisan migrate
    ```

- Attach media to your Eloquent models:

    ```
    <?php
    // Example of attaching media to a model
    $newsItem->addMedia($pathToImage)->toMediaCollection('images');
    ```

These custom Composer packages demonstrate the versatility of Laravel and the Laravel ecosystem, providing solutions for various security-related concerns. While these packages enhance security and functionality, it's essential to keep them up to date and to follow best practices for securing your Laravel applications. We should always review the documentation of each package for the latest usage instructions and features.

CHAPTER 5　SECURITY STANDARDS AND BEST PRACTICES

Secure Authentication and Authorization Mechanisms

Secure authentication and authorization mechanisms are fundamental components of any web application, ensuring that users have access to the right resources while safeguarding sensitive information. In PHP and Laravel, as well as in web development in general, implementing robust authentication and authorization is critical for protecting user data and maintaining the overall security of the application.

Importance of Secure Authentication and Authorization

Secure authentication and authorization are critical components in the development of secure web applications. These mechanisms not only protect sensitive data but also foster user trust, ensure regulatory compliance, and prevent unauthorized access to crucial resources.

Data protection is the foremost reason for implementing secure authentication. By ensuring that only authorized users can access their accounts and sensitive information, we protect user privacy and prevent data breaches. Secure authentication mechanisms, such as multifactor authentication and strong password policies, significantly reduce the risk of unauthorized access, ensuring that personal and confidential data remains secure.

User trust is greatly enhanced by a reliable authentication system. When users know that their data is protected and that the application takes security seriously, their confidence in the application increases. This trust is vital for user retention and satisfaction, as users are more likely to continue using and recommending an application that they perceive as secure.

Compliance with regulatory standards such as the General Data Protection Regulation (GDPR) is another crucial aspect. Many regulations mandate secure authentication and access control measures to protect user data. By adhering to these requirements, we not only avoid legal penalties but also demonstrate our commitment to data security and user privacy. This compliance is essential for maintaining the reputation and credibility of the organization.

Preventing unauthorized access is a fundamental function of robust authorization mechanisms. By ensuring that users can only access resources they are authorized to, we protect sensitive functionalities and data from unauthorized access. This is particularly important in applications with multiple user roles and permissions, where access control policies must be strictly enforced to maintain the integrity and security of the system.

Secure Authentication and Authorization in PHP

Password Hashing: We should use strong cryptographic hashing algorithms like bcrypt to securely store passwords.

```
<?php
// Example password hashing in PHP
$hashedPassword = password_hash($plainPassword, PASSWORD_BCRYPT);
```

Session Management: We should implement secure session management to prevent session hijacking and fixation.

```
<?php
// Example session start and secure settings in PHP
session_start();
session_regenerate_id(true);
```

Let's discuss about some Composer packages for secure authentication and authorization.

CHAPTER 5   SECURITY STANDARDS AND BEST PRACTICES

Laravel Sanctum (for API Authentication)

Laravel Sanctum provides a simple and convenient way to authenticate APIs using token-based authentication.

Usage:

- Install the package using Composer:

```bash
composer require laravel/sanctum
```

- Publish and run migrations:

```bash
php artisan vendor:publish --provider="Laravel\Sanctum\SanctumServiceProvider"
php artisan migrate
```

- Add Sanctum's middleware to your API routes:

```php
<?php
// Example of using Sanctum middleware in routes
Route::middleware('auth:sanctum')->get('/user', function () {
    return Auth::user();
});
```

- Issue API tokens:

```php
<?php
// Example of issuing API tokens
$token = $user->createToken('token-name')->plainTextToken;
```

Laravel Passport (for OAuth2)

Laravel Passport provides a full OAuth2 server implementation for securing API routes and allowing third-party authentication.

Usage:

- Install the package using Composer:

    ```bash
    composer require laravel/passport
    ```

- Run migrations:

    ```bash
    php artisan migrate
    ```

- Install Passport and generate keys:

    ```bash
    php artisan passport:install
    ```

- Use the "Passport" middleware in your routes:

    ```php
    <?php
    // Example of using Passport middleware in routes
    Route::middleware('auth:api')->get('/user', function () {
        return Auth::user();
    });
    ```

Laravel Breeze (for Starter Kits)

Laravel Breeze provides a minimal and customizable starter kit for Laravel applications with secure authentication mechanisms.

Usage:

- Install the package using Composer:

    ```bash
    composer require laravel/breeze --dev
    ```

- Set up and publish Breeze assets:

    ```bash
    php artisan breeze:install
    ```

Laravel Fortify (for Custom Authentication)

Laravel Fortify offers a flexible solution for customizing authentication features and includes features like password reset and two-factor authentication.

Usage:

- Install the package using Composer:

    ```bash
    composer require laravel/fortify
    ```

- Publish Fortify configuration and views:

    ```bash
    php artisan vendor:publish --provider="Laravel\Fortify\FortifyServiceProvider"
    ```

- Customize the configuration and use Fortify features in your application.

CHAPTER 5   SECURITY STANDARDS AND BEST PRACTICES

Additional Techniques and Best Practices
OAuth2 and OpenID Connect

We should implement OAuth2 and OpenID Connect for secure and standardized authentication and authorization, especially in the context of third-party integrations. Let's check OAuth2 implementation using Laravel Passport:

Install Laravel Passport:

```bash
composer require laravel/passport
php artisan migrate
php artisan passport:install
```

Create OAuth2 Server:

```php
<?php
// app/Providers/AuthServiceProvider.php

use Laravel\Passport\Passport;

public function boot()
{
    $this->registerPolicies();

    Passport::routes();

    Passport::tokensExpireIn(now()->addDays(7));
    Passport::refreshTokensExpireIn(now()->addDays(30));
}
```

Then to protect Routes with OAuth2 Middleware:

```php
<?php
// Example of using Passport middleware in routes
Route::middleware('auth:api')->get('/user', function () {
    return Auth::user();
});
```

JWT (JSON Web Tokens)

We should use JWT for stateless authentication and secure transmission of claims between parties. Let's implement its usage:

Install the tymon/jwt-auth Package:

```bash
composer require tymon/jwt-auth
php artisan vendor:publish --provider="Tymon\JWTAuth\Providers\LaravelServiceProvider"
php artisan jwt:secret
```

Configure JWT in "config/auth.php":

```php
<?php
// config/auth.php

'guards' => [
    'api' => [
        'driver' => 'jwt',
        'provider' => 'users',
    ],
],
```

CHAPTER 5 SECURITY STANDARDS AND BEST PRACTICES

Generate and Verify JWT Tokens:

```php
<?php
// Example of generating JWT token
$token = JWTAuth::fromUser($user);

// Example of verifying JWT token
$user = JWTAuth::parseToken()->authenticate();
```

Two-Factor Authentication (2FA)

We should implement 2FA for an additional layer of security, especially for user accounts with elevated privileges.

Install the Laravel 2FA Package:

```bash
composer require pragmarx/google2fa-laravel
```

Enable 2FA in "User" Model:

```php
<?php
// app/User.php

use PragmaRX\Google2FALaravel\Facade as Google2FA;

class User extends Authenticatable
{
    use HasFactory, Notifiable, TwoFactorAuthenticatable;

    // ...

    public function isGoogle2FAEnabled()
    {
        return Google2FA::getGoogle2FASecret($this->id) != null;
    }
}
```

CHAPTER 5   SECURITY STANDARDS AND BEST PRACTICES

Generate and Verify 2FA Tokens:

```php
<?php
// Example of generating 2FA secret and QR code
$google2fa = app('pragmarx.google2fa');
$secret = $google2fa->generateSecretKey();

// Example of verifying 2FA token
$isValid = $google2fa->verifyKey($secret, $user->google2fa_secret, $request->input('2fa_token'));
```

Role-Based Access Control (RBAC)

We should implement RBAC for fine-grained access control, allowing different users to have different levels of access within the application.

Use Laravel Gate for Authorization:

```php
<?php
// app/Providers/AuthServiceProvider.php

use Illuminate\Support\Facades\Gate;

public function boot()
{
    $this->registerPolicies();

    Gate::define('edit-settings', function ($user) {
        return $user->role === 'admin';
    });
}
```

CHAPTER 5 SECURITY STANDARDS AND BEST PRACTICES

Protect Routes with Gate Middleware:

```php
<?php
// Example of using Gate middleware in routes
Route::middleware('can:edit-settings')->group(function () {
    // Routes accessible only to users with 'admin' role
});
```

LDAP Integration

We can integrate with LDAP for centralized authentication and authorization in enterprise environments.

Install the Adldap2/Adldap2-Laravel Package:

```bash
composer require adldap2/adldap2-laravel
```

Configure LDAP in "config/ldap.php":

```php
<?php
// config/ldap.php

return [
    'connections' => [
        'default' => [
            'auto_connect' => env('LDAP_AUTO_CONNECT', false),
            'connection' => Adldap\Connections\Ldap::class,
            'settings' => [
                // LDAP settings
            ],
        ],
    ],
];
```

Authenticate User with LDAP:

```php
<?php
// Example of authenticating user with LDAP
if (Auth::attempt(['username' => $username, 'password' => $password])) {
    // User authenticated
}
```

Implementing secure authentication and authorization is an ongoing process, and it's essential to stay informed about emerging security threats and best practices. Remember to adapt these examples based on your specific use case, application structure, and authentication provider. These are starting points to help you implement the mentioned techniques and best practices in your PHP and Laravel applications.

Security Testing and Vulnerability Assessments

Security testing and vulnerability assessments play a crucial role in identifying and addressing potential security risks within your software applications. Conducting these assessments helps ensure that your systems are robust, resilient, and less susceptible to security threats. Below are the key aspects of security testing, vulnerability assessments, and relevant tools and practices in the context of PHP applications, Composer packages, and cloud environments.

CHAPTER 5   SECURITY STANDARDS AND BEST PRACTICES

Importance of Security Testing and Vulnerability Assessments

Security testing is crucial for keeping our software safe. It helps us find weak spots before bad actors can exploit them, reducing the risk of security breaches. For instance, if we identify a vulnerability in our login system during testing, we can fix it before hackers have a chance to exploit it and gain unauthorized access.

Many industries and regulatory standards also require regular security assessments to ensure we comply with security and privacy regulations. For example, financial institutions must adhere to strict guidelines to protect customer information, and regular security testing helps them meet these requirements.

By proactively addressing security vulnerabilities, we build trust with our users and customers, which helps safeguard our organization's reputation. If users know that we take security seriously and continuously work to protect their data, they are more likely to trust our services. For example, a company that promptly fixes security issues and communicates transparently with its users will be seen as more reliable.

Additionally, finding and fixing security issues early in the development process saves money, as it is much cheaper than dealing with them after a breach has occurred. For example, fixing a bug during development might cost a small amount, but if the same bug is exploited in a live system, it could lead to significant financial losses and damage to the company's reputation. Therefore, early detection and resolution of security issues are not only effective but also economical.

CHAPTER 5   SECURITY STANDARDS AND BEST PRACTICES

Security Testing and Vulnerability Assessment Practices: Static Application Security Testing (SAST)

Static application security testing (SAST) involves analyzing our PHP code for security vulnerabilities without executing the program. This practice is essential for catching potential issues early in the development lifecycle. SAST helps us identify and fix security flaws before the code is deployed, reducing the risk of security breaches in production. By using tools like PHPStan or Psalm, we can ensure our code adheres to security best practices, thereby enhancing the overall security posture of our application.

```bash
# Example using PHPStan
composer require --dev phpstan/phpstan
vendor/bin/phpstan analyse
```

Dynamic Application Security Testing (DAST)

Dynamic application security testing (DAST) involves testing the running application for vulnerabilities by simulating real-world attacks. DAST helps us understand how our application behaves under attack, identifying vulnerabilities that may not be apparent through static analysis alone. Using tools like OWASP ZAP or Arachni, we can detect and fix security issues that arise during the application's runtime, ensuring robust defense mechanisms.

```bash
# Example using OWASP ZAP
docker run -t owasp/zap2docker-stable zap-baseline.py -t http://your-app-url
```

Dependency Scanning

Dependency scanning involves examining our Composer dependencies for known vulnerabilities. Third-party libraries can introduce vulnerabilities into our application. Regular scanning ensures these dependencies are secure and up to date. By integrating tools like OWASP Dependency-Check or Snyk, we can maintain a secure code base and protect against vulnerabilities in third-party code.

```bash
# Example using OWASP Dependency-Check
docker run -it --rm -v "$(pwd):/usr/src" -w /usr/src owasp/dependency-check --scan .
```

Container Image Scanning

Container image scanning involves inspecting Docker images for security vulnerabilities. Containers package our applications along with their dependencies. Scanning these images ensures that all components are secure. Using tools like Clair or Trivy, we can identify and mitigate vulnerabilities within our container images, enhancing the security of our deployments.

```bash
# Example using Trivy
trivy your-docker-image
```

Security Headers

Implementing security headers in our application helps mitigate common web vulnerabilities. Security headers provide an additional layer of protection by controlling how browsers interact with our web content. Tools like securityheaders.com can help us assess and implement secure headers, ensuring our web applications are resistant to common attacks.

CHAPTER 5   SECURITY STANDARDS AND BEST PRACTICES

Automated Security Testing in CI/CD

Integrating security testing into our Continuous Integration/Continuous Deployment (CI/CD) pipeline ensures ongoing security assessment throughout the development process. Automating security tests allows us to detect and address vulnerabilities continuously, preventing security issues from reaching production. By using tools like SonarQube, GitLab CI/CD, or GitHub Actions, we can maintain a secure development workflow and ensure our code is always secure.

```yaml
# Example GitLab CI configuration for SonarQube
sonarqube:
  image: sonarsource/sonar-scanner-cli
  script:
    - sonar-scanner -Dsonar.projectKey=your-project-key
      -Dsonar.sources=.
```

Cloud-Specific Security Testing

Ensuring the security of our applications in the cloud requires specialized practices tailored to the unique aspects of cloud environments. Let's understand some essential cloud-specific security testing practices that help us maintain a secure and robust cloud infrastructure.

Cloud Security Posture Management (CSPM)

Cloud Security Posture Management (CSPM) involves continuously monitoring and assessing the security posture of our cloud environment. CSPM tools help us identify misconfigurations and compliance issues across our cloud resources, ensuring they adhere to best security practices. By leveraging tools like AWS Security Hub or Azure Security Center, we can automate the monitoring process, quickly detecting and addressing potential security threats.

Using AWS Security Hub, we can continuously monitor our cloud environment for security best practices and compliance.

Serverless Security Testing

Serverless security testing focuses on ensuring the security of serverless applications, which often have different security considerations compared to traditional applications. Serverless architectures introduce unique security challenges, such as event data injection and insecure configurations. Specialized tools are needed to address these issues. By using tools like OWASP ServerlessGoat for testing and AWS Lambda Security for monitoring and scanning, we can ensure our serverless applications are secure from various threats.

```bash
# Example using OWASP ServerlessGoat
git clone https://github.com/OWASP/ServerlessGoat.git
cd ServerlessGoat
sls deploy
```

Cloud-Native Security Scanning

Cloud-native security scanning involves using services provided by the cloud provider to scan for vulnerabilities within our cloud resources and applications. Cloud-native tools are designed to integrate seamlessly with the cloud environment, providing efficient and effective security scanning. Utilizing services like AWS CodeScan or Google Container Analysis allows us to identify and mitigate security vulnerabilities in our cloud-native applications, ensuring they are secure and compliant.

```bash
# Example using AWS CodeScan
aws codescan start-scan --region your-region --repository your-repository
```

CHAPTER 5   SECURITY STANDARDS AND BEST PRACTICES

Regular Security Audits

Regular security audits are essential for maintaining a robust security posture. By periodically assessing our systems and applications, we can identify and mitigate vulnerabilities, ensuring ongoing protection against potential threats. Let us review some key practices for conducting regular security audits.

1. Penetration Testing

    Penetration testing involves simulating cyberattacks on our systems to identify vulnerabilities that could be exploited by attackers. Regular penetration tests help us discover and fix security weaknesses before malicious actors can exploit them. By using tools like OWASP OWTF or engaging third-party security experts, we can conduct thorough assessments of our systems, ensuring any vulnerabilities are identified and remediated promptly. Using OWASP OWTF, we can perform penetration tests on our target systems to identify security weaknesses.

    ```bash
    # Example using OWASP OWTF
    git clone https://github.com/owtf/owtf.git
    cd owtf
    ./owtf -s your-target-url
    ```

2. Red Team vs. Blue Team Exercises

    Red team vs. blue team exercises involve simulating real-world attack scenarios (red team) and assessing our defenses (blue team). These exercises provide a practical and dynamic approach to testing our security measures, helping us understand how well our defenses can withstand actual attacks.

Simulating attacks and defenses through red teaming and blue teaming exercises allows us to improve our security strategies, fortify our defenses, and enhance our incident response capabilities. In a red team vs. blue team exercise, the red team attempts to breach the system while the blue team works to detect and prevent these attacks, providing a comprehensive assessment of our security posture.

Continuous Improvement

Continuously improving our security measures is essential to staying ahead of potential threats. By regularly updating our strategies and training our teams, we ensure that our organization remains resilient against evolving security challenges. Let's understand some key practices for continuous improvement in security.

1. Incident Response Planning

   Incident response planning involves developing a detailed plan for how to handle and recover from security incidents. Having a well-defined incident response plan ensures that we can respond to security breaches quickly and efficiently, minimizing damage and recovery time. Regularly updating and testing this plan ensures that all team members know their roles and responsibilities during an incident, leading to a more coordinated and effective response. We can develop an incident response plan that outlines steps to take during a breach, including communication protocols, containment strategies, and recovery procedures.

2. Security Awareness Training

   Security awareness training involves educating our development and operations teams on security best practices. Training helps foster a security-conscious culture within our organization, making every team member aware of potential security risks and how to avoid them. By regularly training our teams, we reduce the likelihood of human error leading to security breaches and ensure that everyone is up to date with the latest security practices. We can conduct regular training sessions and workshops to educate our teams about phishing, secure coding practices, and the importance of strong passwords.

3. Threat Modeling

   Threat modeling involves identifying and prioritizing potential threats and countermeasures for our systems. By understanding potential threats, we can proactively design our systems to mitigate these risks, rather than reacting to them after they occur. Conducting regular threat modeling exercises helps us stay ahead of potential attackers by continuously refining our security measures based on identified threats. We can use tools and frameworks to perform threat modeling exercises, mapping out our system architecture and identifying possible attack vectors and their mitigations.

CHAPTER 5 SECURITY STANDARDS AND BEST PRACTICES

Secure Deployment and DevOps Considerations

Secure deployment and DevOps considerations are integral parts of the software development lifecycle, ensuring that applications are not only developed securely but also deployed and maintained securely. The importance of secure deployment includes safeguarding against various threats, minimizing downtime, and ensuring the continuous delivery of secure and reliable software. Let us understand key considerations and practices for secure deployment and DevOps, both in general and with a focus on PHP and Laravel.

General Secure Deployment and DevOps Considerations

1. Infrastructure as Code (IaC)

Infrastructure as Code (IaC) involves defining and managing infrastructure through code, allowing for automated and consistent deployment. IaC reduces the risk of misconfigurations and ensures that environments are reproducible, which is essential for maintaining consistency across different stages of development and deployment. By using tools like Terraform or Ansible, we can automate the setup and configuration of our infrastructure, ensuring that it is deployed in a controlled and predictable manner.

Example: Using Terraform, we can define our infrastructure in code, making it easy to deploy and manage:

```hcl
resource "aws_instance" "web" {
  ami           = "ami-0c55b159cbfafe1f0"
  instance_type = "t2.micro"
}
```

2. Continuous Integration and Continuous Deployment (CI/CD)

CI/CD pipelines automate the processes of building, testing, and deploying code, ensuring that changes are regularly integrated and deployed. Automating these processes ensures that code changes are tested and deployed quickly and consistently, reducing the risk of errors and improving the overall quality of the software. Utilizing CI/CD tools like Jenkins, GitLab CI, or GitHub Actions helps us streamline our development workflow and ensures that our applications are always in a deployable state.

Example: A simple GitLab CI configuration for automating tests and deployments:

yaml

```yaml
stages:
    - build
    - test
    - deploy

build:
    script:
        - echo "Building the application..."

test:
    script:
        - echo "Running tests..."

deploy:
    script:
        - echo "Deploying the application..."
```

CHAPTER 5   SECURITY STANDARDS AND BEST PRACTICES

3. Immutable Infrastructure

Immutable infrastructure involves creating and deploying complete, stand-alone instances of our applications, which do not change after deployment. This approach reduces the risk of configuration drift and ensures a more secure and stable environment by deploying fresh instances for each update. Building and deploying containerized applications using technologies like Docker helps us achieve immutability and consistency across deployments.

Example: A Dockerfile to build a containerized PHP application:

Dockerfile

```
FROM php:7.4-cli
COPY . /usr/src/myapp
WORKDIR /usr/src/myapp
CMD ["php", "index.php"]
```

4. Secrets Management

Securely managing and storing sensitive information such as API keys and database passwords is crucial for preventing credential exposure. Proper secrets management ensures that sensitive data is stored and accessed securely, reducing the risk of unauthorized access. Using tools like HashiCorp Vault or AWS Secrets Manager allows us to centralize and control access to secrets securely.

Example: Storing and retrieving secrets using AWS Secrets Manager:

bash

```
# Store a secret
aws secretsmanager create-secret --name MySecret --secret-string "my_secret_value"

# Retrieve a secret
aws secretsmanager get-secret-value --secret-id MySecret
```

CHAPTER 5   SECURITY STANDARDS AND BEST PRACTICES

5. Dependency Scanning

Regularly scnning dependencies for known vulnerabilities helps mitigate the risk of using outdated or insecure components. Dependencies can introduce security vulnerabilities if not properly managed. Regular scanning ensures that we are aware of and can address these vulnerabilities promptly. Integrating dependency scanning tools like OWASP Dependency-Check into our CI/CD pipeline helps us maintain a secure code base.

Example: Using OWASP Dependency-Check to scan for vulnerabilities:

bash

```
docker run -it --rm -v "$(pwd):/usr/src" -w /usr/src owasp/
dependency-check --scan .
```

PHP and Laravel-Specific Deployment Considerations

Deploying PHP and Laravel applications securely involves specific practices tailored to the framework and language. These practices help us manage configurations securely, protect our code, and ensure efficient operations. Let us review some key considerations for deploying PHP and Laravel applications securely.

1. Environment Configuration

Securely managing environment-specific configurations is crucial for preventing sensitive information from being exposed. Environment configurations often contain sensitive data like API keys and database credentials. Exposing these in version control can lead to security breaches. By using environment variables and configuration files, we can keep sensitive information out of our code base and version control systems.

CHAPTER 5　SECURITY STANDARDS AND BEST PRACTICES

Example: In Laravel, environment-specific settings are managed using the .env file:

```
DB_CONNECTION=mysql
DB_HOST=127.0.0.1
DB_PORT=3306
DB_DATABASE=your_database
DB_USERNAME=your_username
DB_PASSWORD=your_password
```

2. Code Obfuscation and Encryption

Protecting sensitive parts of our PHP code base by obfuscating or encrypting it helps safeguard our intellectual property and sensitive logic. Code obfuscation and encryption make it difficult for attackers to understand and exploit the code, adding an extra layer of security. Utilizing tools like ionCube or Zend Guard helps protect our PHP code from unauthorized access and reverse engineering.

Example: Using ionCube to encrypt PHP code:

bash

```
# Encrypt PHP code with ionCube
ioncube_encoder --encrypt src/ --output encoded/
```

3. Secure Laravel Configuration

Laravel-specific configuration settings should be secured and properly managed to prevent security vulnerabilities. Insecure configurations can lead to vulnerabilities that attackers can exploit. Regularly reviewing and adjusting configurations helps mitigate these risks. Ensuring that Laravel configuration files, such as .env, adhere to security best practices helps maintain the application's security.

Example: Securing the .env file in Laravel:

```
APP_ENV=production
APP_DEBUG=false
APP_KEY=base64:your_base64_encoded_key
```

4. Laravel Horizon for Queue Management

Laravel Horizon provides a dashboard and monitoring for Laravel queues, ensuring efficient and reliable background job processing. Monitoring and managing queues is essential for maintaining the performance and reliability of background jobs. Using Laravel Horizon helps us visualize queue status, retry failed jobs, and optimize queue performance.

Example: Setting up Laravel Horizon:

Install Horizon via Composer:

```bash
composer require laravel/horizon
```

Publish the Horizon configuration file:

```bash
php artisan horizon:install
```

Run the Horizon dashboard:

```bash
php artisan horizon
```

Secure Deployment Code Practices (Example Using Ansible)

Here's a simple Ansible playbook example for deploying a PHP application securely:

CHAPTER 5   SECURITY STANDARDS AND BEST PRACTICES

yaml

- name: Deploy PHP Application
  hosts: web_servers
  become: yes
  vars:
    app_name: "my_php_app"
    deploy_path: "/var/www/{{ app_name }}"
    release_path: "{{ deploy_path }}/releases/{{ ansible_date_time.date }}"
    shared_path: "{{ deploy_path }}/shared"
  tasks:
    - name: Clone Git Repository
      git:
        repo: "https://github.com/yourusername/your-repo.git"
        dest: "{{ release_path }}"
        version: "master"

    - name: Install Composer Dependencies
      composer:
        command: install
        working_dir: "{{ release_path }}"
        no_dev: yes

    - name: Set Permissions
      file:
        path: "{{ deploy_path }}"
        state: directory
        recurse: yes
        mode: "0755"
        owner: "www-data"
        group: "www-data"

```yaml
- name: Create Symlink to Current Release
  file:
    src: "{{ release_path }}"
    dest: "{{ deploy_path }}/current"
    state: link

- name: Restart PHP-FPM (or Apache/Nginx)
  systemd:
    name: php7.4-fpm
    state: restarted
  become: yes
```

This playbook assumes you have Ansible installed on your deployment server and the required roles and dependencies installed.

General Secure Deployment Code Practices

When we build and deploy software, we need to make sure it's safe and secure. Let's discuss some simple steps we follow to keep our software secure.

First, we use something called SSH keys for authentication. This helps ensure that only authorized users can access our systems. For example, SSH keys are like having a special key to open a locked door. Instead of typing a password every time, we use these keys, and tools like SSH-agent help us manage them securely so that only the right people can open the door.

Next, we set security headers, which are special instructions for our web server to follow. These headers tell the server how to handle various types of content and communication securely.

For example, imagine telling a guard at the door to only let people in who follow certain rules. Content Security Policy (CSP) tells the server what kind of content it can load, and Strict-Transport-Security (HSTS) ensures that the communication between the server and the user is always secure.

CHAPTER 5 SECURITY STANDARDS AND BEST PRACTICES

We also use automated security scans to check our software for any weak spots. These scans automatically look for vulnerabilities in our code. For example, using a metal detector to find hidden dangers helps ensure that our software is free from vulnerabilities before bad guys can exploit them.

Another important practice is to have a plan for backup and rollback. We make automated backups of our data to ensure that we can recover it if something goes wrong. For example, keeping extra copies of important documents helps us revert to the previous, working version of our software, ensuring that everything keeps running smoothly.

Monitoring and logging are systems set up to continuously monitor our software and log important events. This helps us detect and respond to any security incidents quickly. For example, having security cameras and alarms helps us address problems as soon as they happen, keeping our software secure and running smoothly.

When deploying PHP applications on cloud platforms, adopting secure DevOps practices is essential to ensure the resilience and integrity of your systems. Let's discuss some cloud DevOps practices for PHP applications with a focus on security, complete with examples.

Infrastructure as Code (IaC) with CloudFormation or Terraform

One crucial practice is using Infrastructure as Code (IaC) with tools like AWS CloudFormation or HashiCorp Terraform. These tools allow us to define and provision infrastructure as code, enabling version-controlled, repeatable, and secure infrastructure deployments. For instance, a simple Terraform snippet to provision an EC2 instance might look like this:

```hcl
// Example Terraform snippet
resource "aws_instance" "web" {
```

CHAPTER 5   SECURITY STANDARDS AND BEST PRACTICES

```
  ami           = "ami-0c55b159cbfafe1f0"
  instance_type = "t2.micro"
}
```

Containerization with Docker and Kubernetes

Containerization with Docker and orchestration with Kubernetes enhance portability, scalability, and isolation of PHP applications. By containerizing the application, we can ensure consistent environments across development, testing, and production. An example Kubernetes deployment for a PHP application might be the following:

```yaml
# Example Kubernetes Deployment
apiVersion: apps/v1
kind: Deployment
metadata:
  name: php-app
spec:
  replicas: 3
  selector:
    matchLabels:
      app: php-app
  template:
    metadata:
      labels:
        app: php-app
    spec:
      containers:
      - name: php-app
        image: your-registry/php-app:latest
```

Secure Storage Management

For secure storage management, leveraging cloud-native services such as Amazon S3 for object storage and AWS RDS for relational databases is recommended. Data should be encrypted at rest and in transit. Here's an example of using the AWS S3 SDK for PHP to interact with S3:

```php
php
// Example using AWS S3 SDK for PHP
use Aws\S3\S3Client;

$s3Client = new S3Client([
    'version'    => 'latest',
    'region'     => 'us-east-1',
]);
```

Identity and Access Management (IAM)

Implementing the principle of least privilege using Identity and Access Management (IAM) roles and policies is vital. Regularly auditing and rotating access keys further enhances security. An example AWS IAM policy might look like this:

```json
json
// Example AWS IAM Policy
{
  "Version": "2012-10-17",
  "Statement": [
    {
      "Effect": "Allow",
      "Action": "s3:ListBucket",
      "Resource": "arn:aws:s3:::your-bucket"
    },
```

CHAPTER 5   SECURITY STANDARDS AND BEST PRACTICES

```
    {
      "Effect": "Allow",
      "Action": "s3:GetObject",
      "Resource": "arn:aws:s3:::your-bucket/*"
    }
  ]
}
```

Network Security with Virtual Private Cloud (VPC)

Network security can be strengthened by utilizing Virtual Private Clouds (VPCs) to isolate resources and configuring security groups and network ACLs to control inbound and outbound traffic. For example, an AWS security group might be defined as follows:

```json
// Example AWS Security Group
resource "aws_security_group" "example" {
  name        = "example"
  description = "Allow inbound HTTP and SSH traffic"

  ingress {
    from_port   = 80
    to_port     = 80
    protocol    = "tcp"
    cidr_blocks = ["0.0.0.0/0"]
  }

  ingress {
    from_port   = 22
    to_port     = 22
```

CHAPTER 5   SECURITY STANDARDS AND BEST PRACTICES

```
    protocol    = "tcp"
    cidr_blocks = ["0.0.0.0/0"]
  }
}
```

Logging and Monitoring

Logging and monitoring are crucial for maintaining security. Using services like AWS CloudWatch or Google Cloud Monitoring allows us to set up alerts for security-related events and regularly review logs. For example, the AWS CloudWatch SDK for PHP can be used to interact with CloudWatch logs:

```php
<?php
// Example using AWS CloudWatch SDK for PHP
use Aws\CloudWatchLogs\CloudWatchLogsClient;

$cloudWatchLogsClient = new CloudWatchLogsClient([
    'version'   => 'latest',
    'region'    => 'us-east-1',
]);
```

Automated Security Scanning

Integrating automated security scanning tools into the CI/CD pipeline helps identify vulnerabilities early. Tools like GitLab's SAST can be configured to perform static application security testing automatically:

```yaml
# Example GitLab CI configuration for SAST
include:
  - template: SAST.gitlab-ci.yml
```

CHAPTER 5   SECURITY STANDARDS AND BEST PRACTICES

Secrets Management with Cloud Key Management Services

Secrets management using cloud key management services like AWS KMS or Google Cloud KMS ensures secure storage and management of cryptographic keys and secrets. Here's an example of using AWS KMS SDK for PHP:

```php
<?php
// Example using AWS KMS SDK for PHP
use Aws\Kms\KmsClient;

$kmsClient = new KmsClient([
    'version'    => 'latest',
    'region'     => 'us-east-1',
]);
```

Serverless Architectures

Considering serverless architectures with services like AWS Lambda or Google Cloud Functions can abstract infrastructure management and reduce attack surfaces. An example AWS Lambda function might look like this:

```php
<?php
// Example AWS Lambda function (serverless)
exports.handler = async (event) => {
    // Lambda function logic
    return 'Hello from Lambda!';
};
```

CHAPTER 5   SECURITY STANDARDS AND BEST PRACTICES

Backup and Disaster Recovery

Implementing automated backup strategies, snapshotting, and disaster recovery plans is crucial. Regularly testing recovery procedures ensures that you can quickly restore services in case of an incident. For instance, creating a snapshot of an AWS RDS database can be done using the AWS CLI:

```bash
# Example AWS RDS database snapshot
aws rds create-db-snapshot --db-instance-identifier your-db-instance --db-snapshot-identifier your-snapshot-id
```

Summary

This chapter explores essential security standards and best practices for PHP application development. It begins by highlighting the OWASP Top Ten, which identifies the most critical web application security risks, such as injection attacks and cross-site scripting (XSS). The chapter emphasizes secure coding practices and the importance of thorough code reviews to detect vulnerabilities early. Secure authentication and authorization mechanisms, like password hashing and session management, are discussed to safeguard user data and ensure proper access control. The chapter also covers security testing and vulnerability assessments, including static and dynamic testing, to identify and mitigate potential threats. Finally, it addresses secure deployment and DevOps considerations, such as using Infrastructure as Code (IaC), Continuous Integration/Continuous Deployment (CI/CD), and secrets management. By adhering to these practices, developers can significantly enhance the security and resilience of their PHP applications, protecting them from malicious attacks and ensuring compliance with industry regulations.

CHAPTER 6

Protocol Security

In this chapter, we delve into the crucial security aspects of communication protocols frequently employed in PHP applications. Understanding and implementing robust protocol security measures is vital for protecting sensitive data and ensuring secure interactions between users and systems. We will cover the essentials of securing HTTP communications with SSL/TLS and HTTPS, managing user input and data transmission securely, safeguarding API communications using OAuth, JWT, and best practices, and implementing Transport Layer Security (TLS) for email communication. Mastery of these topics is essential for developers aiming to build resilient and secure PHP applications, safeguarding against common threats and vulnerabilities in today's digital landscape.

Securing HTTP Communications: SSL/TLS and HTTPS

The Hypertext Transfer Protocol (HTTP) is the backbone of data communication on the Internet, enabling the transfer of text, links, images, and other multimedia content between web servers and clients like web browsers. HTTP operates on a client-server model, where the client (typically a web browser) requests resources and the server provides the requested information. Each HTTP request is independent, carrying no

CHAPTER 6   PROTOCOL SECURITY

information about previous requests, making it a stateless protocol. While this simplifies the protocol, it often necessitates additional mechanisms like cookies to maintain user state across multiple requests.

In HTTP, each request-response cycle is independent, and once a response is sent, the connection is closed unless explicitly kept alive. HTTP employs various request methods, known as HTTP verbs, each serving a specific purpose: GET retrieves data, POST submits data for processing, PUT updates a resource, and DELETE removes a resource. Resources on the web are identified by Uniform Resource Identifiers (URIs), commonly expressed as URLs (Uniform Resource Locators), which include the protocol (e.g., http://), domain name, path, and optional query parameters.

Both HTTP requests and responses contain headers that provide additional information such as content type, content length, and caching directives. HTTP responses come with status codes indicating the request's outcome, such as 200 OK for success, 404 Not Found for resource not found, and 500 Internal Server Error for server-side errors. HTTP has evolved through versions, with HTTP/1.1 and HTTP/2 being the most widely used, each bringing performance and security improvements.

Security in HTTP is enhanced through HTTPS (Hypertext Transfer Protocol Secure), which adds a layer of encryption using Transport Layer Security (TLS) or its predecessor, Secure Sockets Layer (SSL). This ensures that the data exchanged between the client and server is encrypted, significantly boosting security. Understanding these aspects of HTTP is crucial for developing secure web applications, as it enables efficient and secure data communication between clients and servers.

The process of establishing an HTTP connection over the web in the context of a PHP application involves several steps. Let's break down the process:

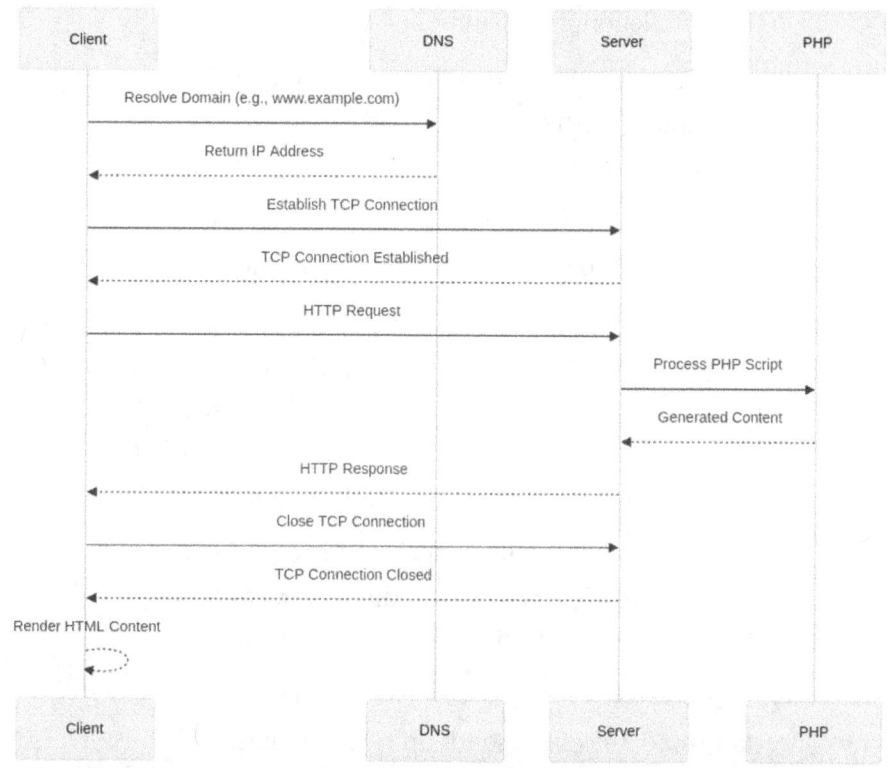

Figure 6-1. *Http Connection workflow lifecycle*

1. Client Request: A user interacts with a web browser or another client application that sends an HTTP request to a web server. The request is typically initiated by entering a URL into the browser's address bar, clicking on a link, or submitting a form.

2. DNS Resolution: If the URL contains a domain name (e.g., www.example.com), the client needs to resolve this domain name to an IP address using the Domain Name System (DNS). The client sends a DNS query to a DNS server to obtain the IP address associated with the domain.

CHAPTER 6   PROTOCOL SECURITY

3. TCP Connection Establishment

   – The client establishes a Transmission Control Protocol (TCP) connection with the server. This involves a three-way handshake:

      – SYN (Synchronize): The client sends a SYN packet to the server, requesting to establish a connection.

         – SYN-ACK (Synchronize-Acknowledge): The server responds with a SYN-ACK packet, indicating acknowledgment of the request and readiness to establish a connection.

         – ACK (Acknowledge): The client sends an ACK packet back to the server, confirming the establishment of the connection.

4. HTTP Request: Once the TCP connection is established, the client sends an HTTP request to the server. The request includes details such as the HTTP method (GET, POST, etc.), the requested resource (specified in the URL), headers, and any applicable data (such as form submissions).

5. Server-Side Processing (PHP): On the server side, if the requested resource is a PHP script, the server's PHP interpreter processes the script. PHP scripts are typically embedded within HTML and generate dynamic content based on the requested parameters.

CHAPTER 6   PROTOCOL SECURITY

6. HTTP Response: The server generates an HTTP response, including a status code, headers, and the actual content. The content may be HTML, JSON, images, or any other type of data depending on the nature of the request.

7. TCP Connection Closure (Optional): The TCP connection may be kept open for additional requests (using the same connection, if the client supports it) or closed after the response is sent, depending on factors like the server's configuration and the presence of HTTP keep-alive headers.

8. Client Rendering: The client (web browser) receives the HTTP response. If the response contains HTML content, the browser renders the page, executing any embedded JavaScript and displaying images and other resources referenced in the HTML.

This sequence of steps repeats for each user interaction with the web application. The dynamic nature of PHP allows for the generation of personalized and context-specific content, enhancing the interactivity and responsiveness of the web application.

CHAPTER 6   PROTOCOL SECURITY

HTTPS

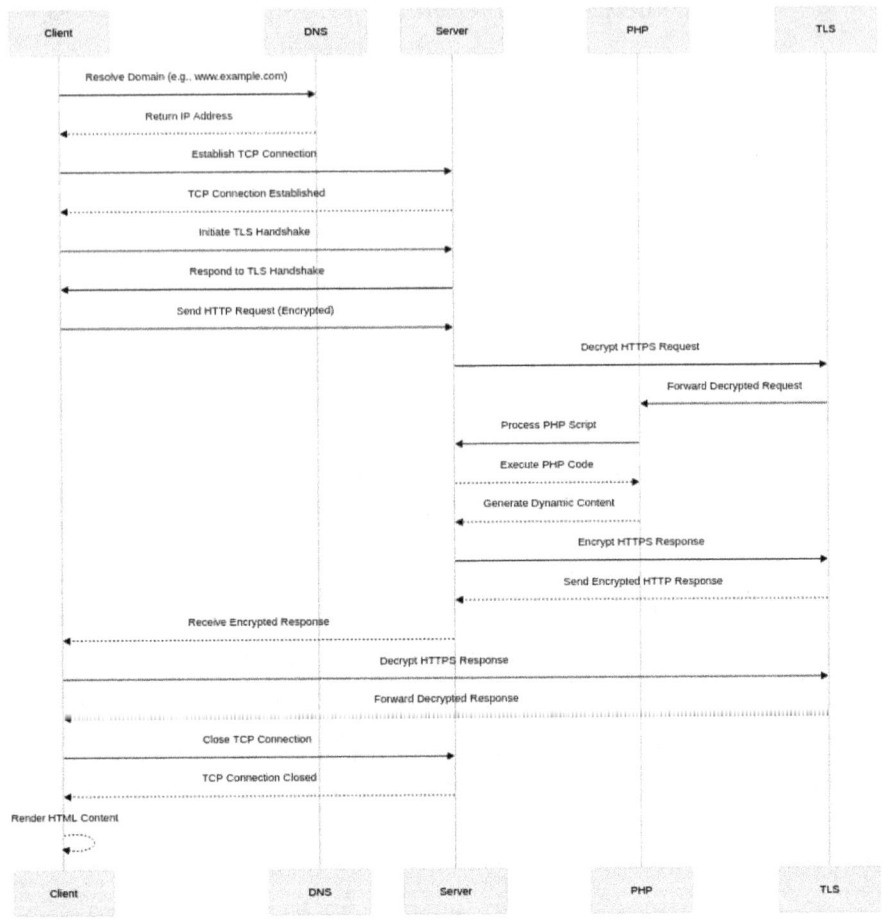

Figure 6-2. *Https Connection workflow lifecycle*

Establishing an HTTPS (Hypertext Transfer Protocol Secure) connection involves additional security measures compared to HTTP. In the context of a PHP application, the process involves securing the communication between the client and server using encryption. Let's discuss an overview of how an HTTPS connection is established in the context of a PHP app, highlighting the differences from HTTP:

1. Client Request: When a user accesses a PHP application over HTTPS, the client (web browser) initiates a secure connection by sending a request to the server using the HTTPS protocol.

2. Server Certificate: The server hosting the PHP application needs to have an SSL/TLS certificate. This certificate is a digital document that verifies the authenticity of the server to the client and facilitates the encryption of data between them. The certificate is typically obtained from a trusted Certificate Authority (CA).

3. SSL/TLS Handshake: The SSL/TLS handshake is a process that occurs at the beginning of an HTTPS connection. During the handshake:

    - The server sends its SSL/TLS certificate to the client.

    - The client verifies the certificate's authenticity using the CA's public key.

    - The client and server negotiate the encryption algorithms and generate shared session keys.

4. Encryption: Once the SSL/TLS handshake is complete, the actual data exchanged between the client and server is encrypted. This ensures that even if intercepted during transit, the data remains unreadable without the proper decryption keys.

5. Secure Data Transfer: The PHP application processes the client's request and generates a response. This response is sent back to the client over the encrypted HTTPS connection, ensuring the confidentiality and integrity of the data during transit.

CHAPTER 6   PROTOCOL SECURITY

Now, let's review the key differences between HTTP and HTTPS. The most significant difference lies in encryption: data exchanged between the client and server in HTTP is transmitted in plain text, meaning it can be easily read if intercepted. In contrast, HTTPS encrypts the data, providing a layer of security that protects sensitive information, such as login credentials or personal details, from being intercepted and misused.

Additionally, HTTP and HTTPS use different URL schemes and port numbers. URLs for HTTP connections begin with "http://", while URLs for HTTPS connections start with "https://", indicating the connection is secured using SSL/TLS encryption. HTTP typically uses port 80 for communication, whereas HTTPS uses port 443 for secure communication. Understanding these differences is crucial for ensuring the security of web applications and the data they handle.

HTTPS adds a layer of security by encrypting the data exchanged between the client and server. This encryption is crucial for protecting sensitive information and ensuring the privacy and integrity of the communication. The use of SSL/TLS certificates, the SSL/TLS handshake, and encrypted data transfer are key components of establishing a secure HTTPS connection in a PHP application.

SSL (Secure Sockets Layer) and TLS (Transport Layer Security) are cryptographic protocols designed to secure communication over a computer network, especially on the Internet. They are commonly used to establish a secure connection between a web browser and a web server, ensuring that the data exchanged between them is encrypted and protected from eavesdropping, tampering, or forgery.

SSL (Secure Sockets Layer) and TLS (Transport Layer Security)

SSL (Secure Sockets Layer)

SSL, developed by Netscape in the mid-1990s, was designed to provide secure communication over the nascent World Wide Web. Despite its initial promise, SSL underwent several iterations due to security vulnerabilities. SSL 1.0 was never publicly released because of these flaws. SSL 2.0, the first public release, also had significant security issues. SSL 3.0, released in 1996, addressed many of these vulnerabilities and became widely adopted.

SSL offers several key features that revolutionized web security. It provides encryption to protect the confidentiality of data during transit, ensuring that intercepted data cannot be easily read. SSL also supports server authentication, which helps verify the identity of the server to the client, preventing man-in-the-middle attacks. Additionally, SSL ensures data integrity, making sure that the data has not been tampered with during transmission. While SSL was widely used, it has been largely replaced by its more secure successor, TLS.

TLS (Transport Layer Security)

TLS was introduced as an improved and more secure successor to SSL, building upon the foundation laid by its predecessor. The first version, TLS 1.0, released in 1999, was similar to SSL 3.0 but included several enhancements. Subsequent versions, TLS 1.1 (2006) and TLS 1.2 (2008), introduced additional security features and improvements. The latest version, TLS 1.3, released in 2018, offers even greater security and performance.

CHAPTER 6   PROTOCOL SECURITY

TLS incorporates several advanced features to enhance security. TLS 1.2 and 1.3 support forward secrecy, ensuring that even if a server's private key is compromised, past communications remain secure. TLS also addresses known vulnerabilities present in earlier versions of SSL, reducing the risk of security breaches. Furthermore, TLS 1.3 introduces a more efficient and secure handshake process, improving both security and performance. Understanding the evolution and features of SSL and TLS is crucial for ensuring secure communication in today's web applications.

SSL/TLS Handshake Process

Figure 6-3.   SSL/TLS handshake process workflow

The SSL/TLS handshake process is a critical sequence that establishes a secure connection between a client and a server, ensuring both parties can communicate securely by agreeing on encryption methods and exchanging cryptographic keys. The process begins with the client initiating the handshake by sending a "ClientHello" message to the server. This message contains information about the cryptographic algorithms and other parameters that the client supports.

CHAPTER 6 PROTOCOL SECURITY

In response, the server sends back a "ServerHello" message, selecting the most secure parameters from the client's list. The server also provides its SSL/TLS certificate, which includes the server's public key and serves as a means of authentication. Following this, the client and server negotiate the key exchange method. This step is essential for establishing shared secret keys that will be used to encrypt the data transmitted between them, with various methods like Diffie-Hellman or RSA being commonly used.

Once the key exchange is successfully negotiated, both parties exchange "Finished" messages. These messages confirm that the handshake process is complete and that both the client and server have verified each other's cryptographic parameters. The "Finished" messages are encrypted, adding an additional layer of security to the handshake process.

With the handshake completed, the client and server can now securely exchange encrypted data. The shared secret keys established during the handshake are used to encrypt and decrypt the information, ensuring the confidentiality and integrity of the data during transmission. Understanding the SSL/TLS handshake process is crucial for implementing secure communications in web applications, as it ensures that the data exchanged remains private and protected from tampering.

In modern web applications, TLS is the standard protocol for securing communications. The terms "SSL" and "TLS" are often used interchangeably, but it's important to note that SSL is considered deprecated, and the use of TLS is recommended for better security.

SSL (Secure Sockets Layer) and its successor TLS (Transport Layer Security) are cryptographic protocols designed to provide secure communication over a computer network, especially the Internet. In a security context, these protocols play a crucial role in ensuring the confidentiality, integrity, and authenticity of data exchanged between clients (such as web browsers) and servers. When used in the context of web browsing, HTTPS (Hypertext Transfer Protocol Secure) is the application of these protocols, indicating a secure communication channel.

CHAPTER 6   PROTOCOL SECURITY

In the realm of Internet security, SSL/TLS and HTTPS play critical roles in safeguarding communication and data exchange. One of the primary functions of SSL/TLS protocols is the encryption of data. These protocols ensure that the information exchanged between a client and server is encrypted, rendering it unreadable to anyone who might intercept the communication. This encryption is vital for maintaining the confidentiality of sensitive information such as login credentials, personal details, and financial transactions.

Data integrity is another crucial role fulfilled by SSL/TLS. Through cryptographic mechanisms, these protocols ensure that the data received by the recipient is identical to the data sent by the sender, preventing tampering or unauthorized modifications during transmission. This guarantees the accuracy and reliability of the data exchanged.

Authentication is a key feature supported by SSL/TLS, where the server's identity is verified to the client. This process helps users trust that they are connecting to the legitimate and intended website, thereby reducing the risk of man-in-the-middle attacks. Secure key exchange is also facilitated during the SSL/TLS handshake process. This ensures that even if communication is intercepted, the data cannot be deciphered without the proper encryption keys.

SSL/TLS also provide robust protection against eavesdropping. The encryption offered by these protocols prevents unauthorized parties from listening in on the communication between the client and server. Without the appropriate encryption keys, any intercepted data remains secure and unreadable.

The implementation of HTTPS, the secure version of the HTTP protocol, applies SSL/TLS to secure communications between a client's web browser and a web server. HTTPS is particularly important for websites handling sensitive information, such as login credentials, payment details, and personal data. The presence of HTTPS and the padlock icon in a browser's address bar signals to users that their connection is secure, building trust and confidence that their data is being transmitted securely.

Also, SSL/TLS help prevent man-in-the-middle attacks through their handshake process and the use of certificates. By authenticating each other, the client and server ensure that they are communicating directly, without intermediaries tampering with the data. This comprehensive security framework provided by SSL/TLS and HTTPS is essential for protecting users and their data in an increasingly digital world.

SSL/TLS and HTTPS are fundamental in creating a secure communication channel on the Internet. They provide a robust framework for encrypting data, ensuring its integrity, and authenticating the parties involved. The adoption of HTTPS is particularly critical for websites handling sensitive information, as it enhances the overall security posture and user trust.

Usage of SSL/TLS/HTTPS in the Context of PHP Application

To implement SSL/TLS and HTTPS in a Laravel application, we'll focus on configuring the web server (such as Apache or Nginx) to manage secure connections. Laravel itself offers features to handle secure communication but relies on the web server for SSL/TLS configuration. Let's walk through the steps and code samples to set up SSL/TLS and HTTPS in our Laravel application.

Web Server Configurations

Nginx Configuration

First, let's configure Nginx to handle HTTPS connections. We need to provide an SSL certificate and configure the server to listen on port 443, which is the default port for HTTPS.

CHAPTER 6   PROTOCOL SECURITY

```
nginx
server {
    listen 443 ssl;
    server_name yourdomain.com;

    ssl_certificate /path/to/your/certificate.crt;
    ssl_certificate_key /path/to/your/private.key;

    # Other SSL/TLS configurations...

    location / {
        # Laravel application configuration...
    }
}
```

In this configuration, we specify the paths to our SSL certificate and private key. These files are crucial because they establish the secure connection between the client and server. The listen 443 ssl; directive tells Nginx to listen for secure connections on port 443.

Apache Configuration

For Apache, we'll set up the virtual host to use SSL and specify the paths to our SSL certificate files.

```
apache
<VirtualHost *:443>
    ServerName yourdomain.com
    DocumentRoot /path/to/your/laravel/public

    SSLEngine on
    SSLCertificateFile /path/to/your/certificate.crt
    SSLCertificateKeyFile /path/to/your/private.key
```

```
    # Other SSL/TLS configurations...

    <Directory /path/to/your/laravel/public>
        # Laravel application configuration...
        AllowOverride All
        Require all granted
    </Directory>
</VirtualHost>
```

Here, we enable SSL with SSLEngine on and specify where our certificate and key files are located. These settings allow Apache to handle secure HTTPS connections on port 443, ensuring encrypted communication.

Laravel Configuration

Next, we need to ensure that our Laravel application recognizes secure connections and generates secure URLs. We'll update the .env file and the config/app.php file.

.env:

```
APP_URL=https://yourdomain.com
```

By setting the APP_URL to use https, we ensure that Laravel generates secure URLs, which is critical for ensuring all links and asset references are secured.

config/app.php:

```
'url' => env('APP_URL', 'http://localhost'),
```

Updating the URL configuration in config/app.php helps Laravel use the correct base URL for all generated links and redirects.

CHAPTER 6   PROTOCOL SECURITY

Forced HTTPS in Laravel

To force HTTPS on specific routes or the entire application, we'll use Laravel's forceScheme middleware. This ensures that all traffic to our application is securely transmitted over HTTPS.

To force HTTPS for the entire application, in the App\Providers\AppServiceProvider class, add the following to the boot method:

```
use Illuminate\Support\Facades\URL;

public function boot()
{
    if (env('APP_ENV') === 'production') {
        URL::forceScheme('https');
    }
}
```

This ensures that our application always uses HTTPS in production, automatically redirecting HTTP requests to HTTPS.

We can also force HTTPS on certain routes using the forceScheme method within our routes:

```php
Route::group(['scheme' => 'https'], function () {
    // Your HTTPS routes go here
});
```

This allows us to selectively enforce HTTPS on routes that require it, providing flexibility in our security settings.

HSTS (HTTP Strict Transport Security)

Enabling HSTS instructs browsers to always use HTTPS, further enhancing security by preventing downgrade attacks and ensuring that users always connect securely.

```
nginx
add_header Strict-Transport-Security "max-age=31536000;
includeSubDomains; preload" always;
```

Adding this header in our Nginx configuration tells browsers to remember to use HTTPS for a specified period (in this case, one year), including all subdomains.

Mixed Content Handling

To avoid mixed content issues, we'll ensure all assets (CSS, JavaScript, images, etc.) are loaded over HTTPS. We can achieve this by using Laravel's asset helper, which generates secure URLs for assets.

```html
<link rel="stylesheet" href="{{ asset('css/app.css') }}">
```

Using the asset helper ensures that all references to assets are secure, preventing mixed content warnings in the browser.

Laravel Mix

If we're using Laravel Mix for asset compilation, we need to ensure that the mix() function generates HTTPS URLs:

```
mix.js('resources/js/app.js', 'public/js').version();
mix.sass('resources/sass/app.scss', 'public/css').version();
```

By versioning our assets, Laravel Mix helps ensure that we always reference the latest versions, and using the mix() function ensures these URLs are generated correctly.

CHAPTER 6   PROTOCOL SECURITY

Testing

Finally, we should test our SSL/TLS configuration and HTTPS setup using online tools like SSL Labs to ensure proper security configurations.

By following these steps, we can set up SSL/TLS and HTTPS for our Laravel application, providing a secure and encrypted communication channel between our server and clients. This ensures that sensitive data remains protected throughout its transmission, enhancing the overall security of our web application.

Securely Handling User Input and Data Transmission

Handling user input and data transmission securely is crucial in ensuring the overall security of PHP and Laravel applications. Without proper security measures, applications become vulnerable to various attacks, such as SQL injection, cross-site scripting (XSS), and data breaches. Let's delve into the importance of securely handling user input and data transmission, providing practical examples within the Laravel framework.

Firstly, preventing SQL injection is a critical aspect of secure user input handling. SQL injection occurs when malicious users insert SQL code into input fields, potentially gaining unauthorized access to the database and manipulating data. In Laravel, we can mitigate this risk by using Eloquent ORM and the Query Builder, which automatically employ prepared statements. For instance, when retrieving a user by email, we use $users = User::where('email', $request->input('email'))->first(); or $users = DB::table('users')->where('email', $request->input('email'))->first();. These methods ensure that user input is safely bound to the query, preventing injection attacks.

CHAPTER 6 PROTOCOL SECURITY

Cross-site scripting (XSS) is another significant threat that can be mitigated by properly handling user input. XSS attacks occur when attackers inject malicious scripts into web pages, which are then executed by other users' browsers. Laravel's Blade template engine provides automatic escaping of variables, ensuring that user-generated content is rendered safely. For example, using <div>{{ $user->name }}</div> in a Blade template ensures that any HTML characters in the user's name are escaped, preventing script execution. This default behavior helps protect our application from XSS vulnerabilities.

Maintaining data integrity during transmission is also vital. Using HTTPS to encrypt data between the client and server ensures that the data cannot be tampered with or intercepted. This is configured in Laravel by setting the APP_URL to https://yourdomain.com in the .env file. By enforcing HTTPS, we guarantee that data remains secure during transit, preserving its integrity.

Cross-site request forgery (CSRF) is another attack that can be prevented by validating and securing user input. CSRF attacks trick a user's browser into making unintended requests on their behalf. Laravel addresses this by including CSRF protection middleware by default. In our routes, we can enable this protection with Route::post('/profile', function () { /* handle form submission */ })->middleware('csrf');. Additionally, Blade templates automatically include a CSRF token in forms using @csrf. This token ensures that the request originates from the authenticated user, thwarting CSRF attacks.

Protecting sensitive information, such as passwords and personal data, is essential for application security. Laravel provides robust tools for this purpose. Passwords should always be hashed using Laravel's Hash facade, as shown with $user->password = Hash::make($request->input('password')); $user->save();. For encrypting other sensitive data, we use Laravel's encryption functions, such as $encrypted = encrypt($request->input('sensitive_data')); and $decrypted = decrypt($encrypted);. These methods ensure that sensitive information is securely stored and transmitted.

Code Samples and Examples in Laravel

1. Input Validation: Laravel provides validation rules to ensure that user input meets specific criteria.

   ```php
   use Illuminate\Http\Request;

   public function store(Request $request)
   {
       $request->validate([
           'username' => 'required|string|max:255',
           'email' => 'required|email',
           'password' => 'required|min:8',
       ]);

       // Process valid input
   }
   ```

2. Sanitizing Input: We can use Laravel's "clean" method to sanitize input.

   ```php
   use Illuminate\Support\Facades\Input;

   $cleanInput = Input::clean($dirtyInput);
   ```

CHAPTER 6　PROTOCOL SECURITY

3. Cross-Site Scripting (XSS) Protection: Laravel's Blade templating engine automatically escapes output, preventing XSS attacks.

   ```php
   // In a Blade view
   {{ $userInput }}
   ```

4. Data Encryption: Laravel provides a convenient way to encrypt and decrypt data.

   ```php
   $encryptedData = encrypt($sensitiveData);
   $decryptedData = decrypt($encryptedData);
   ```

5. Secure Data Transmission (HTTPS): We need to ensure that your Laravel application is served over HTTPS.

   ```nginx
   # Nginx configuration
   server {
       listen 443 ssl;
       server_name yourdomain.com;
       ssl_certificate /path/to/your/certificate.crt;
       ssl_certificate_key /path/to/your/private.key;
       # Other SSL/TLS configurations...

       location / {
           # Laravel application configuration...
       }
   }
   ```

CHAPTER 6 PROTOCOL SECURITY

6. Hashing Passwords: Laravel's "bcrypt" function securely hashes passwords.

   php
   ```
   $hashedPassword = bcrypt($rawPassword);
   ```

7. CSRF Protection: Laravel automatically includes CSRF tokens in forms to prevent CSRF attacks.

   html
   ```
   <form method="POST" action="/profile">
       @csrf
       <!-- Form fields go here -->
   </form>
   ```

By incorporating these secure coding practices into your Laravel application, we enhance its resilience against common security threats associated with user input and data transmission.

CHAPTER 6   PROTOCOL SECURITY

Securing API Communication: OAuth, JWT, and API Security Best Practices

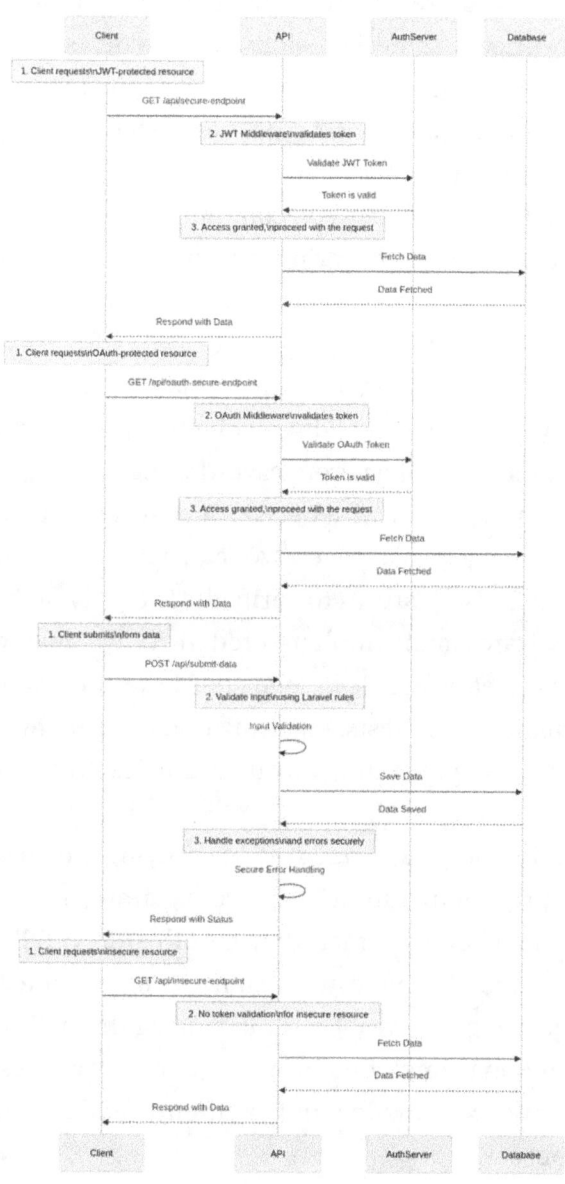

Figure 6-4. *Request-response lifecycle in Secure API Communication*

CHAPTER 6   PROTOCOL SECURITY

Securing API communication is crucial to ensuring the confidentiality, integrity, and authenticity of data exchanged between clients and servers. In the context of PHP and Laravel, using protocols like OAuth and JWT, along with following API security best practices, helps protect against various security threats. Laravel provides robust tools and features for implementing secure API communication. Let's explore the importance of securing API communication and how to handle it using code samples and detailed examples in Laravel.

Confidentiality is essential in API communication to protect sensitive data from unauthorized access during transmission. By encrypting data using HTTPS, we can ensure secure communication. For instance, in Laravel, we can enforce HTTPS by setting the APP_URL to `https://yourdomain.com` in the .env file. This configuration ensures that all data transmitted between the client and server is encrypted, maintaining its confidentiality and protecting it from eavesdroppers.

Integrity is another critical aspect, as it ensures that data is not tampered with during transmission. We can achieve this by using checksums or digital signatures to verify the integrity of the data. In Laravel, middleware can be implemented to verify data integrity. For example, we can create middleware to check the checksum or digital signature of incoming requests, ensuring that the data received is exactly as it was sent, preventing any unauthorized modifications during transit.

Authentication plays a pivotal role in verifying the identity of clients and servers to prevent unauthorized access. Laravel supports various authentication mechanisms, including OAuth and JWT. By using JWT, we can authenticate API requests efficiently. For example, when a user logs in, we can generate a JWT token using the JWTAuth facade. This token can then be included in subsequent API requests to verify the user's identity, ensuring that only authenticated users can access protected resources.

Authorization goes hand in hand with authentication, as it controls access to specific resources based on user roles and permissions. In Laravel, we can leverage OAuth scopes and custom authorization logic to enforce fine-grained access control. For instance, by defining scopes in Laravel Passport, we can restrict access to certain API endpoints based on the user's permissions. This ensures that users can only perform actions they are authorized to, enhancing the security of our application.

Token-based authentication, particularly with JWT, is an efficient way to manage user sessions without relying on server-side storage. With JWT, we can create stateless authentication, where each token contains the necessary information to identify the user. This approach scales well and simplifies session management. For example, when a user logs in, a JWT token is generated and returned to the client. The client then includes this token in the Authorization header of subsequent requests, allowing the server to authenticate the user without maintaining session state.

OAuth 2.0 is essential for enabling secure, delegated access to resources on behalf of users. Laravel Passport simplifies the implementation of OAuth 2.0, allowing third-party applications to access our API securely. By setting up Passport routes, we can handle OAuth authorization flows, issuing access tokens that third-party applications can use to interact with our API on behalf of users.

Following API security best practices is crucial to mitigate common security vulnerabilities. This includes implementing input validation, avoiding information disclosure, and handling errors securely. For example, in Laravel, we can use the built-in validation feature to ensure that user input meets specific criteria before processing it. Additionally, we should handle errors in a way that does not expose sensitive information, logging them securely while providing generic error messages to the client.

CHAPTER 6   PROTOCOL SECURITY

Code Samples and Examples in Laravel

1. Securing API with JWT Authentication

   - Install the "tymon/jwt-auth" package for JWT authentication.

     ```bash
     composer require tymon/jwt-auth
     ```

   - Configure JWT in "config/auth.php".

     ```php
     'guards' => [
         'api' => [
             'driver' => 'jwt',
             'provider' => 'users',
         ],
     ],
     ```

   - Use JWT middleware to protect routes.

     ```php
     Route::middleware('jwt.auth')->get('/api/secure-endpoint', 'ApiController@secureEndpoint');
     ```

2. OAuth in Laravel Using Passport

   - Install the Laravel Passport package.

     ```bash
     composer require laravel/passport
     ```

   - Run Passport migrations and install.

     ```bash
     php artisan migrate
     php artisan passport:install
     ```

- Use Passport middleware for OAuth-protected routes.

  php
  ```
  Route::middleware('auth:api')->get('/api/secure-endpoint', 'ApiController@secureEndpoint');
  ```

3. API Security Best Practices

   - Implement input validation using Laravel's validation rules.

     php
     ```
     $request->validate([
         'username' => 'required|string|max:255',
         'password' => 'required|string|min:8',
     ]);
     ```

   - Avoid information disclosure in error responses.

     php
     ```
     // Disable detailed error messages in production
     'app.debug' => env('APP_DEBUG', false),
     ```

   - Use proper error handling mechanisms.

     php
     ```
     try {
         // Your code here
     } catch (Exception $e) {
         // Handle exceptions securely
         return response()->json(['error' => 'Something went wrong.'], 500);
     }
     ```

These examples showcase the implementation of JWT authentication, OAuth using Passport, and API security best practices in Laravel.

CHAPTER 6   PROTOCOL SECURITY

Implementing Transport Layer Security (TLS) for Email Communication

Implementing Transport Layer Security (TLS) for email communication is essential for securing the transmission of emails between mail servers and clients. TLS ensures that the data exchanged during the email delivery process is encrypted, protecting it from unauthorized access, interception, and tampering. This is crucial for maintaining the confidentiality and integrity of sensitive information communicated via email, such as login credentials, personal details, and attachments.

Key Reasons for Implementing TLS for Email Communication

Confidentiality

TLS encrypts the content of emails during transmission, preventing unauthorized entities from intercepting and reading the message content. This is particularly important for sensitive information shared via email. When an email is sent using TLS, the data is encrypted between the sender's and recipient's email servers, making it extremely difficult for anyone to eavesdrop on the communication.

Integrity

TLS ensures that the email content remains unchanged during transmission. This protects against tampering and manipulation by malicious actors. With TLS, any alteration to the email content during transit can be detected, ensuring that the message received is exactly as it was sent.

CHAPTER 6   PROTOCOL SECURITY

Authentication

TLS provides a mechanism for servers to authenticate each other, ensuring that the email is sent and received by legitimate servers. This helps prevent man-in-the-middle attacks, where an attacker intercepts and possibly alters the communication between two parties without their knowledge. By verifying the identities of the communicating servers, TLS enhances the overall security of email communication.

Compliance

Many regulatory standards and privacy laws, such as GDPR, HIPAA, and others, require the implementation of encryption for certain types of data, including personal and sensitive information. Using TLS for email communication helps organizations comply with these regulations. Implementing TLS ensures that sensitive information is protected in transit, thereby meeting the requirements of various compliance frameworks.

Configuring Laravel for TLS Email Communication

Now, let's go through the steps for implementing TLS for email communication in a Laravel application. Please understand that the actual implementation depends on the email service provider you are using and their support for TLS.

1. Environment Configuration

    - Update your ".env" file with the mail configuration settings.

      ```dotenv
      MAIL_DRIVER=smtp
      MAIL_HOST=your-smtp-server
      ```

CHAPTER 6 PROTOCOL SECURITY

```
MAIL_PORT=587
MAIL_USERNAME=your-email@example.com
MAIL_PASSWORD=your-email-password
MAIL_ENCRYPTION=tls
```

Replace "your-smtp-server", "your-email@example.com", and "your-email-password" with the appropriate values provided by your email service provider.

2. Configuring Laravel Mail Service

   – In your Laravel application, you can configure the mail service in "config/mail.php". Below's an example:

```php
return [
    'driver' => env('MAIL_DRIVER', 'smtp'),
    'host' => env('MAIL_HOST', 'your-smtp-server'),
    'port' => env('MAIL_PORT', 587),
    'from' => [
        'address' => env('MAIL_FROM_ADDRESS',
        'your-email@example.com'),
        'name' => env('MAIL_FROM_NAME',
        'Your Name'),
    ],
    'encryption' => env('MAIL_ENCRYPTION', 'tls'),
    'username' => env('MAIL_USERNAME', 'your-email@example.com'),
    'password' => env('MAIL_PASSWORD', 'your-email-password'),
    'sendmail' => '/usr/sbin/sendmail -bs',
];
```

3. Testing TLS Configuration

    – Send a test email and inspect the email headers to ensure that the "TLS" or "Secure" flag is present, indicating that the email communication is secured.

    ```php
    use Illuminate\Support\Facades\Mail;
    use App\Mail\YourTestMail;
    Mail::to('recipient@example.com')->send(new YourTestMail());
    ```

4. Verify TLS Usage

    – Once the email is sent, we can check the email headers to ensure that the communication is secured using TLS. You can use tools like "dig" or online email header analyzers for verification.

Summary

In this chapter, we explored various aspects of securing communication in PHP and Laravel applications. From securing HTTP communications to implementing secure email transmission, the chapter provided comprehensive insights and practical examples to enhance application security.

Securing HTTP Communications

We began by discussing the importance of securing HTTP communications using SSL/TLS and HTTPS. HTTP is fundamental to data communication on the Web, but it lacks inherent security features. By using HTTPS, which leverages SSL/TLS, we ensure that data exchanged between clients and servers is encrypted. This prevents unauthorized access and protects sensitive information from being intercepted or tampered with during transmission.

CHAPTER 6   PROTOCOL SECURITY

Securely Handling User Input and Data Transmission

Next, we delved into the significance of securely handling user input and data transmission. Improper handling of user input can lead to various vulnerabilities, such as SQL injection, cross-site scripting (XSS), and data breaches. In Laravel, using built-in tools and features like Eloquent ORM, the Query Builder, Blade templates, and middleware, we can mitigate these risks. By enforcing input validation, data integrity checks, and secure authentication mechanisms, we protect our applications from common security threats.

Securing API Communication

Securing API communication is crucial for maintaining the confidentiality, integrity, and authenticity of data exchanged between clients and servers. Protocols like OAuth and JWT, along with best practices in API security, help protect against threats. In Laravel, implementing HTTPS, using JWT for authentication, leveraging OAuth for authorization, and following security best practices ensure that our API communications are robust and secure.

Implementing Transport Layer Security (TLS) for Email Communication

Finally, we covered the implementation of TLS for email communication. TLS is essential for encrypting emails during transmission, ensuring their confidentiality and integrity. By configuring Laravel to use an SMTP server that supports TLS, we can secure our email communications. This is especially important for complying with regulatory standards and protecting sensitive information shared via email.

CHAPTER 7

Incident Response and Security Monitoring

Chapter Goal: Discuss incident response planning, handling security incidents, and implementing security monitoring for PHP applications.

- Developing an Incident Response Plan
- Incident Communication and Escalation Procedures
- Forensic Analysis and Post-incident Analysis
- Implementing Security Monitoring and Intrusion Detection Systems

In today's threat landscape, having a robust strategy for incident response and security monitoring is essential for maintaining the integrity and security of PHP applications. This chapter focuses on the critical aspects of incident response planning, handling security incidents, and implementing effective security monitoring systems. Developing an incident response plan is fundamental to prepare for potential breaches and ensure a swift, organized response. Incident communication and escalation procedures are vital for clear, timely communication during an incident, minimizing confusion and ensuring that all stakeholders are informed and engaged. Forensic analysis and post-incident analysis help organizations understand the root cause of incidents and implement measures to prevent future occurrences. Finally, implementing security monitoring and intrusion detection systems provides continuous oversight, helping to detect and respond to threats in real time. These components are crucial for maintaining a proactive security posture and ensuring the resilience of PHP applications against evolving cyber threats.

Developing an Incident Response Plan

Developing an incident response plan (IRP) is essential for ensuring the security of PHP applications and responding effectively to any security incidents. A well-structured IRP tailored to PHP applications helps organizations prepare for potential threats and manage incidents swiftly and efficiently.

Identifying Stakeholders

First and foremost, identifying stakeholders is a critical step in developing an IRP. Stakeholders include a range of internal and external parties who have a vested interest in the security of the application. Internally, the IT security team, consisting of security analysts, engineers, and administrators, plays a central role in overseeing security measures. The development team, which includes PHP developers, is crucial for ensuring that security monitoring solutions integrate seamlessly with the application's architecture. System administrators, responsible for managing the infrastructure, are key stakeholders in implementing and configuring security monitoring tools at the infrastructure level. Management and executives provide strategic direction, approve budgets, and allocate resources, making their early engagement essential for securing buy-in and support. Additionally, legal and compliance teams ensure that security initiatives comply with relevant laws, regulations, and industry standards, providing guidance on data protection requirements, privacy regulations, and incident response obligations.

External stakeholders are equally important. Third-party vendors and service providers, who may be involved in hosting, cloud services, or other IT-related functions, must be coordinated with to ensure comprehensive security monitoring. Customers and end users of PHP applications have a stake in the security and privacy of their data, and keeping them informed about security measures and incident response processes helps maintain trust and transparency. Regulatory authorities and auditors, who have oversight responsibilities, also play a crucial role in ensuring compliance with security standards and regulations. Engaging with these stakeholders demonstrates compliance and readiness to address security concerns.

External consultants and security experts can also provide specialized expertise and guidance. Their insights help ensure that the chosen solutions align with best practices and industry standards. Engaging stakeholders throughout the IRP development process, soliciting their input, addressing their concerns, and keeping them informed about progress and developments are vital for the success of security initiatives.

After identifying stakeholders, the next step is to develop and document a comprehensive incident response plan. This plan should detail the procedures for detecting, responding to, and recovering from security incidents. It should include clear roles and responsibilities, communication and escalation procedures, and guidelines for forensic analysis and post-incident review. Additionally, the plan should outline the implementation of security monitoring and intrusion detection systems to continuously oversee the application and detect potential threats in real time.

Define Incident Severity Levels

Defining incident severity levels is crucial for prioritizing response efforts, allocating resources effectively, and ensuring a consistent approach to managing security incidents. These levels help us classify incidents

CHAPTER 7 INCIDENT RESPONSE AND SECURITY MONITORING

based on their potential impact on business operations, data integrity, and confidentiality, enabling us to respond appropriately and maintain organizational security.

First, we must identify key impact factors that contribute to the severity of security incidents. These factors include the impact on availability, which assesses how severely an incident disrupts or impairs access to critical systems, services, or resources. Another important factor is the impact on data integrity, evaluating the extent to which an incident affects the accuracy, completeness, or reliability of data. The impact on confidentiality is also critical, determining how sensitive the compromised information is and the risk of exposure. Additionally, we must consider regulatory compliance – whether the incident results in noncompliance with legal or regulatory requirements, potentially leading to severe legal and financial repercussions. Reputational damage is another factor to consider, as incidents harming our organization's reputation, brand, or customer trust require immediate attention. Finally, we need to estimate the potential financial loss resulting from an incident, including both direct costs, such as remediation expenses, and indirect losses, such as lost revenue.

Based on these identified impact factors, we can define a set of severity levels that reflect the varying degrees of severity and urgency associated with security incidents. Commonly used severity levels include critical, high, medium, and low.

Critical incidents have a severe impact on availability, data integrity, or confidentiality, posing an immediate and significant threat to our operations, assets, or reputation. These incidents require urgent response and escalation due to their potential to cause major disruptions or damage. High severity incidents have a substantial impact on one or more key aspects of security, potentially causing significant disruption, damage, or loss if not addressed promptly. These incidents require prompt attention and escalation to prevent further escalation and mitigate harm. Medium severity incidents have a moderate impact on security, causing some disruption or compromise but not posing an immediate or severe threat. These incidents require timely response and investigation to ensure proper resolution and prevent further issues. Low severity incidents have minimal impact or limited scope, posing little or no immediate threat to security or operations. While these incidents still require investigation and remediation, they can be handled with lower priority compared to more critical incidents.

To ensure consistency in assessing and classifying security incidents, we need to establish clear criteria for severity assessment. This involves developing guidelines that consider factors such as the extent of impact, the likelihood of recurrence, the presence of known vulnerabilities, and the potential for escalation. Documenting these severity definitions and criteria in our incident response plan or security policies ensures that all stakeholders understand the definitions and can apply them consistently when assessing and prioritizing incidents.

Training and awareness are essential for effective incident severity classification. We should provide training sessions for incident response team members and other relevant staff on how to identify, assess, and classify security incidents based on severity levels. Fostering a shared understanding of the importance of severity classification helps prioritize response efforts and allocate resources effectively.

Summing it up, continuous review and adjustment of severity definitions and criteria are necessary to keep them relevant and reflective of our organization's security priorities and objectives. Regularly reviewing and updating severity definitions based on lessons learned from incident response activities, changes in the threat landscape, and evolving business requirements ensures that our severity levels remain effective.

Establish Communication Channels

Firstly, impact on availability is a critical factor. We need to consider how the incident disrupts or impairs access to critical systems, services, or resources. Factors to assess include the duration of downtime or service disruption, the number of users or systems affected, the criticality of the affected systems or services to business operations, and the potential revenue loss or operational impact due to downtime. By understanding the extent of disruption, we can prioritize incidents that severely impact our operational continuity.

Next, we evaluate the impact on data integrity. This involves assessing the degree to which the incident compromises the accuracy, completeness, or reliability of data. Criteria to consider include the sensitivity and criticality of the compromised data, the volume of data affected, the potential for data corruption, manipulation, or unauthorized access, and any regulatory or contractual obligations related to data protection and integrity. Understanding these factors helps us prioritize incidents that could lead to significant data integrity issues.

The impact on confidentiality is another essential criterion. We need to assess the sensitivity and confidentiality of the information compromised or at risk of exposure due to the incident. Factors to consider include the type of information exposed, such as personally identifiable information or intellectual property, the scope of exposure, the legal or contractual implications of data exposure, and the reputational damage or loss of trust resulting from data breaches. This assessment helps us prioritize incidents that pose significant risks to our confidential data.

Regulatory compliance requirements must also be considered. We need to determine whether the incident results in noncompliance with legal, regulatory, or industry standards. Considerations include applicable laws and regulations, such as GDPR, HIPAA, or PCI DSS, specific compliance obligations relevant to our industry, potential penalties, fines, or legal consequences for noncompliance, and the requirement for notifying regulatory authorities or affected individuals about security breaches. Ensuring compliance helps us avoid legal and financial repercussions.

The potential for reputational damage is another critical factor. We need to assess the impact of the incident on our organization's reputation, brand image, or customer trust. Criteria to consider include public visibility and media coverage of the incident, customer perception and trust in our ability to protect their data, long-term consequences for customer and brand loyalty, and mitigation measures required to restore public confidence and reputation. Prioritizing incidents that could harm our reputation is essential for maintaining customer trust and market competitiveness.

Financial impact is a significant consideration. We need to evaluate the financial implications of the incident, including direct costs and indirect losses. Factors to consider include the cost of incident response activities, such as investigation, remediation, and legal fees, loss of revenue or business opportunities due to downtime or service disruption, expenses associated with regulatory fines, legal settlements, and customer compensation, and the potential long-term financial impact on our profitability and sustainability. Understanding the financial impact helps us allocate resources effectively.

The likelihood of recurrence is also important. We need to consider the likelihood of similar incidents occurring in the future based on the root causes, vulnerabilities, and risk factors associated with the current incident. Factors to assess include the presence of underlying security weaknesses or vulnerabilities, the effectiveness of existing controls and mitigation measures, historical trends and patterns of similar incidents, and the potential for exploitation by threat actors. This helps us prioritize incidents that could recur and implement measures to prevent future occurrences.

We determine the overall severity assessment by evaluating these criteria and assigning an appropriate severity level using a predefined scale, such as critical, high, medium, or low. We consider the cumulative impact of multiple factors and exercise judgment to assign a severity level based on our organization's risk tolerance and priorities. By doing so, we ensure that our incident response efforts are prioritized effectively, minimizing the impact of incidents and maintaining a consistent and effective approach to incident management.

When establishing criteria for severity assessment, it's essential to involve key stakeholders from relevant departments, such as IT security, legal, compliance, and executive management. Collaboratively define criteria that are tailored to the organization's unique risk landscape, business objectives, and regulatory environment. Regularly review and update the criteria to ensure their relevance and effectiveness in guiding incident response efforts.

Create an Incident Response Team (IRT)

Creating an incident response team (IRT) is essential for effectively managing security incidents and minimizing their impact on the organization. The IRT consists of individuals with specific roles and responsibilities dedicated to detecting, responding to, and recovering from security incidents.

To begin, we need to identify team members based on their expertise, skills, and responsibilities. Key roles within the IRT may include an Incident Coordinator who oversees the incident response process, coordinates team activities, and communicates with stakeholders. A Technical Lead is crucial for leading technical investigations, analyzing evidence, and coordinating with IT and security teams to contain and mitigate incidents. A Forensic Analyst conducts forensic analysis of compromised systems, identifies the root cause of incidents, and preserves digital evidence for investigation. The Communication Liaison manages communication with internal stakeholders, external parties, and the media during security incidents. Additionally, a Legal Advisor provides legal guidance on compliance, data protection, and incident reporting obligations. IT and Security Personnel, who are technical experts responsible for implementing security controls, monitoring systems, and responding to incidents, are also vital team members.

Next, it is important to define roles and responsibilities clearly. This ensures accountability and effective collaboration within the team. We need to document the expectations, duties, and authority levels associated with each role within the IRT. This clarity helps in seamless functioning during an incident when swift and decisive action is required.

Establishing a reporting structure within the IRT is another critical step. We need to define the lines of authority, escalation paths, and communication channels for reporting incidents and sharing updates. This structure facilitates smooth communication and decision-making during security incidents, ensuring that everyone knows their role and who to report to.

Providing training and resources to team members is essential for them to fulfill their roles effectively. We should offer training sessions on incident response procedures, tools, and techniques. Additionally, providing access to incident response tools, documentation, and relevant resources ensures that the team is well equipped to handle any incident.

We must also develop incident response procedures by creating documented guidelines outlining the step-by-step process for detecting, analyzing, containing, and recovering from security incidents. These procedures should define the steps for reporting incidents, assessing severity, coordinating response efforts, and communicating with stakeholders.

Conducting tabletop exercises and simulated incident scenarios helps test the effectiveness of the IRT and incident response procedures. These exercises allow the team to practice coordination, communication, decision-making, and technical skills in a controlled environment, preparing them for real incidents.

Setting up the necessary incident response infrastructure is vital for supporting incident response activities. This includes incident management platforms, collaboration tools, forensic analysis tools, and communication channels. Having the right infrastructure in place ensures that the team can respond quickly and effectively to incidents.

Regularly reviewing and updating the composition, roles, procedures, and capabilities of the IRT is crucial to reflect changes in the organization's technology, threat landscape, and business requirements. Incorporating lessons learned from incident response activities and feedback from team members ensures continuous improvement.

Maintaining up-to-date contact information for IRT members, including alternate contacts and after-hours contact details, ensures that team members can be reached promptly in case of a security incident, including outside normal business hours. This readiness is essential for timely incident response.

Promoting collaboration and coordination within the IRT and across organizational departments fosters a culture of teamwork and effective communication. Encouraging regular communication, knowledge sharing, and cross-training enhances the team's effectiveness and resilience.

Document PHP Application Architecture

Documenting the PHP application architecture is crucial for understanding its structure, components, dependencies, and security considerations. Proper documentation ensures that developers, system administrators, and security professionals have a clear understanding of how the application is designed and deployed, facilitating effective maintenance, troubleshooting, and security assessments.

We need to start with an overview of the application architecture. This includes providing a high-level overview of the PHP application architecture, detailing its purpose, scope, and key functionalities. Describing the role of the application within the organization and its interaction with other systems and services offers a broad understanding of its significance and operational context.

Next, we need to identify and describe the components and modules of the application. This involves listing the various components, modules, and subsystems that make up the PHP application, such as front-end

CHAPTER 7   INCIDENT RESPONSE AND SECURITY MONITORING

interfaces, back-end logic, databases, APIs, third-party libraries, and external integrations. Documenting the functionality, purpose, and responsibilities of each component ensures that every part of the application is well understood.

Illustrating the data flow and interaction between different components is another crucial step. We should use diagrams, flowcharts, or sequence diagrams to visualize how data is processed, transmitted, and stored within the application. Identifying input sources, processing logic, data storage mechanisms, and output destinations helps in understanding the application's data lifecycle.

We also need to document the database schema and structure used by the PHP application. Providing an overview of the database tables, fields, relationships, and constraints is essential. Descriptions of table structures, data types, primary and foreign keys, and indexing strategies should be included to ensure comprehensive database documentation.

Describing the deployment architecture of the PHP application is vital. This includes the server infrastructure, hosting environment, and deployment configurations. We need to document details such as server specifications, operating systems, web server software (e.g., Apache, Nginx), PHP runtime environment, and caching mechanisms to give a clear picture of the deployment setup.

Documenting the security controls and mechanisms implemented within the PHP application architecture is critical for protecting against common security threats and vulnerabilities. This should cover authentication mechanisms, access controls, encryption methods, input validation, output encoding, and session management techniques.

Identifying third-party dependencies and libraries used by the PHP application is also necessary. We should document the versions, licenses, and integration points of third-party components and include information about how these dependencies are managed, updated, and secured.

CHAPTER 7　INCIDENT RESPONSE AND SECURITY MONITORING

We need to document the configuration settings and parameters relevant to the PHP application. This includes settings related to performance optimization, security hardening, error handling, logging, and debugging. Specifying recommended configurations and best practices for securing and optimizing the application ensures consistency and reliability.

If the PHP application exposes APIs, we need to document the API endpoints, methods, parameters, and response formats. Providing examples and usage guidelines for interacting with the APIs securely and effectively is crucial for integration purposes.

Maintaining version control and change history for the documentation is essential. Using version control systems such as Git to manage changes, updates, and contributions ensures that documentation is accurate and up to date. Keeping a record of changes helps track the evolution of the application architecture.

Including accessibility and usability guidelines ensures that the application is user-friendly and compliant with web standards. Documenting accessibility considerations, usability principles, and design patterns helps meet the needs of diverse users.

We need to review and update the documentation regularly. Reflecting changes, updates, and enhancements in the documentation ensures that it remains a valuable resource for developers, administrators, and stakeholders. Keeping the documentation current and relevant is essential for maintaining its usefulness and accuracy.

Through documenting the PHP application architecture comprehensively, organizations can enhance their understanding of the application's design, functionality, and security posture. Well-documented architectures facilitate collaboration, troubleshooting, and security assessments, ultimately leading to more robust and resilient PHP applications.

CHAPTER 7   INCIDENT RESPONSE AND SECURITY MONITORING

Implement Monitoring and Logging

Implementing monitoring and logging mechanisms is crucial for detecting and responding to security incidents, performance issues, and other anomalies in PHP applications. Let's discuss detailed steps on how to implement monitoring and logging effectively.

We need to select monitoring tools that are capable of monitoring PHP applications, web servers, databases, and related infrastructure components. Tools like Nagios, Zabbix, Prometheus, or Datadog offer features for monitoring PHP-specific metrics and performance indicators, ensuring comprehensive oversight of our systems.

Next, we need to define our monitoring objectives clearly. These objectives may include monitoring for performance bottlenecks, system resource utilization, application errors, security events, and abnormal behavior patterns. Having clear objectives helps us focus our monitoring efforts and ensures we are capturing relevant data.

Identifying key metrics is essential for effective monitoring. We should identify the performance metrics and indicators that are relevant to our PHP application, such as CPU usage, memory utilization, disk I/O, network traffic, response times, error rates, and throughput. Monitoring these metrics helps us understand the health and performance of our application.

We need to configure monitoring agents by installing and configuring them on the servers hosting our PHP applications. These agents collect data about system performance, resource utilization, and application behavior, transmitting it to the monitoring server for analysis. This setup allows for real-time monitoring and quick identification of issues.

Setting up Application Performance Monitoring (APM) solutions is crucial for gaining insights into the performance of PHP code execution, database queries, external API calls, and other application-level activities. APM tools like New Relic or Dynatrace provide detailed instrumentation and monitoring capabilities, helping us optimize application performance.

CHAPTER 7   INCIDENT RESPONSE AND SECURITY MONITORING

We need to monitor PHP logs by configuring PHP to log errors, warnings, and other relevant events to log files. Enabling PHP error logging in the php.ini configuration file and specifying the desired log level (e.g., E_ALL for logging all errors) ensures that we capture all relevant information. Regularly monitoring PHP error logs helps us identify and address application errors, warnings, or exceptions.

Monitoring web server logs is also essential. We should monitor access logs and error logs generated by the web server (e.g., Apache, Nginx) hosting our PHP applications. Analyzing access logs helps us track incoming requests, client IP addresses, user agents, and response codes, while monitoring error logs provides insights into server errors, HTTP status codes, and potential security issues.

Implementing security logging is critical for capturing security-relevant events and activities within the PHP application. Logging security-related events such as authentication failures, access control violations, SQL injection attempts, and other suspicious activities helps us detect and respond to security threats. Integrating with security information and event management (SIEM) systems for centralized security logging and analysis enhances our security posture.

We need to centralize logging by sending logs from PHP applications, web servers, databases, and other components to a centralized logging server or platform. Using tools like Elasticsearch, Logstash, and Kibana (ELK stack) or Splunk for log aggregation, storage, and analysis ensures that all logs are easily accessible and can be analyzed collectively.

Implementing log rotation and retention policies is necessary to manage log files effectively and prevent them from consuming excessive disk space. Configuring log rotation based on size or time and archiving or deleting old logs according to retention policies ensures compliance with data retention requirements and keeps our logging system efficient.

Setting up alerting and notifications is vital for timely incident response. We need to configure alerting mechanisms to notify system administrators or operations teams when predefined thresholds or conditions are met. Setting up alerts for critical events, performance degradation, security incidents, or abnormal behavior patterns detected through monitoring and logging ensures that we can respond promptly to issues.

We need to regularly review and analyze logs to identify performance issues, security incidents, or other anomalies requiring attention. Using log analysis tools and dashboards to visualize trends, patterns, and correlations in log data helps generate actionable insights and supports continuous improvement of our application reliability and security.

Define Incident Response Procedures

Defining incident response procedures is critical for ensuring a swift, organized, and effective response to security incidents in PHP applications. These procedures outline the step-by-step actions to be taken when an incident occurs, including detection, analysis, containment, eradication, recovery, and post-incident activities. Let's focus upon a few detailed steps for defining incident response procedures.

We need to start with incident categorization. This involves defining categories or types of security incidents that the procedures will address. Categories may include unauthorized access, data breaches, denial-of-service attacks, malware infections, or website defacement. Categorization helps us prioritize and respond appropriately to different types of incidents.

Incident detection and reporting is the next critical step. We need to establish procedures for promptly detecting and reporting security incidents. This includes defining how incidents will be detected, who is responsible for monitoring and reporting incidents, and the channels through which incidents should be reported, such as an incident response hotline, email, or a ticketing system.

We also need to outline the initial response and triage steps to be taken upon receiving a security incident report. This involves designating an incident coordinator or first responder responsible for coordinating the initial response efforts. Conducting a preliminary assessment to determine the nature, scope, and severity of the incident is crucial at this stage.

Incident escalation and notification procedures are essential for escalating incidents to higher management or specialized response teams as needed. We need to establish criteria for determining when to escalate incidents based on severity, impact, and complexity. Notifying relevant stakeholders, including IT security teams, management, legal counsel, and regulatory authorities, as required, ensures that the appropriate resources are mobilized.

Preserving evidence is a critical part of the incident response. We need to establish procedures for preserving digital evidence relevant to the incident. This includes defining how evidence should be collected, documented, and stored to maintain its integrity and admissibility for forensic analysis or legal purposes. Ensuring that evidence handling procedures comply with chain of custody requirements and best practices is vital.

Containment and mitigation procedures are necessary to prevent further harm or spread of the incident. We need to outline containment measures such as isolating affected systems, blocking malicious activities, or implementing temporary security controls to limit the incident's impact on the organization.

Defining forensic analysis and investigation procedures helps us understand the root cause of incidents. We need to specify techniques and tools for collecting, analyzing, and interpreting digital evidence to identify the root cause, extent of compromise, and tactics used by threat actors. Ensuring that forensic analysis procedures follow industry best practices and legal requirements is crucial.

Incident recovery and restoration procedures outline the steps for restoring affected systems, data, and services to normal operation following a security incident. Recovery steps may include restoring from backups, applying patches or updates, and implementing corrective actions to address vulnerabilities exploited during the incident.

Communication and coordination protocols ensure that stakeholders are kept informed about incident response activities. We need to establish channels for internal and external communication, including incident status updates, progress reports, and post-incident reviews. Ensuring timely and transparent communication helps maintain trust and confidence in the organization's response efforts.

Post-incident analysis and lessons learned sessions are essential for evaluating the effectiveness of incident response procedures and identifying areas for improvement. We need to document findings, recommendations, and action items for enhancing incident response capabilities and mitigating future risks.

Documentation and reporting requirements are necessary for recording incident response activities, findings, and outcomes. We need to document incident details, actions taken, evidence collected, and lessons learned in incident reports or post-incident reviews. Maintaining accurate and comprehensive records is essential for regulatory compliance, legal purposes, and continuous improvement.

We need to provide training and awareness programs for incident response team members and other relevant staff on incident response procedures, roles, and responsibilities. Conducting regular drills, simulations, and tabletop exercises helps test the effectiveness of procedures and ensures readiness to respond to security incidents.

Test Incident Response Plan

Testing the incident response plan (IRP) is a crucial step to ensure its effectiveness in real-world scenarios and to identify any gaps or weaknesses that need to be addressed. A few detailed steps for elaborating on testing the incident response plan.

CHAPTER 7   INCIDENT RESPONSE AND SECURITY MONITORING

We need to begin by understanding the types of testing available. Tabletop exercises involve key stakeholders simulating various security incidents and walking through the steps outlined in the IRP. These exercises are discussion based and focus on decision-making, communication, and coordination among team members. Functional testing involves performing tests on specific components or procedures within the IRP to ensure they operate as intended, such as testing incident detection, notification, escalation, containment, eradication, and recovery procedures. Scenario-based testing requires developing realistic scenarios representing different types of security incidents, such as data breaches, malware infections, or denial-of-service attacks, and simulating these scenarios to test the response capabilities of the incident response team. Red team exercises involve a team of skilled professionals simulating real-world attacks or security breaches to test the organization's detection and response capabilities, identifying vulnerabilities and weaknesses in the IRP and security controls. Lastly, drills and simulations test specific aspects of the incident response plan, such as communication procedures, incident escalation, evidence preservation, or coordination with external stakeholders.

Next, we need to focus on scenario development. Developing realistic scenarios that reflect our organization's threat landscape, industry sector, and potential security risks is essential. Scenarios should be diverse, challenging, and relevant to our operations and assets, considering insider threats, external attacks, system failures, or natural disasters.

Exercise planning is crucial for organizing the logistics and details of the testing exercises. This includes scheduling, identifying participants, defining roles and responsibilities, scenario briefings, simulation environment setup, and evaluation criteria. Ensuring that all participants understand their roles and expectations during the exercises is essential for a successful test.

Conducting the exercises involves facilitating the testing exercises according to predefined scenarios and objectives. We need to provide participants with scenario briefings and instructions for responding to the simulated incidents, encouraging active participation, collaboration, and decision-making among team members.

Observation and evaluation of the performance of participants and the effectiveness of the incident response procedures during the exercises is critical. We need to assess how well the team identifies, analyzes, and responds to the simulated incidents, as well as their adherence to established protocols and best practices. Collecting feedback from participants about their experiences, challenges encountered, and areas for improvement in the incident response plan and procedures helps in identifying areas that need enhancement.

Debriefing and lessons learned sessions should be conducted after each testing exercise to review the outcomes, discuss observations, and identify lessons learned. Documenting key findings, strengths, weaknesses, and recommendations for enhancing the incident response plan and capabilities is vital. Using the lessons learned from testing exercises to refine and improve the incident response plan, procedures, training programs, and security controls ensures continuous improvement.

Iterative improvement is an ongoing process. We need to continuously review, update, and refine the incident response plan based on insights gained from testing exercises, real-world incidents, changes in the threat landscape, and organizational feedback. Regularly conducting testing and exercises to validate the effectiveness of the IRP and maintaining readiness to respond to evolving security threats is essential for staying ahead of potential incidents.

By rigorously testing the incident response plan through these methods, we can ensure that our team is prepared to detect, respond, and recover from security incidents promptly and effectively. This proactive approach helps in minimizing the impact of incidents and continuously improving our security posture.

CHAPTER 7 INCIDENT RESPONSE AND SECURITY MONITORING

Incident Reporting and Escalation

Incident reporting and escalation are crucial aspects of incident response, ensuring that incidents are promptly communicated, assessed, and escalated to the appropriate stakeholders for further action. Let's connect on a few detailed steps for establishing effective incident reporting and escalation procedures.

We need to start by establishing incident reporting procedures. This involves defining clear procedures for reporting security incidents within the organization, specifying the channels, methods, and contact points through which incidents should be reported, such as a dedicated incident response hotline, email address, or online reporting portal. It's also important to specify the information required in incident reports, including the nature of the incident, affected systems or assets, the time and location of the incident, and any initial actions taken to mitigate or contain the incident.

Incident triage and classification are essential for prioritizing response efforts. We need to develop criteria for triaging and classifying reported incidents based on their severity, impact, and urgency. Establishing categories or levels of incidents (e.g., low, medium, high, critical) helps in allocating resources effectively. Defining the roles and responsibilities of incident responders or triage teams responsible for assessing reported incidents, verifying their validity, and determining appropriate response actions ensures that incidents are handled systematically.

Next, we need to define incident escalation procedures. This involves establishing escalation paths and procedures for escalating incidents to higher levels of management or specialized response teams when necessary. Criteria for determining when incidents should be escalated based on severity, complexity, and potential impact on the organization need to be well defined. Identifying individuals or teams responsible for making escalation decisions and specifying the communication channels through which incidents should be escalated ensures a streamlined process. Ensuring that escalation procedures are well documented, understood by all stakeholders, and regularly reviewed and updated is crucial for effectiveness.

Notification requirements must be specified to ensure relevant stakeholders are informed about security incidents. We need to determine who should be notified, including internal stakeholders (e.g., IT security teams, management, legal counsel) and external parties (e.g., regulatory authorities, law enforcement, customers, vendors). Establishing communication protocols and notification templates for sending incident notifications, including the content, format, and timing of notifications, ensures consistency. Compliance with legal, regulatory, and contractual obligations regarding incident reporting and disclosure is essential.

Incident response coordination is necessary to ensure a unified and effective response. We need to coordinate incident response efforts across organizational departments and teams. Designating an incident coordinator or incident response team responsible for orchestrating response activities, communicating with stakeholders, and coordinating remediation efforts helps in maintaining order. Fostering collaboration and communication among incident responders, IT teams, security personnel, legal counsel, and other relevant stakeholders facilitates timely and coordinated incident response.

Documentation and tracking of all reported incidents, including their classification, status, response actions, and outcomes, is essential for accountability and improvement. Using incident tracking systems or incident management platforms to log and track incident reports, updates, and resolution activities ensures that all details are recorded accurately. Maintaining accurate and comprehensive incident records is important for regulatory compliance, legal purposes, and post-incident analysis. Documenting the timeline of events, response actions taken, lessons learned, and recommendations for improving incident response processes helps in continuous improvement.

Also we need to focus on continuous improvement. Continuously evaluating and refining incident reporting and escalation procedures based on lessons learned from incident response activities, feedback from stakeholders, and changes in the threat landscape is crucial. Conducting regular reviews and assessments of incident response processes to identify areas for improvement and enhance organizational readiness to respond to security incidents effectively ensures that our procedures remain relevant and effective.

Post-incident Analysis and Improvement

Post-incident analysis and improvement are critical components of the incident response lifecycle. They enable organizations to learn from security incidents, identify areas for improvement, and enhance their incident response capabilities. Let's discuss a few detailed steps for conducting post-incident analysis and implementing improvements:

> Incident Debriefing: We need to conduct a post-incident debriefing session with the incident response team and relevant stakeholders. This session should review the incident response process, actions taken, and outcomes. Discussing what went well during the response, as well as areas for improvement or lessons learned, is essential for gaining insights into the effectiveness of the response.
>
> Root Cause Analysis (RCA): Performing a root cause analysis helps identify the underlying causes and contributing factors that led to the security incident. We need to investigate the technical, human, and organizational factors that may have contributed to the incident, such as software vulnerabilities, misconfigurations, or inadequate security controls.

Lessons Learned Documentation: Documenting lessons learned from the incident response process is crucial. This includes findings from the root cause analysis, observations, and recommendations for improving incident response procedures, policies, and practices. Capturing insights into what worked effectively, what could have been done better, and how similar incidents can be prevented in the future helps build a knowledge base for ongoing improvement.

Incident Response Review: Reviewing the effectiveness of incident response procedures, protocols, and tools used during the incident is necessary. We need to evaluate how well the incident response plan was followed, whether response actions were timely and appropriate, and if any gaps or deficiencies were identified in the response process.

Identify Improvement Opportunities: Based on the findings from the post-incident analysis and lessons learned documentation, we need to identify specific actions or initiatives to address root causes, strengthen incident response capabilities, and enhance the organization's overall security posture. This step involves determining what changes are needed to prevent future incidents.

Implement Corrective Actions: Implementing corrective actions and remediation measures to address the root causes and contributing factors identified during the post-incident analysis is crucial. This may involve updating security policies and procedures, enhancing security controls, implementing new technologies or tools, or providing additional training and awareness programs for staff.

Continuous Improvement Culture: Fostering a culture of continuous improvement within the organization is vital. Encouraging open communication, collaboration, and feedback sharing among incident responders and stakeholders helps empower team members to contribute ideas, suggestions, and insights for improving incident response processes and practices.

Incident Response Plan Updates: We need to update the incident response plan based on lessons learned from the incident and improvements identified during the post-incident analysis. Incorporating any changes, updates, or enhancements to incident response procedures, roles, responsibilities, and communication protocols ensures the organization is better prepared for future incidents.

Training and Skills Development: Providing training and skills development opportunities for incident response team members and relevant staff enhances their knowledge, skills, and capabilities in incident detection, response, and mitigation. Offering training sessions, workshops, and simulations reinforces best practices and lessons learned from past incidents.

Regular Review and Assessment: Conducting regular reviews and assessments of incident response processes, procedures, and capabilities ensures ongoing effectiveness and alignment with evolving security threats and organizational requirements. Continuously monitoring and measuring incident response metrics and key performance indicators helps track progress and identify areas for further improvement.

Training and Awareness

Training and awareness initiatives are essential components of a comprehensive cybersecurity strategy. These initiatives ensure that employees and stakeholders are equipped with the knowledge, skills, and awareness necessary to mitigate security risks and respond effectively to cyber threats. Here are detailed points to consider for establishing an effective training and awareness program.

We need to develop and implement security awareness training programs. These programs should educate employees about common cybersecurity threats, best practices, and organizational security policies. Training topics may include phishing awareness, password security, social engineering, malware detection, and data protection. Educating employees on these topics helps them recognize and avoid common security pitfalls.

Role-based training is crucial for addressing the specific responsibilities and security requirements of different job roles within the organization. By customizing training content and delivery methods to each role, we can ensure that employees understand the unique security challenges and compliance requirements relevant to their positions.

Conducting regular training sessions is essential for reinforcing key security concepts and practices among employees. These sessions can include workshops or webinars, offering interactive and engaging training materials such as videos, quizzes, case studies, and simulations to enhance learning effectiveness and retention.

Incorporating hands-on exercises and simulations into training programs gives employees practical experience in identifying and responding to security threats. Simulated phishing exercises, tabletop exercises, or red team/blue team scenarios can simulate real-world security incidents and test employees' response capabilities.

Launching awareness campaigns promotes a culture of cybersecurity awareness and vigilance throughout the organization. Using posters, newsletters, email reminders, intranet announcements, and other communication channels raises awareness about cybersecurity risks, trends, and best practices.

Providing specialized executive and leadership training ensures that executives, senior management, and business leaders understand cybersecurity risks, governance requirements, and their role in supporting cybersecurity initiatives. Emphasizing the importance of leadership buy-in and support for cybersecurity initiatives across the organization is crucial for fostering a top-down approach to security.

Offering technical training for IT and security teams enhances their skills and expertise in areas such as network security, threat detection, incident response, penetration testing, and security operations. Technical training and certification programs help ensure that our technical staff are well prepared to handle complex security challenges.

Compliance training programs ensure that employees understand their obligations and responsibilities under relevant data protection regulations, industry standards, and organizational policies. Training on regulatory requirements such as GDPR, HIPAA, PCI DSS, and SOC 2 compliance helps us maintain compliance and avoid legal penalties.

Providing training on remote work and BYOD security is increasingly important as more employees work remotely or use personal devices for work purposes. Educating employees about the risks associated with remote work environments, secure remote access methods, and measures to protect sensitive data when working outside the corporate network is crucial for maintaining security.

Encouraging continuous learning and development helps employees stay abreast of emerging cybersecurity threats, technologies, and best practices. Providing access to online training resources, webinars, conferences, and industry certifications supports ongoing skill development and professional growth.

Establishing metrics and performance measurement allows us to measure the effectiveness of security awareness training programs and track employees' knowledge, behavior changes, and security awareness levels over time. Using metrics to assess training program effectiveness, identify areas for improvement, and demonstrate ROI to stakeholders ensures that our training efforts are impactful.

Soliciting feedback and evaluation from employees regarding the effectiveness of security training programs is vital. Conducting periodic evaluations and surveys to assess employees' knowledge, attitudes, and behaviors related to cybersecurity helps us incorporate feedback into future training initiatives and continuously improve our training programs.

Legal and Regulatory Compliance

Ensuring that the incident response plan complies with relevant legal and regulatory requirements is a critical aspect of cybersecurity, particularly for organizations handling sensitive data or operating in regulated industries. Let's discuss a few detailed points to consider for maintaining legal and regulatory compliance:

Understanding Applicable Laws and Regulations: We need to identify and understand the legal and regulatory requirements relevant to our organization based on its industry, geographic location, and the type of data it handles. Common regulations include the General Data Protection Regulation (GDPR), Health Insurance Portability and Accountability Act (HIPAA), Payment Card Industry Data Security Standard (PCI DSS), Sarbanes-Oxley Act (SOX), and various industry-specific regulations.

Data Protection and Privacy Laws: Complying with data protection and privacy laws that govern the collection, processing, storage, and transfer of personal data is essential. We need to ensure that personal data is collected and processed lawfully, transparently, and for specified purposes, and that individuals' privacy rights are respected.

Security Standards and Frameworks: Adhering to security standards and frameworks provides guidelines and best practices for securing information systems and protecting sensitive data. Examples include the National Institute of Standards and Technology (NIST) Cybersecurity Framework, ISO/IEC 27001, and the Center for Internet Security (CIS) Controls.

Risk Management and Compliance Programs: Implementing risk management and compliance programs helps assess and mitigate cybersecurity risks, monitor compliance with legal and regulatory requirements, and demonstrate due diligence to regulators, auditors, and stakeholders.

Data Breach Notification Requirements: Understanding the data breach notification requirements imposed by relevant laws and regulations is critical. We need to develop incident response procedures for promptly detecting, investigating, and reporting data breaches to regulatory authorities, affected individuals, and other stakeholders as required by law.

Vendor and Third-Party Compliance: Ensuring that vendors, suppliers, and third-party service providers comply with applicable legal and regulatory requirements when handling data or providing services on behalf of the organization is crucial. Implementing contractual agreements, due diligence processes, and oversight mechanisms helps manage third-party risks effectively.

Recordkeeping and Documentation: Maintaining accurate and up-to-date records and documentation demonstrates compliance with legal and regulatory requirements. We need to document security policies, procedures, risk assessments, audit trails, incident response activities, and other compliance-related activities to provide evidence of due diligence and regulatory compliance.

Compliance Audits and Assessments: Conducting regular compliance audits and assessments evaluates the effectiveness of cybersecurity controls, processes, and practices in meeting legal and regulatory requirements. Engaging internal or external auditors to assess compliance with applicable laws, regulations, and industry standards is essential.

Training and Awareness Programs: Providing training and awareness programs educates employees about legal and regulatory requirements, their responsibilities for compliance, and the potential consequences of noncompliance. Ensuring that employees understand the importance of adhering to security policies, procedures, and guidelines helps maintain regulatory compliance.

Legal Counsel and Compliance Advisors: Seeking guidance and support from legal counsel, compliance advisors, or cybersecurity consultants with expertise in regulatory compliance and data protection laws is essential. Consulting with legal experts to interpret complex legal requirements, assess compliance risks, and develop strategies for achieving and maintaining compliance ensures we are on the right track.

Continuous Monitoring and Improvement: Implementing continuous monitoring and improvement processes helps us stay abreast of changes in legal and regulatory requirements, emerging cybersecurity threats, and industry best practices. Regularly reviewing and updating security policies, procedures, and controls addresses evolving compliance obligations and mitigates new risks.

Transparency and Accountability: Fostering a culture of transparency and accountability within the organization by promoting open communication, ethical behavior, and a commitment to compliance with legal and regulatory requirements is crucial. Encouraging employees to report compliance concerns, security incidents, or potential violations of policies and regulations helps maintain a compliant and secure environment.

Incident Communication and Escalation Procedures

Incident communication and escalation procedures are critical components of an effective incident response plan. Let's contemplate upon a detailed outline of how we can develop these procedures in an interactive and discussable manner.

Define Communication Channels

We can ensure effective incident communication by establishing primary and secondary communication channels. These might include email, phone calls, instant messaging platforms, and collaboration tools. Having multiple communication channels means we can share information promptly and reliably, even if one channel fails.

Designate Communication Roles

We need to assign specific roles within the incident response team for communication tasks. Roles such as incident coordinator, communication liaison, and spokesperson should have clearly defined responsibilities and authority levels. This clarity helps avoid confusion about who handles different communication aspects during an incident.

Incident Reporting Process

It's essential to define a process for reporting security incidents, including who should report incidents, what information should be included in incident reports, and to whom reports should be submitted. By encouraging timely and accurate reporting, we can facilitate swift response actions. Clear guidelines streamline the reporting process and ensure that critical details are captured.

Internal Communication Procedures

We should outline how internal communication will be managed during a security incident. This involves notifying relevant stakeholders within the organization, such as IT teams, senior management, legal counsel, and human resources. Establishing a clear internal communication procedure ensures that all necessary parties are informed and can collaborate effectively.

External Communication Procedures

When it comes to external communication, we need to define protocols for interacting with parties such as customers, partners, regulators, law enforcement agencies, and the media. We should establish guidelines for what information can be shared externally, who is authorized to communicate with external parties, and how to maintain confidentiality and integrity. Proper external communication helps us manage public perception and comply with regulations.

Incident Severity Classification

We can define criteria for classifying incident severity levels based on their impact on business operations, data integrity, and confidentiality. Establishing thresholds for escalating incidents to higher management or external authorities based on severity levels helps us prioritize response efforts and ensure appropriate escalation.

Escalation Matrix

An escalation matrix is crucial for outlining the chain of command and escalation paths for different types of security incidents. We need to specify who should be notified at each level of escalation and under what circumstances escalation is necessary. This matrix ensures that incidents are handled at the appropriate level of authority.

Response Time Objectives (RTOs) and Service-Level Agreements (SLAs)

By establishing response time objectives (RTOs) and service-level agreements (SLAs) for acknowledging, investigating, and resolving security incidents, we can set clear expectations for incident response times and performance. It's important to ensure that these response times are realistic and aligned with the severity and impact of the incident.

Incident Notification Templates

We should prepare pre-approved incident notification templates for internal and external communication. These templates should include essential information such as the nature of the incident, its impact, actions taken, and contact information for further inquiries. Having templates ready speeds up the communication process and ensures consistency.

Training and Awareness

Providing training and awareness programs for incident response team members and other relevant staff on effective communication practices during security incidents is essential. Conducting drills and simulations ensures that team members are familiar with their roles and responsibilities. Regular training helps us ensure that the team is prepared and confident in handling real incidents.

Documentation and Post-incident Analysis

We need to document all communication activities, including incident reports, notifications, responses, and follow-up actions. Conducting post-incident reviews helps us assess the effectiveness of communication procedures and identify areas for improvement. Thorough documentation and analysis refine the communication process and enhance future incident response.

Legal and Regulatory Compliance

Ensuring that our incident communication procedures comply with applicable legal and regulatory requirements, such as data breach notification laws, privacy regulations, and industry standards, is crucial. Consulting legal counsel helps us ensure that our communication practices adhere to legal obligations and minimize legal risks. Compliance helps protect the organization from legal repercussions and ensures transparency.

Forensic Analysis and Post-incident Analysis

Forensic analysis and post-incident analysis are crucial components of incident response, aimed at understanding the root causes of security incidents, identifying gaps in security controls, and implementing measures to prevent recurrence. Let's discuss the below approaches to follow for these processes:

1. Forensic Analysis

    Preservation of Evidence: We need to ensure the preservation of digital evidence immediately upon detecting a security incident. This includes system logs, network traffic captures, memory dumps, and any other artifacts that may help in reconstructing the events leading to the incident. Preserving evidence helps maintain its integrity for analysis and legal proceedings.

    Forensic Imaging: Creating forensic images of affected systems and storage devices is essential to capture their exact state at the time of the incident. Using specialized tools and techniques ensures the integrity and authenticity of these forensic images, which are crucial for accurate analysis.

    Analysis of Digital Artifacts: Conducting an in-depth analysis of digital artifacts helps uncover evidence of unauthorized access, malicious activities, or data breaches. This involves examining file system metadata, registry entries, event logs, network connections, and other forensic artifacts to understand the nature and scope of the incident.

Timeline Reconstruction: Developing a timeline of events leading up to and following the security incident is crucial. This timeline, based on forensic evidence, helps us understand the sequence of actions taken by threat actors and their impact on the affected systems and data.

Malware Analysis: If malware is suspected, performing malware analysis is necessary to understand its behavior, capabilities, and propagation methods. Analyzing malware samples in a controlled environment helps avoid further contamination and assess the extent of compromise.

Forensic Reporting: Documenting findings from forensic analysis in a detailed forensic report is vital. This report should include the methodology used, evidence collected, analysis results, and conclusions drawn. Ensuring that the forensic report is accurate, comprehensive, and suitable for legal and investigative purposes is essential.

2. Post-incident Analysis

    Root Cause Analysis: We need to conduct a thorough investigation to identify the root causes of the security incident. This involves examining vulnerabilities in systems, misconfigurations, human errors, insider threats, and other factors contributing to the incident.

    Gap Analysis: Assessing existing security controls and practices helps identify gaps that allowed the incident to occur or escalate. Determining whether security policies, procedures, and technical controls need to be enhanced or updated to address identified weaknesses is critical for future prevention.

Lessons Learned: Extracting lessons learned from the incident response process helps identify strengths and weaknesses in the organization's response capabilities. We should pinpoint areas for improvement in incident detection, response, communication, and coordination.

Recommendations for Improvement: Based on the findings of the post-incident analysis, we need to develop recommendations for enhancing the organization's security posture and resilience. Prioritizing actionable steps to address identified weaknesses and mitigate future risks is essential.

Incident Response Plan Updates: Updating the incident response plan and associated documentation based on lessons learned from the incident is crucial. Incorporating improvements in procedures, communication protocols, escalation paths, and forensic analysis techniques enhances the organization's readiness to respond to future incidents.

Training and Awareness: Providing training and awareness sessions for incident response team members and other relevant stakeholders based on the findings of the post-incident analysis is necessary. Ensuring that personnel are equipped with the knowledge and skills required to effectively respond to security incidents in the future is essential.

Continuous Improvement: Establishing mechanisms for continuous improvement in incident response capabilities, such as regular reviews, exercises, and simulations, helps maintain readiness. Fostering a culture of security awareness and proactive risk management throughout the organization is key to ongoing security enhancement.

Implementing Security Monitoring and Intrusion Detection Systems

Implementing security monitoring and intrusion detection systems (IDS) is crucial for proactively identifying and responding to security threats in PHP applications. Let's plan a comprehensive guide to effectively implementing these systems.

First, we need to define our monitoring objectives. By identifying the goals of our security monitoring efforts, such as detecting unauthorized access attempts, identifying abnormal behavior patterns, and protecting sensitive data, we can ensure that our monitoring activities are focused and effective.

When selecting monitoring tools, we should choose those capable of monitoring PHP applications, web servers, databases, and network infrastructure. Tools like web application firewalls (WAFs), intrusion detection systems (IDS), security information and event management (SIEM) systems, and log management platforms are essential. By choosing the right tools, we can ensure that we have the necessary capabilities to monitor and protect our environment effectively.

Next, let's implement logging mechanisms. We need to configure PHP applications, web servers, and database logging to capture relevant security events and activities. By enabling logging of authentication

CHAPTER 7   INCIDENT RESPONSE AND SECURITY MONITORING

attempts, access control decisions, application errors, SQL queries, and other critical events, we can maintain a comprehensive record of activities that can be analyzed for signs of security incidents.

Deploying web application firewalls (WAFs) is another crucial step. By installing and configuring WAFs to inspect and filter incoming HTTP requests to PHP applications, we can help prevent common web application attacks such as SQL injection, cross-site scripting (XSS), and remote code execution. Properly configured WAFs act as a protective barrier, shielding our applications from malicious traffic.

We also need to set up network intrusion detection systems (NIDS). By deploying NIDS sensors strategically within our network infrastructure to monitor traffic and detect suspicious activities, we can enhance our ability to detect and respond to network-based threats. Configuring NIDS rules to identify known attack patterns and anomalies is vital for maintaining network security.

Defining monitoring policies tailored to the specific security requirements and risk profile of our PHP applications is essential. By establishing rulesets and thresholds for triggering alerts based on the severity of security events and their impact on business operations, we can prioritize and manage alerts effectively.

Configuring alerting mechanisms ensures that security personnel or incident response teams are notified in real time when security events or anomalies are detected. By delivering alerts via email, SMS, instant messaging, or integrating with incident response platforms, we can enable swift action to mitigate potential threats.

To stay updated on emerging threats, malware signatures, and malicious IP addresses, we should integrate threat intelligence feeds into our monitoring and IDS systems. Leveraging threat intelligence enhances the accuracy and effectiveness of our intrusion detection rules, helping us stay ahead of potential attackers.

CHAPTER 7   INCIDENT RESPONSE AND SECURITY MONITORING

Performing regular security monitoring is crucial. By continuously monitoring PHP application logs, network traffic, and system activities for signs of security breaches or suspicious behavior, we can promptly investigate anomalies and respond to mitigate potential threats before they escalate.

We need to conduct periodic audits and reviews of our security monitoring configurations, IDS rulesets, and alerting mechanisms. By ensuring their effectiveness and alignment with evolving security requirements, we can keep our defenses robust and adaptive. Updating monitoring policies and configurations based on lessons learned from incident response activities is key to maintaining a strong security posture.

Integrating our security monitoring and IDS systems with our incident response processes and procedures is essential. By defining escalation paths, response workflows, and mitigation strategies for addressing security incidents detected through monitoring activities, we can ensure a coordinated and efficient response.

We should monitor and evaluate the performance of our security monitoring and IDS systems over time. By measuring key metrics such as detection accuracy, alert response times, and incident resolution rates, we can use performance data to identify areas for improvement and optimize our security monitoring capabilities.

Summary

In this chapter, we focus on implementing security monitoring and intrusion detection systems (IDS) to proactively identify and respond to security threats in PHP applications. We begin by defining our monitoring objectives, such as detecting unauthorized access attempts, identifying abnormal behavior patterns, and protecting sensitive data. Selecting appropriate monitoring tools is essential, including web application firewalls (WAFs), IDS, security information and event management (SIEM) systems, and log management platforms.

CHAPTER 7   INCIDENT RESPONSE AND SECURITY MONITORING

Implementing robust logging mechanisms for PHP applications, web servers, and databases is crucial for capturing relevant security events and activities. Deploying WAFs helps prevent common web application attacks like SQL injection and cross-site scripting (XSS), while setting up network intrusion detection systems (NIDS) enhances our ability to detect and respond to network-based threats. Defining tailored monitoring policies and configuring real-time alerting mechanisms ensures that security personnel or incident response teams are promptly notified of security events.

Integrating threat intelligence feeds into our monitoring and IDS systems keeps us updated on emerging threats and enhances the accuracy of our detection rules. Regular security monitoring, including continuous analysis of logs, network traffic, and system activities, is essential for early detection and mitigation of potential threats. Periodic audits and reviews of our security monitoring configurations, IDS rulesets, and alerting mechanisms help maintain their effectiveness and alignment with evolving security requirements.

Forensic analysis and post-incident analysis are crucial for understanding the root causes of security incidents and implementing measures to prevent recurrence. Preservation of evidence, forensic imaging, and in-depth analysis of digital artifacts aid in reconstructing events and uncovering unauthorized activities. Post-incident analysis involves conducting root cause analysis, identifying gaps in security controls, and extracting lessons learned to enhance future incident response capabilities.

Incident communication and escalation procedures ensure effective communication and coordination during security incidents. Defining communication channels, designating communication roles, and establishing incident reporting processes facilitate timely and accurate information sharing. Both internal and external communication protocols need to be clearly outlined to maintain confidentiality and manage public perception.

CHAPTER 7   INCIDENT RESPONSE AND SECURITY MONITORING

Training and awareness programs for incident response team members and relevant staff are vital for enhancing their knowledge and skills. Providing regular training sessions, hands-on exercises, and simulations helps prepare the team for real incidents. Continuous improvement mechanisms, including regular reviews, exercises, and simulations, foster a culture of security awareness and proactive risk management throughout the organization.

CHAPTER 8

Future Trends in PHP Application Security

As the digital landscape continuously evolves, so do the security challenges that PHP applications face. This chapter delves into the future trends of PHP application security, offering a comprehensive overview of the emerging threats and attack techniques that developers need to be aware of. This chapter also explores the latest advancements in security tools and technologies, highlighting the critical role of AI and machine learning in fortifying PHP applications. Additionally, it examines the integration of large language models (LLMs) and generative AI technologies into PHP security measures. The chapter also addresses the unique security considerations for microservices and serverless architectures, providing actionable insights for safeguarding next-generation PHP applications.

Emerging Security Threats and Attack Techniques

In the realm of PHP application security, emerging threats and sophisticated attack techniques are constantly evolving as technology advances. Staying ahead of these threats requires an ongoing commitment to understanding and mitigating potential vulnerabilities.

CHAPTER 8 FUTURE TRENDS IN PHP APPLICATION SECURITY

One such threat is Server-Side Request Forgery (SSRF), where attackers manipulate inputs sent to the server, tricking it into making unintended requests. In PHP applications, this can be particularly dangerous if attackers gain access to internal resources or bypass firewalls. Similarly, injection attacks like SQL injection and command injection remain significant threats. Despite being older, these attacks exploit vulnerabilities in user input handling by injecting malicious code or commands, aiming to gain unauthorized access to databases or execute arbitrary commands on the server.

Cross-site scripting (XSS) is another persistent threat, involving the injection of malicious scripts into web pages viewed by other users. These vulnerabilities often stem from improper input validation and output encoding in PHP applications, allowing attackers to execute scripts within other users' sessions, potentially leading to data theft or unauthorized actions. Security misconfigurations in servers, frameworks, or dependencies can also open the door to various vulnerabilities. Common issues include default settings, unnecessary services or ports left open, and inadequate access controls, all of which can be exploited by attackers.

As APIs become increasingly prevalent in modern web applications, securing them is crucial. API security threats include authentication and authorization vulnerabilities, insecure data transmission, and inadequate rate limiting or access controls, which can lead to data breaches or service disruptions. Additionally, insecure cryptographic implementations, such as weak encryption algorithms or improper key management, expose sensitive data to attackers. It's essential to use strong cryptographic algorithms and follow best practices for key generation, storage, and transmission in PHP applications.

Supply chain attacks represent another growing concern, where attackers target the software supply chain by injecting malicious code into PHP packages or dependencies. This can lead to the distribution of compromised libraries or frameworks, potentially affecting numerous PHP applications that rely on them. Moreover, botnets and automated

CHAPTER 8   FUTURE TRENDS IN PHP APPLICATION SECURITY

attack tools continuously scan for vulnerabilities in PHP applications and exploit them at scale. These attacks can include brute-force attempts on authentication mechanisms, automated exploitation of known vulnerabilities, and reconnaissance activities to identify potential targets.

To mitigate these emerging threats, we must prioritize proactive security measures. This includes adopting secure coding practices, conducting regular security assessments and audits, timely patching and updates, secure configuration management, and ongoing security awareness training for our development teams. Additionally, leveraging security tools and frameworks specifically designed for PHP application security can help us detect and mitigate vulnerabilities more effectively. By staying vigilant and informed, we can better protect our PHP applications against these evolving threats.

Advancements in Security Tools and Technologies

Advancements in security tools and technologies have been crucial in addressing the evolving landscape of cybersecurity threats, including those faced by PHP applications. These innovations help developers and security teams better protect their applications from an ever-growing array of vulnerabilities and attack techniques.

One significant advancement is the integration of security plug-ins within Integrated Development Environments (IDEs) such as Visual Studio Code, PhpStorm, and Eclipse. These plug-ins assist developers in identifying and remediating security issues directly within their coding environment, offering features like code analysis, vulnerability scanning, and real-time security feedback. This integration allows for immediate detection and correction of potential vulnerabilities during the development process.

CHAPTER 8 FUTURE TRENDS IN PHP APPLICATION SECURITY

Static application security testing (SAST) tools have also become more advanced, analyzing source code or compiled binaries to identify security vulnerabilities, coding errors, and compliance issues without executing the application. Modern SAST tools are highly effective in detecting a wide range of vulnerabilities in PHP code, including injection flaws, XSS, and insecure cryptographic implementations, helping developers address issues early in the development lifecycle.

Dynamic application security testing (DAST) tools play a crucial role in identifying vulnerabilities by simulating attacks against running web applications. These tools are particularly valuable for testing the security posture of PHP applications in production environments, uncovering issues such as SQL injection, XSS, and insecure configurations that might be missed by static analysis alone.

Interactive application security testing (IAST) tools combine elements of both SAST and DAST by instrumenting the application during runtime to provide real-time security feedback to developers. This hybrid approach offers better accuracy and coverage compared to traditional testing methods and is especially suited for dynamic languages like PHP.

Runtime Application Self-Protection (RASP) solutions offer another layer of defense by monitoring application behavior during runtime to detect and prevent attacks in real time. Deployed alongside PHP applications, RASP solutions can protect against a variety of threats, including injection attacks, XSS, and security misconfigurations, by dynamically responding to potentially malicious activities.

As containerization becomes more prevalent in PHP application deployment, specialized container security tools have emerged to secure containerized environments. These tools provide features such as vulnerability scanning, runtime protection, and compliance monitoring for PHP containers deployed in Docker, Kubernetes, and other container orchestration platforms, ensuring the security of applications even in modern deployment scenarios.

API security gateways have also become essential, providing centralized security controls for APIs, including authentication, authorization, encryption, and rate limiting. These gateways help protect PHP applications from API-specific threats such as injection attacks, data exposure, and unauthorized access to sensitive endpoints, enhancing the overall security of API interactions.

Machine learning and AI-based security solutions are increasingly being integrated into security tools, enhancing threat detection, anomaly detection, and behavioral analysis. These advanced capabilities enable PHP application security teams to identify and respond to sophisticated attacks more effectively, leveraging the power of artificial intelligence to stay ahead of emerging threats.

DevSecOps tools and practices emphasize integrating security into the software development lifecycle (SDLC) from the outset. By automating security testing, compliance checks, and vulnerability management processes, DevSecOps tools enable continuous security improvements for PHP applications throughout development, testing, and deployment stages. This approach ensures that security is not an afterthought but a fundamental aspect of the development process.

The Role of AI and Machine Learning in PHP Application Security

Artificial intelligence (AI) and machine learning are increasingly pivotal in bolstering PHP application security. These advanced technologies contribute in several key ways, enhancing the ability to detect, prevent, and respond to security threats effectively.

AI and machine learning algorithms excel at threat detection and prevention by analyzing vast amounts of data from PHP applications, including logs, traffic patterns, and user behavior. These algorithms learn from historical data to identify patterns associated with known attacks and can proactively prevent them in real time, ensuring that potential threats are detected before they cause harm.

Behavioral analysis is another critical application of AI in PHP security. AI-powered systems monitor the behavior of applications and users to establish baselines of normal activity. Any deviation from these baselines, such as unusual access patterns, unexpected API calls, or abnormal data transfer volumes, can trigger alerts for further investigation, helping to identify potential security incidents or breaches early.

Machine learning techniques are also invaluable for vulnerability detection and patch management. These techniques can analyze PHP code bases to uncover security vulnerabilities such as SQL injection flaws, XSS vulnerabilities, or insecure configurations. By scanning code repositories and identifying patterns associated with known vulnerabilities, AI-powered tools assist developers in prioritizing and addressing security issues during the development lifecycle.

When security incidents occur, automated response and remediation powered by AI can significantly enhance incident management. AI algorithms can analyze the situation, assess the severity of the threat, and take appropriate actions, such as blocking suspicious IP addresses, quarantining compromised user accounts, or rolling back unauthorized changes, all without human intervention.

In terms of user authentication and access control, AI-based systems can strengthen mechanisms by analyzing various factors such as user behavior, device characteristics, and contextual information to determine the legitimacy of login attempts. Machine learning algorithms can optimize access control policies based on user roles, privileges, and historical access patterns to prevent unauthorized access to sensitive resources.

AI-powered security solutions also enable adaptive security controls. These systems can dynamically adjust security controls and policies based on evolving threats and changing environmental conditions. By continuously analyzing threat intelligence feeds, security trends, and system performance metrics, AI algorithms can optimize security configurations for PHP applications, effectively adapting to new attack vectors and mitigating emerging risks.

To sum it up, AI and machine learning technologies are crucial in phishing and fraud detection. They can analyze email and web traffic to detect phishing attempts, fraudulent activities, and social engineering attacks targeting PHP application users. By examining email content, sender reputation, and user interaction patterns, AI-powered security solutions can identify and block malicious emails and URLs before they reach users, reducing the risk of successful phishing attacks.

Integrating LLMs and Generative AI Technologies into PHP Application Security

Integrating large language models (LLMs) and generative AI technologies into PHP application security offers numerous benefits. These advanced AI techniques can enhance security strategies in several impactful ways, contributing to a more robust defense against evolving threats.

Natural Language Processing for Security Intelligence is one area where LLMs, such as GPT (Generative Pre-trained Transformer) models, excel. These models can process and analyze vast amounts of security-related text data, including security advisories, threat intelligence reports, and cybersecurity blogs. By understanding and summarizing this information, LLMs can provide valuable insights into emerging threats, attack techniques, and best practices. This helps security teams stay informed and make data-driven decisions to enhance PHP application security.

Automated Security Documentation and Policy Generation is another significant application of generative AI. These techniques can automatically generate security documentation, policies, and guidelines for PHP application development and deployment. By analyzing

CHAPTER 8 FUTURE TRENDS IN PHP APPLICATION SECURITY

existing security standards, compliance regulations, and organizational requirements, generative AI models can produce customized security documentation tailored to specific PHP application architectures, coding practices, and deployment environments. This ensures consistent and comprehensive security measures are implemented throughout the development lifecycle.

In the realm of Code Generation and Analysis, generative AI algorithms can assist developers in generating secure PHP code by providing code snippets, templates, and best practice recommendations. By analyzing code repositories, open source projects, and security guidelines, generative AI models can generate PHP code that adheres to security principles, avoids common vulnerabilities, and follows secure coding practices. This reduces the likelihood of introducing security flaws during development.

Anomaly Detection and Behavior Modeling is another critical area where LLMs and generative AI techniques can significantly impact. These AI models can train on historical data and user behavior profiles to model normal behavior patterns and detect anomalies in PHP application traffic, user interactions, and system activities. By identifying deviations from expected behavior, these models can alert security teams to potential security incidents, such as unauthorized access attempts, data exfiltration, or malicious activities, enabling timely detection and response to potential threats.

For Adversarial Testing and Red Teaming, LLMs and generative AI algorithms can simulate adversarial attacks against PHP applications to identify vulnerabilities, weaknesses, and blind spots in security defenses. By generating realistic attack scenarios, crafting exploit payloads, and performing penetration testing exercises, these AI-powered red teaming techniques help organizations proactively identify and remediate security issues before they can be exploited by real attackers. This improves the overall resilience of PHP applications against cyber threats.

Integrating LLMs and generative AI technologies into PHP application security strategies augments existing security measures, enhances threat detection capabilities, and empowers developers and security teams to build and maintain more secure PHP applications effectively. By leveraging the capabilities of these advanced AI techniques, organizations can strengthen their defenses, mitigate emerging risks, and protect critical assets from cyber threats.

Securing Microservices and Serverless Architectures

Securing microservices and serverless architectures presents unique challenges due to their distributed nature and dynamic infrastructure. Adopting best practices is essential to address these challenges effectively and ensure robust security across the system.

Implement Proper Authentication and Authorization

It's crucial to use robust authentication mechanisms such as OAuth 2.0 or JSON Web Tokens (JWT) to authenticate users and services within the microservices or serverless ecosystem. Implementing fine-grained access controls and role-based authorization helps restrict access to sensitive resources based on user roles and permissions, enhancing security.

Secure Communication Channels

Encrypting communication between microservices or serverless functions using Transport Layer Security (TLS) ensures data confidentiality and integrity. Utilizing service mesh frameworks like Istio or Linkerd can enforce mutual TLS authentication and implement network policies for secure communication between services, further securing the infrastructure.

Apply the Principle of Least Privilege

Following the principle of least privilege involves granting only the minimum permissions required for each microservice or serverless function to perform its intended function. Avoiding overly permissive IAM (Identity and Access Management) roles or service accounts minimizes the impact of potential security breaches.

Implement Defense in Depth

Applying multiple layers of security controls, including network security, host-based security, and application-level security mechanisms, protects microservices and serverless architectures from various attack vectors. Utilizing web application firewalls (WAFs) and API gateways helps filter and monitor incoming traffic for malicious activities.

Monitor and Logging

Centralized logging and monitoring solutions track activities and detect anomalies within microservices and serverless environments. Using logging frameworks like the ELK stack (Elasticsearch, Logstash, Kibana) or centralized logging services like AWS CloudWatch or Google Cloud Logging allows for the collection, analysis, and visualization of logs for security analysis and incident response.

Continuous Vulnerability Management

Regularly scanning microservices and serverless functions for security vulnerabilities using automated tools like Docker Security Scanning, Clair, or AWS Inspector is essential. Applying timely security patches and updates to underlying operating systems, container images, and third-party dependencies mitigates known vulnerabilities.

Secure Deployment and Configuration

Secure deployment pipelines and configuration management practices ensure that microservices and serverless functions are deployed securely. Utilizing infrastructure as code (IaC) tools like Terraform or AWS CloudFormation helps define and enforce security controls such as resource isolation, network segmentation, and encryption settings.

Implement Rate Limiting and Throttling

Protecting microservices and serverless functions from brute-force attacks, denial of service (DoS), and distributed denial-of-service (DDoS) attacks involves implementing rate limiting and throttling mechanisms. Using API management platforms or CDN (Content Delivery Network) services enforces rate limits and mitigates the impact of excessive traffic.

Container and Function Security

Securing containerized microservices involves adhering to container security best practices, such as image signing and verification, runtime isolation using container namespaces and seccomp profiles, and regular vulnerability scanning. For serverless architectures, leveraging built-in security features provided by serverless platforms, such as AWS Lambda's execution environment isolation and function-level IAM permissions, is crucial.

CHAPTER 8   FUTURE TRENDS IN PHP APPLICATION SECURITY

Security Testing and Compliance

Integrating security testing, including static application security testing (SAST), dynamic application security testing (DAST), and penetration testing, into the CI/CD (Continuous Integration/Continuous Deployment) pipeline helps identify and remediate security issues early in the development lifecycle. Ensuring compliance with industry regulations and standards, such as GDPR, HIPAA, and PCI DSS, by implementing appropriate security controls and conducting regular audits and assessments is also vital.

Summary

This chapter explores the importance of securing modern PHP applications against cyber threats. With the increasing use of machine learning (ML) and generative AI, developers can now leverage these technologies to enhance security measures and improve threat detection capabilities. Anomaly Detection and Behavior Modeling enable timely identification of potential security incidents, such as unauthorized access attempts or data exfiltration. Adversarial Testing and Red Teaming allow organizations to simulate attacks and identify vulnerabilities in their applications.

The chapter also delves into securing microservices and serverless architectures, which present unique challenges due to their distributed nature and dynamic infrastructure. Implementing proper authentication and authorization, secure communication channels, and applying the least privilege principle are essential best practices for these architectures. Defense-in-depth strategies, including network security, host-based security, and application-level security mechanisms, can protect microservices and serverless environments from various attack vectors.

CHAPTER 8　FUTURE TRENDS IN PHP APPLICATION SECURITY

Monitoring and logging solutions help track activities and detect anomalies within microservices and serverless environments. Continuous vulnerability management involves regular scanning of applications for security vulnerabilities using automated tools like Docker Security Scanning or AWS Inspector. Implementing secure deployment pipelines, configuration management practices, and infrastructure as code (IaC) tools can ensure that microservices and serverless functions are deployed securely.

Finally, the chapter highlights the importance of rate limiting and throttling to protect against brute-force attacks, DoS, and DDoS attacks. Container and function security best practices, such as image signing and verification, runtime isolation using container namespaces and seccomp profiles, can secure containerized microservices. Security testing and compliance measures, including static application security testing (SAST) and penetration testing, are integrated into the CI/CD pipeline to identify and remediate security issues early in the development lifecycle.

Index

A, B

Access Control Lists (ACLs), 138–140
ACLs, *see* Access Control Lists (ACLs)
Advanced Persistent Threats (APTs), 23
AI, *see* Artificial intelligence (AI)
API, *see* Application programming interface (API)
APM, *see* Application Performance Monitoring (APM)
Application Performance Monitoring (APM), 359
Application programming interface (API), 338–341
Application security (AppSec)
    AI/machine learning, 393–395
    authentication/authorization, 4
    compliance/regulations, 6
    cybersecurity threats/attack vectors, 19–23
    developer's perspective, 1
    generative AI technologies, 395–397
    incident response, 5
    information security, 1
    lifecycle approach, 3
    LLMs/GPT, 395–397
    microservices/serverless architectures, 397–400
    security tools and technologies, 391–393
    PHP security landscape, 14, 15
        core language, 14
        ecosystem, 15
        frameworks, 15
    principles, 24
        authentication/authorization, 25
        design, 24
        handle errors/logging, 27
        incident response plan, 29
        patch management/security updates, 28
        regular testing and reviews, 29
        secure code, 25
        secure communication, 28
        session management, 26
        upload files, 27
    protecting sensitive data, 5
    threats/sophisticated attack techniques, 389–391

INDEX

Application security (*cont.*)
    secure development, 4
    security protocols, 7–12
    security testing, 4
    software applications, 2
    vulnerabilities, 2, 15 (*see also* Security vulnerabilities)
AppSec, *see* Application security (AppSec)
APTs, *see* Advanced Persistent Threats (APTs)
Artificial intelligence (AI), 393–395

C

CI/CD, *see* Continuous integration and continuous deployment (CI/CD)
Cloud Security Posture Management (CSPM), 294
CMS, *see* Content management systems (CMS)
Composer packages in Laravel
    authentication, 272
    authorization, 271
    debugbar, 273
    dusk (browser testing), 278
    full-text search, 274
    intervention Image, 277
    log activity, 277
    media management, 279
    nova (admin panel), 276
    telescope, 275

Content management systems (CMS), 38
Content Security Policy (CSP), 151, 165
    coding practices/reviews, 260, 266
    validation techniques, 79
Continuous integration and continuous deployment (CI/CD), 9, 294, 300, 400
Cross-site request forgery (CSRF), 3, 21, 168, 178–182, 333
    coding practices/reviews, 259, 265
    cookies/sessions, 106–110
    Laravel security features, 205
    OWASP Top Ten, 254
    sanitization, 83
    validation techniques, 73, 77–79
    vendor security, 159
Cross-site scripting (XSS), 3, 20
    application security, 390
    coding practices/reviews, 266
    handling user input/data transmission, 333
    Laravel security features, 183–186
    OWASP Top Ten, 251
    PHP configuration settings, 70
    sanitization, 83
    validation techniques, 72
    vendor security, 159
    web application security, 151
    web security (*see* Web security)

INDEX

CSP, *see* Content Security Policy (CSP)
CSPM, *see* Cloud Security Posture Management (CSPM)
CSRF, *see* Cross-site request forgery (CSRF)
Cybersecurity threats/attack vectors
   APT attack, 23
   credential theft, 22
   cryptojacking, 22
   CSRF attacks, 21
   DDoS/DoS, 20
   insider threats, 21
   IoT vulnerabilities, 22
   Malware, 19
   MitM techniques, 21
   phishing attacks, 19
   social engineering, 21
   SQL injection, 20
   supply chain attacks, 23
   XSS attacks, 20
   zero-day vulnerabilities, 22

D

DAST, *see* Dynamic application security testing (DAST)
Database-driven authorization, 136
Database operations
   authentication/authorization, 120
   data encryption, 122
   environment, 122
   error handling, 121
   input validation/sanitization, 119
   logging/monitoring, 122
   parameterized queries, 119
   patches, 121
   privileges, 120
   query parameters, 120
   request-response cycle, 117, 118
   store database credentials, 120
DDoS, *see* Distributed Denial-of-Service (DDoS)
Denial-of-service (DoS), 20, 36
Development (DevOps)/deployment
   automated security scanning tools, 311
   backup/disaster recovery, 313
   CI/CD pipelines, 300
   CloudFormation/HashiCorp Terraform, 307
   cloud key management services, 312
   code obfuscation and encryption, 303
   containerization, 308
   Docker/Kubernetes, 308
   environment configurations, 302
   IaC, 299
   IAM implementation, 309
   immutable infrastructure, 301
   Laravel configuration, 303
   lifecycle, 299
   logging and monitoring, 311

INDEX

Development (DevOps)/
    deployment (*cont.*)
  network security, 310
  queue management, 304–306
  scanning dependencies, 302
  secrets management, 301, 312
  serverless architectures, 312
  software secure, 306
  storage management, 309
Distributed Denial-of-Service
    (DDoS), 20
DoS, *see* Denial-of-service (DoS)
Dynamic application security
    testing (DAST), 292, 392, 400

E

End of Life (EOL), 34, 35
EOL, *see* End of Life (EOL)

F

File handling/uploads
  authorization/
    authentication, 117
  directory outside, 115
  double extensions, 116
  file size, 115
  file types, 114
  proper permissions, 115
  randomized directory
    structure, 116
  rename uploaded files, 114
  request-response cycle, 110–112

  secure processing/storage,
    112, 113
  uploads directory, 117
  validate and sanitize file
    names, 116
Framework security, *see* Laravel
    security features

G

Generative Pre-trained
    Transformer (GPT), 395
GPT, *see* Generative Pre-trained
    Transformer (GPT)

H

Handling user input/data
    transmission
  CSRF attacks, 333
  protecting sensitive
    information, 333
  source code, 334–336
  SQL injection, 332
  XSS attacks, 333
HSTS, *see* HTTP Strict Transport
    Security (HSTS)
HTTP, *see* Hypertext Transfer
    Protocol (HTTP)
HTTPS, *see* Hypertext Transfer
    Protocol Secure (HTTPS)
HTTP Strict Transport Security
    (HSTS), 221, 223, 225, 330
Hypertext Transfer Protocol (HTTP)

INDEX

client rendering, 319
client request, 321
client request/DNS
  resolution, 317
data communication, 315
differences, 320, 322
encryption, 316, 321
GET/POST/PUT/DELETE, 316
HTTPS (*see* Hypertext Transfer
  Protocol Secure (HTTPS))
request/response, 318
secure data transfer, 321
server certificate, 321
server-side processing, 318
SSL/TLS handshake, 321
SSL/TLS layers, 322
TCP connection closure, 319
TCP connection
  establishment, 318
workflow lifecycle, 316, 317, 320
Hypertext Transfer Protocol
  Secure (HTTPS)
internet security, 325

I

IaC, *see* Infrastructure as
  Code (IaC)
IAM, *see* Identity and Access
  Management (IAM)
IAST, *see* Interactive application
  security testing (IAST)
Identity and Access Management
  (IAM), 309–310

IDEs, *see* Integrated Development
  Environments (IDEs)
IDOR, *see* Insecure Direct Object
  References (IDOR)
IDS, *see* Intrusion detection
  systems (IDS)
Incident communication and
  escalation procedures
  definition, 377
  documentation/analysis, 380
  escalation matrix, 379
  external procedures, 378
  internal procedures, 378
  legal and regulatory
    requirements, 380
  notification templates, 379
  reporting process, 378
  roles, 377
  RTOs/SLAs, 379
  severity levels, 379
  training and awareness
    programs, 380
Incident response plan (IRP),
  153–155, 348
  communication
    channels, 351–354
  data flow and interaction, 357
  data integrity, 352
  deployment architecture, 357
  escalation/notification
    procedures, 362
  identifying stakeholders, 348, 349
  incident severity levels, 349–351
  IRT creation, 354–356

407

INDEX

Incident response plan (IRP) (*cont.*)
  legal/regulatory
    requirements, 373–377
  monitoring/logging
    implementation, 359–361
  PHP application
    architecture, 356–358
  post-incident analysis/
    improvement, 368–371
  reporting/escalation, 366–368
  response procedures, 361–363
  testing, 363–365
  training/awareness, 371–373
Incident response team
  (IRT), 354–356
Infrastructure as Code (IaC),
  299, 307, 399, 401
Insecure Direct Object References
  (IDOR), 252
Integrated Development
  Environments (IDEs), 391
Interactive application security
  testing (IAST), 392
Internet of Things (IoT), 22
Intrusion detection systems (IDS),
  127, 128, 386
  applications, 347
  communication/escalation
    procedures, 377–380
  forensic analysis, 381
  IRP (*see* Incident response
    plan (IRP))
  post-incident
    analysis, 382–384

IoT, *see* Internet of Things (IoT)
IRP, *see* Incident response plan (IRP)
IRT, *see* Incident response
  team (IRT)

J, K

JSON Web Tokens (JWT), 338, 397
JWT, *see* JSON Web Tokens (JWT)

L

Laravel security features
  authentication/
    authorization, 283–285
  authorize method, 196, 198
  Blade views, 194
  controller, 193, 194
  flow diagram, 190
  password hashing/
    protection, 189
  policies, 195, 198
  resource controller, 192
  routes, 192
  setting up, 190, 191
  coding practices/reviews, 262
  composer packages, 271–279
  configuration/
    deployment, 224–231
    application security, 226–231
    HSTS implementation, 225
    HTTPS/communication, 225
    production environments, 225
    protecting sensitive
      information, 224

408

INDEX

secure configuration, 227
vulnerabilities, 224
web server
  configuration, 228
CSRF protection, 178–182
file uploads, 205–211
HTTPS/secure configuration
  Apache configuration, 218
  application security, 216, 217
  configuration, 219, 220
  HSTS, 221, 222
  Nginx configuration, 218
  SSL certificate, 217
middleware, 215
  additional protection, 212
  creation, 213
  implementation, 213, 214
  routes/route groups, 215
protocol security, 329
routes/middleware/
    controllers, 232
  access control/
    authorization, 233
  defense/security
    policies, 233
  input validation/
    sanitization, 233
  logging and
    monitoring, 234–238
securing database
  operations, 241–246
security best practices, 238–240
  authorization checks, 239
  error handling, 240

middleware, 239
  parameters, 240
  policies, 239
  RBAC approach, 239
  route grouping, 240
session security
  configuration, 201
  controller/routes, 201
  CSRF protection, 203
  detailed explanation,
    199, 200
  encryption, 203
  flash data, 203
  middleware, 202
SQL injection
  vulnerabilities, 189–192
XSS protection, 183–186
Large language models (LLMs),
    389, 395–397
LFI, *see* Local File Inclusion (LFI)
LLMs, *see* Large language
  models (LLMs)
Local File Inclusion (LFI)
  vendor security, 159

M

Machine learning (ML), 393, 400
  AI (*see* Artificial
    intelligence (AI))
Man-in-the-middle (MitM)
  attacks, 21
MFA, *see* Multifactor
  authentication (MFA)

409

INDEX

MitM attacks, *see* Man-in-the-middle (MitM) attacks
ML, *see* Machine learning (ML)
Multifactor authentication (MFA), 26, 135

N

Network intrusion detection systems (NIDS), 385, 387
NIDS, *see* Network intrusion detection systems (NIDS)

O

Object-Relational Mapping (ORM), 187, 188
Open Web Application Security Project (OWASP) Top Ten
    access controls, 253
    authentication mechanisms, 252
    CSRF attacks, 254
    IDOR implementation, 252
    injection vulnerabilities, 251
    security misconfigurations, 252, 253
    sensitive information, 253
    third-party components, 254
    unvalidated redirects and forwards, 255
    XSS vulnerabilities, 251
ORM, *see* Object-Relational Mapping (ORM)

OWASP Top Ten, *see* Open Web Application Security Project (OWASP) Top Ten

P, Q

PHP (Hypertext preprocessor)
    AppSec (*see* Application security (AppSec))
    configuration, 40–56
    configuration settings, 63–71
    cookies, 57–58
    data storage/management, 57
    file handling/uploads, 110–117
    initialization/handling, 57
    input validation, 71–81
    sanitization, 83–88
    secure database access, 117
    security measures, 60–63
    sessions, 89–110
    version (*see* Version control, PHP)
    visual representation, 31, 32
    web security (*see* Web application security)
PHP configuration
    common settings, 43
    directives, 42
    display error messages, 47
    display_startup_errors controls, 47
    error log file, 48
    error reporting, 46

INDEX

error reporting settings, 44
expose_php, 45
file inclusion, 50
file uploads, 51, 52
ignore_repeated_errors, 49
key aspects, 41
log_errors, 48
max_file_uploads, 55
modules/extensions, 43
per-directory, 42
php.ini, 41
post_max_size, 54
runtime, 42
security, 43
session management, 56
settings/parameters, 40
SQL injection, 50
upload_max_filesize
    setting, 53
upload_tmp_dir directory, 53
PHP configuration settings
    allow_webdav_methods
        controls, 66
    doc_root/open_basedir, 64
    extension_dir, 65
    html_errors, 70
    include_path, 65
    max_execution_time, 68
    memory_limit, 68
    mime_magic.magicfile, 66
    report_memleaks, 69
    session.gc_maxlifetime, 67
    session.referer_check, 68
    track_errors, 69

PHP security measures
    access controls, 61
    classes, 63
    cookies, 59
    disable_functions, 62
    enable_dl, 61
    session.cache_expire, 60
    session cookie lifetime, 59
    session.hash_function/session.
        hash_bits_per_
        character, 60
    session.sid_bits_per_
        character, 60
    session.sid_length, 60
    strict mode, 59
PHP session cookies
    attributes, 107–110
    configuration files, 58, 59
    fundamental concepts, 88
    handling cookies, 107
    request-response cycle, 91
    storing sensitive data, 110
    websites, 89
PHP sessions
    avoid storing sensitive
        data, 99–101
    CSRF protection, 106–110
    destroying sessions, 101–103
    fundamental concepts, 88
    handling ID, 93
    protect session data, 98, 99
    regenerating IDs, 93–95
    request-response
        cycle, 90, 91

INDEX

PHP sessions (*cont.*)
   security perspective, 96–98
   set parameters, 95, 96
   setting/management, 93
   steps, 91, 92
   timeout, 103–106
   variables, 106
   websites, 89, 90
PoLP, *see* Principle of least privilege (PoLP)
Principle of least privilege (PoLP), 129–131
Protocol security, 315
   Apache configuration, 328
   API communication, 338
      authentication, 338
      authorization, 339
      OAuth 2.0, 339
      protect sensitive data, 338
      request-response cycle, 337
      source code, 340, 341
      token-based authentication, 339
   force HTTPS, 330
   handling user input/data transmission, 332–336
   HSTS, 330
   HTTP request, 315–322
   Laravel application, 329
   Laravel Mix, 331
   mixed content issues, 331
   SSL/TLS, 323–327
   testing, 332
   TLS/email communication, 342–345
   web server/Nginx configuration, 327

R

RASP, *see* Runtime Application Self-Protection (RASP)
RBAC, *see* Role-Based Access Control (RBAC)
RCA, *see* Root cause analysis (RCA)
Remote file inclusion (RFI)
   vendor security, 159
Response time objectives (RTOs), 379
RFI, *see* Remote file inclusion (RFI)
Role-Based Access Control (RBAC), 130, 135, 136
   authentication/authorization, 288
   Laravel security features, 239
Root cause analysis (RCA), 368
Runtime Application Self-Protection (RASP), 392

S

Sanitization techniques
   cross-site scripting attacks, 83
   CSRF attacks, 83
   data tampering, 84
   file uploads, 84
   filtering characters, 86

fundamental best practice, 85
htmlspecialchars(), 86
long-term maintenance/
    security, 85
reducing attack surface, 84
remove/escape control
    characters, 88
request-response cycle, 83
SQL injection, 83, 86
strip_tags() function, 85
upload files, 87
URLs, 87
user experience, 84
SAST, *see* Static application security
    testing (SAST)
SDLC, *see* Software development
    lifecycle (SDLC)
Secure authentication and
    authorization
    components, 280
    data protection, 280
    JWT (JSON web tokens), 286
    Laravel Fortify, 284
    LDAP integration, 289
    OAuth2 and OpenID
        connect, 285
    passport (OAuth2), 283
    password hashing, 281
    RBAC, 288
    Sanctum, 282
    session management, 281
    starter kit (Laravel Breeze), 283
    two-factor authentication
        (2FA), 287

Secure coding practices and
    code reviews
    application development, 256
    authentication/
        authorization, 262
    automated testing, 270
    checklist-based reviews, 270
    code reviews, 267–269
    cross-site request forgery
        (CSRF), 265
    CSP headers, 260, 266
    CSRF tokens, 259
    database connections, 260
    data validation and
        sanitization, 259
    dependency injection, 266
    Eloquent ORM, 264
    error handling, 258
    file uploads, 258
    handling passwords, 257
    HTTPS, 267
    input validation/
        sanitization, 256
    Laravel security, 262
    middleware, 262
    password recovery, 260
    peer reviews, 269
    policies/gates, 264
    risk mitigation, 255
    secure coding practices, 256
    security issues, 256
    security linters and
        scanners, 270
    session management, 257, 265

INDEX

Secure coding practices and code reviews (*cont.*)
  session security, 261
  SSL/TLS, 261
  static code analysis, 269
  validation, 263
Secure Sockets Layer (SSL), 143, 217, 261, 316
  features, 323
  handshake process workflow, 324
  meaning, 323
  ServerHello/Finished message, 325
  TLS (*see* Transport Layer Security (TLS))
Securing database operations
  authorization features, 244
  database credentials, 246
  detailed code, 241
  Eloquent ORM, 241
  hide error details, 246
  parameterized queries, 243
  query builder, 245
  validation, 242
Securing microservices/serverless architectures
  authentication/authorization, 397
  communication channels, 398
  container/function security, 399
  defense in depth, 398
  deployment/configuration management, 399
  least privilege, 398
  logging and monitoring solutions, 398
  rate limiting and throttling, 399
  security testing/compliance, 400
  vulnerabilities, 399
Security information and event management (SIEM), 360, 384, 386
Security monitoring
  IDS (*see* Intrusion detection systems (IDS))
Security monitoring system
  implementation, 384
  integration, 386
  logging mechanisms, 384
  NIDS sensors, 385
  objectives, 384
  tools, 384
Security protocols
  code reviews, 9
  functional requirements, 9
  healthcare applications, 7
  integration, 8
  potential risks/vulnerabilities, 8
  regulations, 7
  roles/responsibilities, 10–12
  secure coding techniques, 8
  shift left, 7, 8, 10
  threats/vulnerabilities, 9
Security standards, PHP, 249
  authentication/authorization, 280–290

coding practices/
    reviews, 255–270
continuous monitoring, 250
deployment/DevOps, 299–313
Laravel packages, 271–279
OWASP Top Ten (*see* Open Web
    Application Security
    Project (OWASP) Top Ten)
secure coding practices, 250
testing/vulnerability
    assessments, 290–298
Security testing and vulnerability
    assessments
    automation, 294
    cloud-native scanning, 295
    container image scanning, 293
    continuous improvement, 297
    CSPM tools, 294
    DAST, 292
    dependency scanning, 293
    incident response planning, 297
    issues, 291
    penetration testing, 296
    red team *vs.* blue team
        exercises, 296
    regular security audits, 296
    risk management, 291
    SAST, 292
    security awareness training, 298
    security headers, 293
    serverless, 295
    threat modeling, 298
Security vulnerabilities, 15
    data breaches, 16

demage impact, 18
disrupt normal operations, 17
impact users, 17
legal problems, 17
long-lasting effects, 18
mitigation costs, 18
operational inefficiencies, 19
reputation damage, 16
substantial financial losses, 16
Server-Side Request Forgery
    (SSRF), 390
Service-level agreements (SLAs), 379
SIEM, *see* Security information and
    event management (SIEM)
SLAs, *see* Service-level
    agreements (SLAs)
Software development lifecycle
    (SDLC), 3, 7, 393
SQL injection
    vulnerabilities, 189–192
SSL, *see* Secure Sockets Layer (SSL)
SSRF, *see* Server-Side Request
    Forgery (SSRF)
Static application security testing
    (SAST), 392, 400, 401
    testing/vulnerability
        assessments, 292

T

TCP, *see* Transmission Control
    Protocol (TCP)
TLS, *see* Transport Layer
    Security (TLS)

415

INDEX

Transmission Control Protocol (TCP), 318
Transport Layer Security (TLS), 143, 217, 261, 315, 316, 397
  authentication, 326
  cryptographic protocols, 325
  data integrity, 326
  email communication, 342
    authentication, 343
    compliance frameworks, 343
    confidentiality, 342
    environment configuration, 343
    integrity, 342
    mail service, 344
  features, 324
  fundamental model, 327
  meaning, 323
  web applications, 325

U

Uniform Resource Identifiers (URIs), 316
URIs, *see* Uniform Resource Identifiers (URIs)

V

Validation techniques
  allowed/denied list, 76
  attack surfaces, 74
  compliance standards, 73
  CSP headers, 79
  CSRF attack, 77-79
  CSRF tokens, 73
  database security, 73
  data filtering/validation functions, 74
  data integrity, 73
  development process, 74
  escape output, 76
  file uploads, 80
  HTTP security headers, 80
  injection attacks, 72
  logic abuse, 73
  parameterized queries/statements, 77
  parameter manipulation, 72
  regular expressions (regex), 75
  request-response cycle, 71
  sensitive information exposure, 72
  user base, 74
  XSS attacks, 72
Vendor security
  assess/trust security, 157
  security strategies, 157-161
  third-party libraries/services, 158
  web applications, 159-161
Version control, PHP
  best practices, 35
  compatibility challenges, 37, 38
  End of Life (EOL), 34, 35
  performance/efficiency benefits, 36

security updates, 33
vendor/application, 38-40
Virtual Private Clouds (VPCs), 310
VPCs, *see* Virtual Private Clouds (VPCs)

W

WAFs, *see* Web application firewalls (WAFs)
Web application firewalls (WAFs), 146, 147, 385, 386, 398
Web application security
 application security, 128
 authentication, 133, 134
 authorization, 133, 135
 database-driven authorization, 136
 defense in depth, 127, 128
 design phase, 152
 encryption, 140-142
 error handling, 145
 firewalls/IDS/policies, 128
 incident response plan (IRP), 153-155
 input validation, 131, 132
 least privilege principle, 129-131
 MFA implementation, 135
 middleware/access control lists, 138-140
 network security, 127
 openssl functions, 143, 144
 OWASP ZAP/Nessus, 148

patch management, 149
pinciples, 127
principles, 126
RBAC implementation, 135, 136
regular security testing, 147, 148
request-response cycle, 126
secure coding practices, 132, 133
secure session management, 137, 138
security design, 152, 153
security headers, 151
sensitive information, 142
server security, 127
session management, 145, 146
TLS/SSL, 143
user education, 155-157
username/password, 134
validation/sanitization, 150, 151
vendors, 157-161
WAFs, 146, 147
Web security
 anti-CSRF token, 172
 bypass authentication, 169
 CSP directives, 165
 CSRF attacks, 168
 data exposure, 169
 data manipulation, 168
 financial transactions, 169
 hijacking, 169
 HTTP protocol, 167
 JavaScript generation, 166
 legal and compliance issues, 170

INDEX

Web security (*cont.*)
   output encoding, 164
   POST requests, 173
   referer header, 172
   reputation damage, 170
   request-response lifecycle, 163, 164
   same-site attribute, 173
   security libraries, 167
   security testing, 167
   security training, 167
   significant implications, 161, 162
   statements/parameterized queries, 166
   unauthorized actions, 168
   user's session, 174
   validation/sanitization, 165
   XSS (*see* Cross-site scripting (XSS))

X, Y

XSS, *see* Cross-site scripting (XSS)

Z

Zero-day vulnerabilities, 22

GPSR Compliance

The European Union's (EU) General Product Safety Regulation (GPSR) is a set of rules that requires consumer products to be safe and our obligations to ensure this.

If you have any concerns about our products, you can contact us on

ProductSafety@springernature.com

In case Publisher is established outside the EU, the EU authorized representative is:

Springer Nature Customer Service Center GmbH
Europaplatz 3
69115 Heidelberg, Germany

www.ingramcontent.com/pod-product-compliance
Lightning Source LLC
LaVergne TN
LVHW010333260326
834688LV00036B/689